THE DOLLS OF YESTERDAY

THE DOLLS OF YESTERDAY

by ELEANOR ST. GEORGE

"The cabinet stood ajar and a large doll, rather oldish and with a rivet in her neck, peeped out and said: 'Suppose we play at human beings—that would be so charming!' "

Hans Christian Andersen—"THE MONEY BOX."

BONANZA BOOKS · NEW YORK

To the memory of "Mrs. Nellie," "Mrs. Frankie," and "Mrs. Gertie"—three little girls of the Long Ago who played "house" in grandfather's orchard—and to their "Make Believe Neighbors" the "Doodle family," on whom the eye of grown-up never rested.

FOREWORD

THIS BOOK is the outgrowth of my own pleasure in the doll-collecting hobby and my own sense of the need for more information more readily available to the average collector. There is little printed matter on the subject of dolls, and that little mostly "out of print" and selling, when it can be obtained, at rare book prices. Since this is true, the chief source of information must be found in the study of old dolls themselves. This book could not have been written without the cordial co-operation of more than five hundred collectors throughout the United States. It is their book.

For inspiration, constant encouragement, and patient answering of questions, and for her unselfish sharing of the knowledge she has gained through years of handling and repairing thousands of dolls annually, our first acknowledgment and gratitude go to Mrs. Emma C. Clear of the Humpty Dumpty Doll Hospital, Redondo Beach, California.

To Harold A. Rugg, assistant librarian of the Baker Memorial Library at Dartmouth College, Hanover, New Hampshire, for making available the full resources of that splendid library; to Miss Alice T. Neef and the reference staff for reference work; and to John Davenport Crehore of Washington, D. C., for research in the Library of Congress; to the Royal Ontario Museum, Charles M. Currelly, Curator, of Toronto, for pictures and information; to Pearl McCarthy Sabiston, art editor of the *Toronto Globe and Mail,* to the Charles W. Bowers Memorial Museum and Mrs. F. E. Coulter, Curator, of Santa Ana, California; to the Witt Memorial Museum of San Antonio, Texas; and to Charles D. Martin, genealogical expert, also of San Antonio, for making available information and photographs.

Our special thanks go to Mrs. Coolidge for the unpublished photograph of her son John in the President's baby carriage; to Mr. Herbert Ellis, son of Joel Ellis, and Mr. Henry Taylor, son of Luke Taylor, for catalogues and information on the subject of the Springfield, Vermont, dolls; to George W. Schoenhut of Hanover, New Hampshire, grandson of Albert Schoenhut, for information, and to Mr. Otto F. Schoenhut of Philadelphia, son of Albert

Schoenhut, for a complete set of photographs of the Schoenhut dolls from his collection of the firm's catalogues. We are deeply indebted to Mrs. Kenneth Colburn of Pasadena, California, for the unpublished photographs of the Eugene Field doll collection, which were a wedding gift to her from Eugene Field's daughter, Mrs. W. O. Engler of Altadena, California; to the *Journal of American Folklore* for permission to reproduce the text of the "Ballad of Fair Charlotte."

To Kenneth L. Spring and Isabel Stark Cole for photographic work; to Miss Jennie L. Abbott, Librarian of Doll Collectors of America Inc., for the loan of rare books from her personal collection; to Staff Sergeant Charles Mears, U.S.A., who sent us dolls from England; to Mrs. Ralph E. Wakeman of Claremont, New Hampshire; Mrs. Cyrus M. Beachy of Wichita, Kansas; Mrs. William Walker, Louisville, Kentucky; Mrs. Winifred Harding, Woodstock, Vermont; Mrs. Sadie Fraser of Woodstock; Mrs. Norman Craven, Detroit, Michigan, and Quechee, Vermont; and Mrs. Earle E. Andrews of Winchester, Massachusetts, all of whom sent me dolls to study. Special thanks are due to Mrs. Elsie Clark Krug of Baltimore for her generous gift of a rare type of Jumeau doll for the book. Thanks also to Miss Gertrude Gordon of New York for help in many ways.

They and many others have been of great assistance.

The two years of work on the book have been enriched by warm friendships formed with many whom we know only by correspondence and by the knowledge we have gained of other interesting hobbies of those we have contacted, which range from the world's finest collection of the first coinage minted in the New World, that of Emperor Charles V and his mother, "the Mad Johanna," to a project for establishing the golden palomino horse of the Spanish conquistadors into a separate breed. Doll collectors are seldom one-idea people.

ELEANOR ST. GEORGE

Quechee, Vt.
January, 1948

CONTENTS

CONTENTS

ILLUSTRATIONS

THE DOLLS OF YESTERDAY

DOLL COLLECTING

DO YOU KNOW what a "pious rent" is? Do you know the difference between a "snood" and a "chignon" or "waterfall"? The origin of Irish crochet lace? Who set the fashion for bobbed hair and why? The origin of hairnets? Do you like a "Whodun-it" mystery? An amazing spy story? These queries are just a hint of the variety of interest one may find in doll collecting.

Of course there have been doll collections and collectors for a good many years, but the real tide of the doll hobby began to rise in the early 1930's. Except for the tulip craze in Holland, it is doubtful if any hobby has ever grown more rapidly than this one. Some part of the credit for this amazing growth is due to *Hobbies*, the magazine for collectors, which established its Dollology department in 1936 and has since been an important medium for the exchange of doll knowledge and experiences among collectors.

Doll collecting is distinctly an adult pastime. Women collect dolls for beauty, for associations, and for the memories they invoke of dolls they had in their own childhood.

Not many men *collect* dolls, but men of all walks of life are fascinated by such a collection. It is interesting to observe their reactions. The Polish farmer's eyes light up as he sees the old china-head dolls:

Pictures of dolls discussed in this chapter will be found following page 12.

"Missus, that's the kind of dolls we had in Poland—my sisters and the other girls had these." Of course they did with Poland so near to pre-war Germany where the china dolls were made. A Detroit executive spends most of an evening studying the ingenious mechanical structure of a Joel Ellis wooden doll made in Springfield, Vt. A British naval commander, who is visiting some neighbors, lingers over the replicas of such royal ladies as Empress Eugenie and Queen Victoria. "What a beautiful lace on this one's petticoat," he exclaims. (Fancy her puritanical Majesty Victoria having the quality of her lingerie made the subject of parlor conversation!) The superintendent of the local woolen mill, the Jewish junk man (university educated), the town manager (who is a civil engineer), the doctor, the minister, begin with an indulgent smile; then, as their attention is called to the fine points of the collection—the old papier mâché doll that is almost a duplicate of an N. Currier print, the modern Parians of George and Martha Washington by Mrs. Clear, the old wooden Pedlar doll from England, the American made Greiners, the French and German bisques, the English made wax dolls—they grow more and more interested in the materials, the ceramics, the historical associations, until, after an hour or more of absorbed interest, they end by saying, just a bit sheepishly: "I wish my little girl could see all these dolls—she'd be crazy about them!"

But the chances are good that she would not be at all. Modern children are apt to be politely bored with the antique dolls. Perhaps it is because these differ so much from the modern dolls to which they are accustomed. More probably it is because dolls do not mean to the child of today what they meant to her mother and grandmothers of the sixties, seventies, eighties or nineties when a doll was a lifetime possession—perhaps her only toy. Around it the little girl of those eras built a whole imaginary world in which the colored buttons from grandmother's button box were lovely jewels—rubies, sapphires and emeralds; the crystals from a discarded hanging lamp, strung on yarn, were diamond necklaces, bracelets, rings, and earrings of purest ray serene; and grandmother's majolica butter-leaves or some bits of broken crockery salvaged from the chip yard were the finest of china.

Today there are movies, radios, a multiplicity of ingenious and realistic toys to distract the child's attention from dolls and they leave little—far too little—to the imagination.

Besides the collectors of antique dolls there has grown up an even larger group who collect frankly modern dolls, folk types from various countries, state dolls, character dolls, story book dolls, copies of famous paintings, portrait dolls of historic characters, past and present; religious dolls, dolls of unusual materials such as shells, sponges, beads, wishbones, corn husks, etc. The types are endless and in time these, too, will become antiques. Of such dolls there are many fine and interesting collections numbering hundreds, even thousands, of items. Dr. Madeline Donnelly, a busy public health official of Gladwin, Mich., finds her recreation in a fine collection of one thousand dolls from all parts of the world.

Such collections have served to increase interest in foreign countries and folk customs; have been useful in teaching geography and history when exhibited in schools and libraries; in stimulating missionary interest when displayed in churches. One enterprising doll collector has taken her dolls into the field of commercial advertising and tours the country displaying a group of her dolls in certain types of stores as an advertisement for their merchandise.

Mrs. Margaret Sahli of Hays, Kansas, has assembled a remarkable collection of over two hundred nun dolls representing the various religious orders of the Catholic Church. She sent large German bisque dolls to convents throughout the United States, Mexico and Canada, that they might be accurately garbed by the order they represent. The purposes of this collection are, of course, educational and vocational.

To supply the demand for collectors' material, both antique and modern, there have grown up three national doll houses and endless smaller specialty doll shops, while general antique dealers throughout the country buy and sell such antique dolls as come their way—dolls which a few years ago they would have passed by unheeded. Some antique dealers *buy* dolls but do not *sell* them, being themselves afflicted with the divine madness of the doll hobby. Two of the largest private collections of old dolls in Vermont are owned by antique dealers—Mrs. Winifred Harding of Woodstock and Mrs. Rose Parro of Waterbury.

3

THE DOLLS OF YESTERDAY

There are two national doll collectors' associations and many small local clubs.

Doll hospitals, where skilled workers restore seemingly hopeless wrecks to pristine beauty, have multiplied.

Doll dressmaking is an increasing profession by which many a woman of skill and taste is adding to a perhaps too limited income. Attics are being combed for old silks and costumes of Civil War vintage to supply authentic materials, and the colored fashion plates of *Godey's* and *Peterson's* have taken on a new importance.

The collecting of antique dolls is naturally self-limiting by reason of the relative scarcity of the objects collected, for, as yet, no great amount of faking or reproducing of old dolls has appeared—as has happened in other lines. The antique furniture that is reputed to have "come over in the Mayflower," for example, would have required our entire war-time merchant marine to carry it all across the ocean. It is not yet so with old dolls.

The eagerness of some doll collectors, however, has had one unfortunate effect in developing an increasing inflation of prices which, in the end, may be more self-limiting—even to the extent of destroying the hobby itself. Indeed there are several well-known collectors who have already abandoned dolls and turned to other less competitive hobbies. The absurdity of any doll selling for hundreds—or even a thousand dollars—has been just too much for their common sense and sense of fitness.

However, one may still have all the joys of collecting and the happiness that comes from an interest outside one's daily grind, without spending fabulous sums. As Scotch grandmother used to say: "Better a small bush than no shelter."

A few dolls may be more fun than a thousand and much less bother to care for and house. They need not be rare Parians either, for much of the joy of a collection of any kind lies in the finding and acquiring. Where does one *find* antique dolls? Almost anywhere. Dolls are where you find them. For instance, Miss Grace Woodworth of Colorado Springs, Colo., found the interesting Spanish Gentleman shown following page 12 in the stuffing of an upholstered chair!

Another collector, Mrs. F. R. Gibis of West St. Paul, Minn., has acquired about seventy-five old china-head dolls by the simple expedient of advertising in Midwestern farm papers.

In Amarillo, Texas, the next door neighbor of Mrs. Louis E. Lahn one day noticed some small boys playing "shinny" with some object in the alley back of her house. Finally, after kicking the object into her back yard they went away. Sometime later, going out to empty some potato parings in the garbage can, she saw that the object was a large broken china doll-head. Remembering that Mrs. Lahn collected old dolls, she picked up the head and took it indoors, intending to give it to Mrs. Lahn. But she did not do so immediately. In fact, she was a little ashamed to offer anything so dilapidated and dirty. A few days later, however, she showed it to Mrs. Lahn, who gratefully accepted the find and sent it out to the famous Humpty Dumpty Doll Hospital of Redondo Beach, Calif., for restoration. It was found to be a fine head, was mended, missing parts supplied, as were body and legs and arms of china. Mrs. Clear, who owns the hospital, being a friend of young Mrs. Lahn, had the doll suitably costumed and entered it in Mrs. Lahn's name at the annual Doll Show at Charles W. Bowers Memorial Museum, Santa Ana, Calif. The "Cinderella of the Alley" won two blue ribbons in the show.

Priorities and a pressure cooker brought us "Martha Victoria," a lovely French Fashion Doll of the 1870's—but *that* is another story.

Without too much expense, one may become a specialist in penny dolls, paper dolls, rag dolls, advertising dolls like "Rastus," the Cream of Wheat Chef, Aunt Jemima of the pancake flour, etc.; doll clothes, doll millinery, doll customs in many countries; doll scrap books, pictures of famous paintings and old tintypes in which dolls appear; poems about dolls, doll music—the possibilities are endless, and the dividends of interest and pleasure are rich indeed.

FROM THE CRADLE OF INVENTIONS

SPRINGFIELD, VERMONT, where but yesterday thousands were employed turning out machine tools for the war industries of the nation, is an old town. Its first white settler, John Nott, who had an Indian wife, bought land from the Indians in 1752. Other settlers came from Northampton, Mass., the next year, and Governor Bennings Wentworth of New Hampshire granted the town's charter in 1761.

Abundant water power from the Black River, abundant timber on the surrounding hills, shaped the character of the town's industrial future and determined, to a large extent, the type of inventions that were the basis of its manufactures. In no other town of its size in New England has Yankee ingenuity and inventive genius flourished as here.

Two men of genius, Joel A. H. Ellis, a prolific inventor, and Luke Taylor, a great mechanic as well as inventor, were responsible for the town's most remembered products—the wooden dolls of the 1870's and early 1880's—now so much sought for by doll collectors and collectors of Americana.

Joel A. H. Ellis died in 1888 and Luke Taylor died in 1898, but there are those still living, sons of these two men, who have first-hand knowledge of the making of the dolls. To collect and pass on this information is the purpose of this chapter.

Pictures of dolls discussed in this chapter will be found following page 12.

6

FROM THE CRADLE OF INVENTIONS

Herbert Ellis of West Somerville, Mass., second son of Joel Ellis, now almost eighty-five years old, has written a privately printed monograph on the Ellis dolls and has been very kind and helpful in clearing up disputed points by correspondence.

Joel A. H. Ellis was born in Barnard, Windsor County, Vt., in 1830. On the death of his mother when he was thirteen years old, he went to Springfield and lived successively with three of her brothers: George Woodbury of Springfield, Joel Woodbury of North Springfield, and Daniel Woodbury of Perkinsville. From the latter he gained his first knowledge of mechanics.

Joel Ellis patented thirteen inventions, ranging from a steam shovel for excavating roads to a child's carriage or cab, which gained for him the local nickname of "Cab" Ellis. A replica of this cab in iron, which was used on the factory building as a weathervane, is still preserved in Springfield. At various times he made and marketed a jointed wooden doll, doll carriages, the first toy carts ever to come on the market, the first violin and guitar cases ever made for sale in America.

Many of these ventures failed financially, for Ellis appears to have been more proficient as an inventor than a practical businessman. Luck was not always with him either. The great flood of 1869 carried away his entire plant, stock and tools with a loss of $40,000. Reorganized as the Vermont Novelty Works, these shops were destroyed by fire in 1878 and again rebuilt.

Wooden dolls in America did not originate with Joel Ellis in Springfield, but this was probably the first time they were ever made here commercially. The Joel Ellis doll had but a brief history. It was manufactured only during the year 1873.

The patent for the mortise-and-tenon joint was granted to Joel Ellis, May 20, 1873. Some months before, while the patent was pending, Ellis had organized a company for the manufacture of the dolls, known as The Co-operative Manufacturing Co., with Joel A. H. Ellis, President; A. H. Whitmore, Secretary and Treasurer; and Charles D. Brink, Superintendent. A saw and planing mill on the banks of the Black River was purchased and a two-story building was erected near-by. Machinery was installed. There were sixty employees, of which about one-third were women. When the patent was granted, Ellis turned it over to the company in exchange for capital stock.

The distinctive features of the Ellis doll were that the mortise-and-tenon friction joint, which was the patented feature, allowed the doll to assume and hold all sorts of acrobatic poses, intriguing to any child, and being of wood, it was supposed to be unbreakable.

The dolls were made wholly of rock maple, kiln-dried on the premises, except the hands and feet, which were of metal. Herbert Ellis, in his monograph, gives very complete details of the process of manufacture. For many of these details he acknowledges indebtedness to his brother Hartley Ellis who worked on the dolls. Because they are so recorded, it is only necessary to give the briefest outline here.

The bodies, arm and leg sections were turned on lathes and assembled with steel pins. At the neck a tenon was turned on the body which fitted a hole bored in the head. The head was stationary. Wrists and ankles ended in similar tenons. The feet were malleable cast iron, with a small hole to receive the ankle tenon to which it was fastened with a steel pin. The hands were cast with molten metal in small molds into which the wrist tenons were thrust before the metal was poured.

The heads were made of kiln-dried maple on the end of the grain, pressed into form in steel dies under 2000 pounds pressure in a hydraulic press. Strips of wood 4 feet long by 2½ inches by 2¾ inches were run through a four-sided planing machine to round them for the top and sides of the head and to form the neck sections; they were then cut into blocks the right size for the individual heads. One side of the block was then sharply pointed in another machine so that the nose could be formed.

The dies of fine steel were in two sections, one having the features, the other, the back of the head and hair. These dies were about an inch apart when put under the press, but soon came together, forming a perfect head. When taken out, a slight burr at the joining was removed with a sharp knife by one of the women operatives. The hole was drilled in the head to fit the tenon on the body, and the head was glued to the body.

The assembling and painting of the dolls were done by women. Before assembling, the lower legs and forearms were dipped in flesh-colored paint and dried and hardened in the kiln.

Later the feet were dipped in black paint to color the shoes. All of the Ellis dolls have black feet. All other, later Springfield dolls except the so-called Martin doll have blue feet—a sort of bright Dutch blue. The bodies, with

Courtesy of Herbert Ellis.

Joel Ellis Toys—Toy piano and stool.
Catalogue of 1866.

heads attached, were dipped to the shoulders in flesh-colored paint and similarly hardened. Young women painted the hair light or dark, traced the eyebrows and eyelashes, colored lips and cheeks.

The delicate job of painting the eyes was entrusted to two young artists, the Misses Abbie and Emma Woodbury, daughters of Deacon Joel Woodbury of North Springfield, one of the uncles with whom Joel Ellis spent his orphaned boyhood. Miss Emma Woodbury, the younger sister, later became a successful miniature painter and was for some years connected with the Department of Fisheries in Washington, D. C., copying in water colors the

9

minute scales of living fish. The two sisters spent the last years of their lives together. Herbert Ellis, in a personal letter to this writer, adds this little human interest touch to their history:

"My father's cousins, the Woodbury sisters, died at their home in Rochester, N. Y., two or three years ago, upon the same day from natural causes, neither knowing that the other was near death. They were eighty-five and eighty-seven years of age."

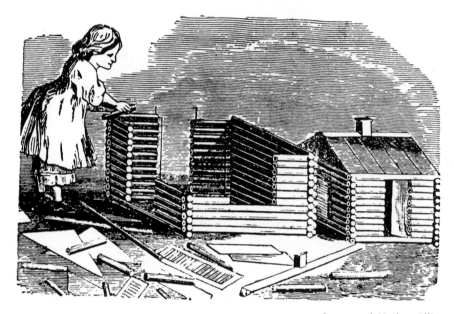

Courtesy of Herbert Ellis.

Joel Ellis Toys—Log cabin. Catalogue of 1866.

The Joel Ellis dolls were made in three sizes: small, medium and large (twelve, fifteen and eighteen inches), which sold at the wholesale prices of $9, $10.50 and $13.50 a dozen. Mr. Ellis does not remember how many were made—several hundred dozens, he thinks. Nearly all were white, the proportion of blondes and brunettes being about equal. Some few Negro dolls were painted for special orders. Note that he says *painted*.

Some writers have assumed that the Negro Ellis dolls had negroid features but this is incorrect. Queried on this point, Mr. Ellis replied:

10

"As to the Negro Joel Ellis dolls: there was but one style of doll head made in the three sizes, Nos. 1, 2, 3. The expense of making the steel dies was considerable. The Negro dolls were made as ordered, i.e. *painted*—and not made up for stock as were the regular faces."

Herbert Ellis says that the largest size was never so popular as the smaller sizes. Probably the reason for this lies in the fact that a doll of this size in solid rock maple would be uncomfortably heavy for a small child to handle.

Joel Ellis Toys—Rail fence. Catalogue of 1866.

(An 18-inch Ellis doll weighs about two pounds.) At any rate, this largest size is very scarce today and none of the Ellis dolls are very plentiful—as collectors know.

The year 1873 developed into a year of depression and financial panic. This, together with the fact that, as Herbert Ellis records in his monograph, the reception of the doll by the trade, while generous, was not sufficient to inspire confidence in its future, caused the company to abandon its manufacture and no more were ever made.

But these dolls were not the only products of the factory. When the twenty-six-year-old Joel Ellis returned to Springfield in the year 1856 and organized the firm of Ellis, Britain and Eaton, near-by timber-lands were purchased and suitable buildings erected, and the business, which included among its principal products baby carriages or "cabs," grew to be the largest manufacturing plant in Springfield, sending their goods even to California in sailing ships around Cape Horn.

In making the children's carriages, many kinds of lumber were used. Says Herbert Ellis: "The sides and bottoms of the body were maple—dash-boards and backs were bent basswood. The wheel hubs, spokes and wood axles were maple, the front tongues and rear perambulator handles were oak and the bows for carriage tops were made of ash. For boxing when shipping, strong cases were made of unplaned hemlock with maple or oak corner braces inside." All this timber was cut on the company's wood lots and dried and seasoned under their own sheds.

Certain toys predated the baby cab. The very first articles put out by the company were toy carts which Mr. Ellis describes as "consisting of a small body attached to an axle, two spoked wheels and a tongue in front, all made of wood. There was a little rim around the top edge of the body of the cart, the sides and ends were slanted inward toward the bottom so the bodies nested closely together in packing. . . . The bodies and wheels were painted in bright colors and varnished and the tongues were varnished on the plain wood."

Then followed four-wheel toy wagons, doll gigs with tops, and doll perambulators with four wheels and a top, and a double handle at the back. The manufacture of the baby cabs and perambulators—the first ever made in this country—was next started. Different models sold as low as $3.50 and as high as $25. The late President Calvin Coolidge rode in an Ellis baby cab in his infancy. The unpublished picture of his son John in the same carriage came to us through the courtesy of Mrs. Grace Coolidge. The carriage is now in the Ford Museum at Dearborn, Mich., a gift of President Coolidge to Henry Ford.

As time went on, new lines of toys were added, many of them designed to make use of what would otherwise have been waste wood. Among the articles added were doll beds, dining tables, doll's rocking chairs; some were made

Odd and unusual old dolls exhibited at Santa Ana Doll Show, 1946, at Charles W. Bowers Memorial Museum, Santa Ana, California. *Courtesy of the Museum.*

The so-called "Countess Dagmar" type in china. Displayed in daguerreotype setting designed by Mrs. F. E. Coulter, Curator of the Charles W. Bowers Memorial Museum, Santa Ana, California, and patented by her. *Doll loaned by Mrs. Ruby Selby.*

Left, Spanish doll found in stuffing of an upholstered chair. *Miss Grace Woodworth, Colorado Springs, Colorado. Right,* China doll found in an alley. *Collection of Mrs. Louis E. Lahn, Amarillo, Texas.*

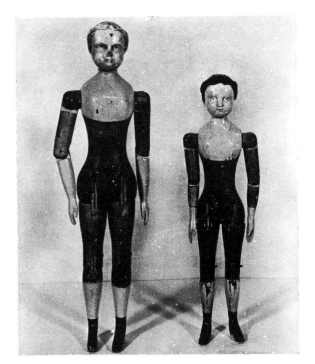

Left, Joel Ellis dolls, 1873. *Collection of Mr. and Mrs. John M. Pierce, Springfield, Vermont. Right*, Weather-vane from Joel Ellis factory. Preserved in Springfield, Vermont.

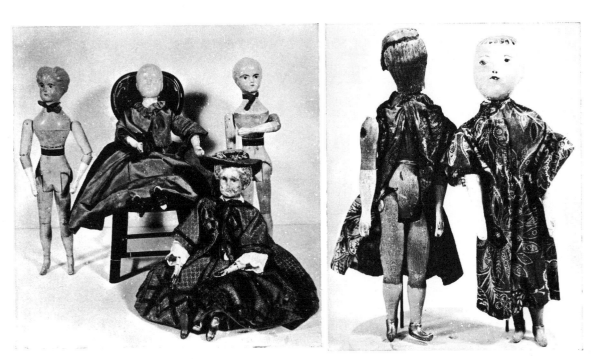

NOVELTY TYPES OF MASON AND TAYLOR DOLLS

Left, Baby doll in center—*collection of Miss Ruth Ellison, Springfield, Vermont.* Twins, "Willie" and "Tillie"—*collection of Mr. and Mrs. John M. Pierce, Springfield, Vermont.* Doll on floor—regular type Mason and Taylor doll with Johnson head. *Right*, Witch and Wizard dolls. *Collection of Mr. and Mrs. John M. Pierce, Springfield, Vermont.*

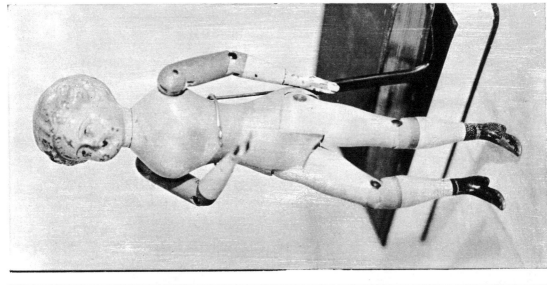

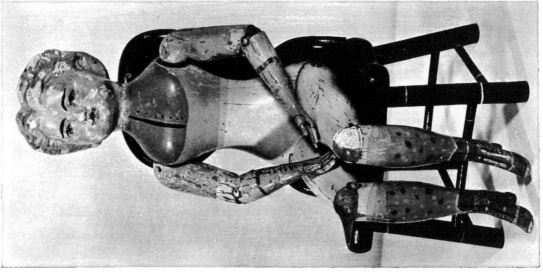

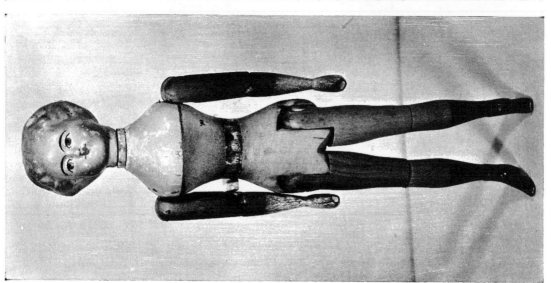

Left, Mason and Taylor doll with wooden "spoon" hands, 1880. *Collection of Mr. and Mrs. John M. Pierce, Springfield, Vermont. Center,* 17-inch pattern doll of the Martin doll (which is about 12 inches tall)—*The Springfield, Vermont, Public Library.* Chair made by Ellis. *Right,* Martin doll, 1879, made by Mason and Taylor on machines invented and made by Luke Taylor; rarest of the Springfield dolls. This specimen came from Ludlow, Vermont.

TYPES OF SPRINGFIELD DOLL

A. Joel Ellis doll. B. Mason and Taylor—Witch and Wizard doll. C. Rare "Martin" doll by Mason and Taylor. D. Mason and Taylor doll with metal hands. E. Joel Ellis doll showing method of attaching head. F. Early Mason and Taylor doll with wooden "spoon" hands.

Left, "Peg Wooden," old manikin doll from Springfield, Vermont. *Collection of Miss Blanche Mosse, Denison, Texas. Right,* "Pity Sakes" and "Old Pinkie," wooden dolls. *Collection of Mrs. Cyrus M. Beachy, Wichita, Kansas.*

Left, Old wooden doll made into pincushion. Belonged to descendants of William Dawes, who rode with Paul Revere, April 18, 1775. *Right,* Old New Hampshire wooden doll. *Courtesy of Mrs. Ralph E. Wakeman, Claremont, New Hampshire.*

Old wooden Negro doll. *Collection of Miss Alma Robeck, Annapolis, Maryland.*

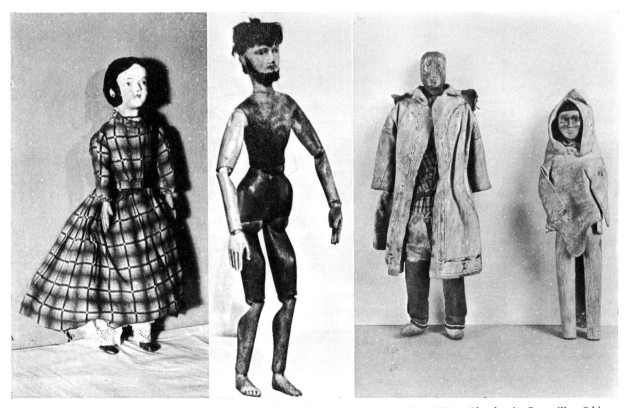

Left, Old wooden doll. Hair probably later than doll. *Collection of Mrs. Nina Shephard, Granville, Ohio.*
Center, Wooden Abraham Lincoln doll, Rochester, New York, 26 inches tall. *Courtesy of Mrs. William F.*
Harvey, Cortland, New York. Right, Wooden Indians from Connecticut. *Collection of Mrs. Chester Dimick,*
Gales Ferry, Connecticut.

Alice in Wonderland plywood toys by Ila Fifield, East Calais, Vermont.

Left, "Colonial Lady" and *right,* "Paul Revere." Both made by Mrs. H. A. Foster, Stowe, Vermont.

Redwood bark dolls by Mrs. Edith Groshong,
Fields Landing, California.

Left, Wooden Poppets from the Kentucky Mountains. *St. George Collection.* Right, Mrs. Ruggles, Practical
Nurse, made in Pennsylvania mountains. *Collection of Mrs. Cyrus M. Beachy, Wichita, Kansas.*

"*Schoenhut Doll*"

Welcome American Invention

1911 First

...ILLUSTRATED CATALOGUE...

DOLLS The A. Schoenhut Company

SOLE MANUFACTURERS

Philadelphia, Penna., U. S. A.

PATENTED IN THE
UNITED STATES AND
FOREIGN COUNTRIES

Cover of first catalogue of Schoenhut Dolls, 1911. Last dolls appeared in 1928 catalogue.

INGENIOUS CONSTRUCTION OF THE "Schoenhut Doll"

NOTICE:—NO rubber cord is used.

NO more loose joints.

NEVER needs restringing.

NO Broken Heads.

The "SCHOENHUT DOLL" is made of All Wood from Head to Foot, and is painted with Enamel Oil Colors, can be washed with a fine sponge or soft cloth.

SEE the Patent STEEL SPRING HINGES having

DOUBLE SPRING TENSIONS and

SWIVEL connections.

All parts tightly held together, at the same time all joints are very flexible, and move smoothly, and will stay in any correct position placed.

All our Dolls have Wrist and Ankle Joints.

Entirely made of Wood.

Even the head is solid wood.

Hands and Feet made of Hardwood.

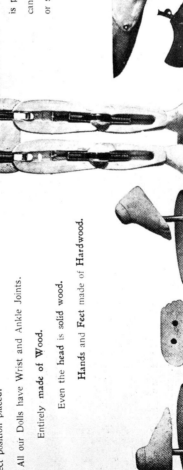

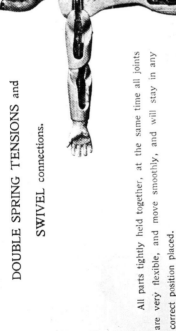

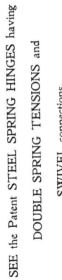

The feet of all "Schoenhut Dolls" are made of hardwood and have two holes in the soles to receive the post of our unique Metal Stand that goes with every Doll.

The shoes and stockings have two holes in the soles to correspond with those in the feet.

The one hole is straight to hold the foot resting flat, and the other hole is oblique to hold the foot in a tiptoe position.

See illustrations above.

Only one stand is necessary to support the Doll on one foot or the other.

Construction of Schoenhut Dolls.

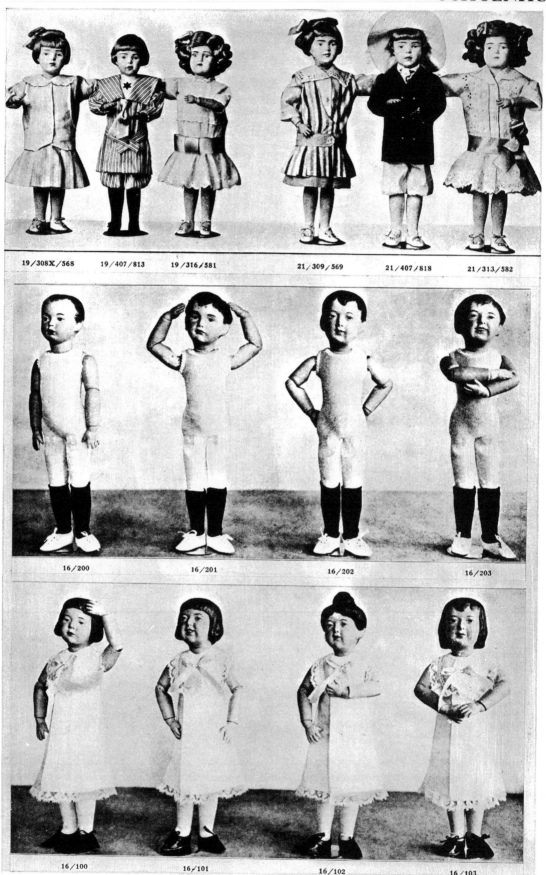

19/308X/568   19/407/813   19/316/581   21/309/569   21/407/818   21/313/582

16/200   16/201   16/202   16/203

16/100   16/101   16/102   16/103

Top, 1915 dolls, 19 and 21 inches. *Center,* Boys—undressed, carved wooden hair, 16 inches. *Bottom,* Girls with carved wooden hair, 16 inches.

DOLLS

"TOOTSIE WOOTSIE"

15/50   15/51   15/52

"SCHNICKEL-FRITZ"

15/77   15/75   15/76

19/175   19/175/1   19/175/2   19/175/3   19/175/4

Top, "Tootsie Wootsie," 15 inches. *Center*, "Schnickel-Fritz," 15 inches. *Bottom*, Schoenhut Manikin—for students of art or window display figures. . . .

Fully Jointed With Elastic Cord

Heads on These Dolls Copyright Dec. 31, 1913

14/107/550   (Fully Jointed)   17/108/551   13/107/552   (With Nature Arms and Legs)   15/108/553

13/107   15/108   14/107   17/108   14/107/554   17/108/555

Top, 1915 infant dolls, with painted hair or mohair wigs. *Center*, 1924 dolls jointed with elastic cord—last effort. *Bottom*, 1915 infant dolls with painted hair or mohair wigs. With nature arms and legs. Also with jointed arms and legs.

Size 22"

New! SCHOENHUT STUFFED DOLLS

WITH MAMMA VOICES

Hollow Wooden Heads, Strong and Durable
Fine Real Mohair Wigs   Very Prettily and Stylishly Dressed

Top, left, Walkable doll, 1919, with painted hair or mohair wigs. 11 inches and 17 inches. *Right,* Dolls with moveable, sleeping, all-wood eyes, 1921. "Doll faced" sizes 15, 17, 19½ and 22 inches tall. *Bottom,* Last Schoenhut doll, 1924

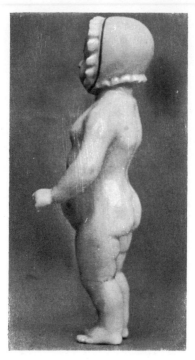

Left, Group of Penny dolls—china, bisque, and wooden. *Collection of Miss Alma Robeck, Annapolis, Maryland.* *Right,* 12-inch "Frozen Charlotte." *Collection of Mrs. Velma Fuller Von Bruns, Bristol, Vermont.*

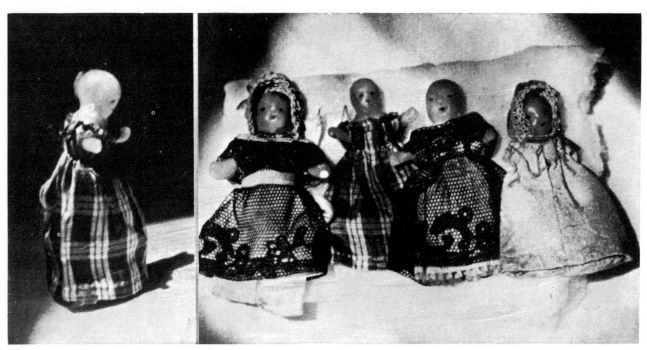

Left, Wax Penny doll, detail. *Right,* Wax Penny dolls, 1828. Belonged to granddaughter of William Dawes, who rode with Paul Revere.

without rockers to be used in sets with the dining table. Another interesting item was a toy piano and stool which sold for $20. All these articles of toy furniture were finished in imitation rosewood.

The pictures of the doll cabs and toys included herewith are copies of woodcuts from the *Seventh Annual Catalogue and Supplement* for the year 1866, which, like the earlier editions, was written and compiled by Joel Ellis himself. The title page of this catalogue reads:

SEVENTH ANNUAL
DESCRIPTIVE PRICE LIST
and
ILLUSTRATED CATALOGUE
of
CHILDREN'S CARRIAGES,
TOYS, & C.
made by
ELLIS, BRITAIN AND EATON
at the
VERMONT NOVELTY WORKS,
Springfield, Vermont
FOR 1866.

It bears the imprint:

NEW YORK
French and Wheat, Steam Printers, no. 18 Ann Street
1866.

On the back cover is listed the amount of sales in 219 towns and cities in the United States plus $261 worth of goods sold to Australia and $37.50 worth sold in London, England—a total for the year 1865 of $100,748.04—certainly a respectable business for a firm in a small Vermont town.

OTHER SPRINGFIELD DOLLS

SPRINGFIELD'S next venture in doll-making seems to have been the Mason and Taylor doll in 1879 and the early 1880's. The chief improvement of this over the Ellis doll lay in the improved joint patented by George W. Sanders of Springfield, December 7, 1880. The joint of the Ellis doll consisted of a slot into which a double tenon was slightly sprung to create a certain amount of friction, the tenon being held in the slot by a pin.

The Sanders patent was a combination of a ball and socket type with a mortise and tenon with recesses and stops. It was a stronger and more durable joint than that of the Ellis dolls.

There is a tradition in Springfield that George Sanders, who was a cabinet-maker of sorts, did not *invent* this joint. It is supposed that C. C. Johnson purchased the idea from the real inventor, whoever he was, and furnished money for Sanders to have it patented. U. S. Patent Office records show that the patent was assigned by Sanders to W. H. H. Slack of Springfield, Vt.

Henry E. Taylor, a son of Luke Taylor who made the Mason and Taylor dolls, still lives in Springfield where he has lived most of his life. He has represented the town in the State Legislature for several terms. He is nearly eighty years old.

Pictures of dolls discussed in this chapter will be found following page 12.

"Yes," said Mr. Taylor in an interview, "I worked on the Mason and Taylor doll when I was a boy, mornings and nights, before and after school, and during vacations.

"My father was a natural mechanic and he could not only make anything of wood, but could invent and make machinery needed for the work. He leased quarters in the old clothespin shop owned by Smith, Mason and Co., and this is where the Mason and Taylor dolls were manufactured. He did all sorts of custom wood-turning, and also wood-turning for Joel Ellis, who at that time was making toys, dice boxes, checkerboards and all sorts of games. Sometimes on a Saturday, he would take the team and deliver to Mr. Ellis' shop barrels of checkers, dice boxes, drum sticks, and so on.

"Henry Mason, one of the partners of Smith, Mason and Co., was a travelling man. Often after his trips through the country he would bring back some article to be manufactured. On one occasion I remember he brought back some folding camp chairs, and asked my father if he could make them. For a number of years after that, we manufactured those camp chairs.

"That also is the way the Mason and Taylor doll came to be manufactured. Mr. Mason brought the design for the dolls, and asked my father if he could make them, and father replied:

" 'Yes, if you want to go to the expense of making the special machinery it will require.'

"Mason gave him orders to go ahead. Father made most of the machinery himself. Each separate part of the doll required a special machine.

"The body of the doll was made of soft wood—poplar—and was turned from a square block of wood on a machine similar to those used in making shoe lasts. This lathe left the body somewhat pitted, and these irregularities were smoothed off on a sanding belt about $2\frac{1}{2}$ inches wide. I have done this part of the work many times, holding the body of the doll against the moving belt and turning it until all parts were smooth and finished.

"The arms and legs were made of rock maple or beech, and the feet were made of lead or pewter run onto the ankles through a mold. Some early dolls had rather crude wooden hands in one with the arms, which they called 'spoon hands.' Later the hands were molded on the molten lead or pewter. The hip joints of the earlier dolls were fastened with wooden pins, but later steel screws were used for the purpose.

"On May 31, 1881, Mason and Taylor patented a neck joint of wood with an iron pin through it, which was grooved in such a manner as to permit the head to turn. This is one of the features of the Mason and Taylor doll.

"They may have used some china or papier mâché heads in the beginning, but most of the heads were of a model design, consisting of a wooden core covered by composition. This paste was made of glue, rosin, plaster of Paris and I've forgotten what else, of the consistency of cookie paste. It was rolled out with a rolling pin and cut out with a round cookie cutter. Two of these circles were used for each head, one being put into each half of the mold which consisted of two four-inch-square blocks. Though simple, it would be difficult to explain without a diagram."

Mr. Taylor's reminiscences should serve to clear up much of the confusion that exists in the minds of collectors on the subject of the post-Ellis Springfield dolls. Most of this confusion has arisen because of the number of patents for doll parts granted to Springfield men—Martin, Sanders, Mason and Taylor and Johnson—between the years 1879 and 1882. It was at first thought that each of these patents represented a different doll-making enterprise and a different type of doll.

Mr. Taylor says that he has no recollection of any dolls having been made in Springfield other than the Joel Ellis and the Mason and Taylor dolls. This is confirmed by the finding by Mrs. Enid Pierce, a close student of existing Springfield dolls, of two Mason and Taylor dolls in their original wrappings, each of which wears around its waist a black paper band on which is printed the dates of all of the various patents. All Mason and Taylor dolls still show traces of having had a similar band around their waists. The single exception to this rule is the "Witch and Wizard doll," for the good reason that this special model had none of the patented features. It was cheaply made, 10½ inches tall, with the standard Mason and Taylor body; legs and arms, without knee and elbow joints, were shapely and graceful. The legs were fastened to the body at the hips with wooden pins and the arms were fastened to the shoulders with metal pins. Wooden spoon hands like those on the earliest

Mason and Taylor dolls were used and the blue feet had a special type of metal shoe with toes that turned up. The heads, attached by the toggle joint which enabled the doll to be decapitated without losing its head, were rather flat on top and oriental in features. These dolls—the only ones dressed at the factory—came clad in red kimonos flowered in Oriental designs.

In the group picture following page 12 are shown two unusual or novelty types of Mason and Taylor dolls. Seated on the Joel Ellis chair in the center is a "baby" doll owned by Miss Ruth Ellison of Springfield, Vt. It has a Johnson head, Sanders joints, hands of composition with plump wrists and baby hands. The feet are also composition. On either side of the "baby" stand the twins, "Tillie" and "Willie" which Mrs. John M. Pierce of Springfield bought in their original wrappings from an elderly workman formerly employed in the factory.

"Willie," the boy twin, has quite a distinct type of face.

One of the weak points in all the Springfield dolls is the paint. Few examples of either the Ellis or the Mason and Taylor dolls can be found today with the paint on heads and hands in original condition. Another weakness is noted in the metal feet and hands which are often missing. It is of interest to note that the hands of the two groups are different in that the hands on the Ellis dolls are held with fingers curved while those of the Mason and Taylor dolls are practically straight.

The "Martin doll," which is the rarest of all the Springfield dolls—only very, very few of them have come to light—is unquestionably the first product of the Mason and Taylor enterprise. It is identical with the other Mason and Taylor dolls in materials, proportions and workmanship and must have been made on the same machines—which Mr. Taylor tells us were made by his father, Luke Taylor. They differ chiefly in having the hemispherical joints patented by Frank D. Martin of Springfield, April 29, 1879. This patent says: "The upper part or top end of the arms fitting into the socket of the shoulder is held in position by means of an elastic or spiral spring passing transversely through the top of the trunk from shoulder to shoulder." A "pattern doll" 17½ inches tall owned in Springfield, Vt., has the steel spring but the specimen owned by this writer, which is entirely in original condition, is 12 inches tall and has the elastic. Mason and Taylor controlled this patent as is shown by the fact that its date appears with the others on the paper waistbands.

The Martin dolls have the metal feet and hands similar to the Ellis dolls, and like those of the Ellis doll, the feet are black. These dolls have immovable heads, 6½ inches in circumference, which is a half inch more than the later Johnson head used on the later Mason and Taylor dolls. Mr. Henry Taylor has said that they "may have used some papier mâché and china heads in the beginning." None with china heads have so far come to light.

In the 1943 supplement to Doll Collectors of America Inc.'s *American Made Dolls and Figurines*, there is pictured a colored Springfield doll owned by Mrs. Winifred Harding of Woodstock, Vt., which is described as representing "a native of India" and as having been "made in 1874 by the H. H. Mason Co." In the light of Mr. Taylor's first-hand information, both maker and date of this doll now have to be revised.

There is no record to show that H. H. Mason ever had anything to do with the manufacture of dolls earlier than 1879, when, as a partner in the firm of Smith, Mason and Co., he brought the doll design to Luke Taylor with the question: "Can we make this doll?"

Mrs. Harding's doll has all the patented features of the Mason and Taylor doll—Sanders joint, Johnson head and the movable neck joint patented by Mason and Taylor (probably invented by Luke Taylor). On the black band around its waist is printed: *"Improved joint patented April 29, 1879."*

This is the Martin patent date so the doll could not have been made any earlier, and since it was the Sanders and not the Martin joint that was used on it, it must have been made later than that date. Moreover, it was, clearly, made on the machines which had been made and installed by Luke Taylor. It would therefore seem to be one of the "novelty dolls" and one of the "Negro dolls" which according to Mr. Taylor were made by Mason and Taylor.

On the testimony of the sons of Springfield's two great doll-makers (and two of the three sons, Hartley Ellis and Henry E. Taylor, actually worked on the dolls) it seems that all wooden dolls made at Springfield may be classified as either "Joel Ellis" or "Mason and Taylor." This certainly simplifies a complicated question and solves a heretofore dark mystery. The solution is a rather simple one, too—going back to original sources while those who can speak with authority on the subject are still in our midst.

EARLY WOODEN DOLLS

T HE OLD HAND-CARVED wooden dolls have a charm all their own, an individuality as varied as the long-dead hands that wrought them. Except for rag dolls, colonial children had little else than these. Pioneer fathers whittled them out in the evenings by the light of the log fires, along with the wooden dowels that held together the logs and rafters of their houses and barns—just as they hewed and whittled out bowls, trenchers, wooden spoons, sap spouts and other necessary utensils. The Yankee, particularly the Vermont Yankee, has always been a skilled and industrious whittler.

Generally these early dolls were crude and unadorned but occasionally one finds attempts to "pretty" them, as with the corkscrew curl down either side of the face of the old Salem doll shown following page 12. This doll was found by Mrs. Ralph E. Wakeman in Claremont, N. H. The owner, a woman past eighty-five, had had it as long as she could remember and said it had been her mother's.

"Pity Sakes" and "Old Pinkie"—delightful names—are in the collection of Mrs. Cyrus M. Beachy of Wichita, Kansas. "Pity Sakes," wooden throughout and of frail structure, is supposed to have been made for some little Pennsylvania Dutch girl. Her hands and feet are stubs, to avoid breakage.

Pictures of dolls discussed in this chapter will be found following page 12

"Old Pinkie," says Mrs. Beachy, "is of European origin and is 'sure enough' *old*. Her legs and arms are slender sticks of wood wrapped with very old newspapers. The legs and arms are tacked to a wooden torso that is nearly V-shaped. Blotches of red paint are on her cheeks. Her cotton dress is older than it looks in the picture. She wears an odd affair of cloth on her head as a bonnet."

Miss Blanche Mosse of Denison, Texas, has an 18-inch wooden manikin which she calls "Peg Wooden" because he is put together with wooden pegs. It was given her by a friend who lived in Springfield, Vt., who said it was brought there by John Nott in 1752. As stated elsewhere, John Nott was the first settler of Springfield, Vt. "Peg Wooden" has ball joints, and can sit or stand and curl his legs, feet, arms and hands into almost any position. A similar doll is in the collection of Mrs. John T. Buchanan of Omaha, Nebr. These dolls are probably artist's models of the seventeenth and early eighteenth century. (Compare the artist's manikin made by Schoenhut in 1915.)

Of New England origin are two old Indian dolls in the collection of Mrs. Chester Dimick, Gales Ferry, Conn. The brave is 11½ inches tall; the squaw, 14 inches. The squaw has cloth arms; the brave has no arms. The face of the man is well carved; he has black painted hair, and wears a doeskin coat with a parka or hood, but no trousers or moccasins. The squaw, not so well carved, has no hair. She wears bead-trimmed doeskin trousers, calico waist, doeskin coat with painted decorations, doeskin moccasins, red wool stockings, and a wool cap with bead trim.

Another very quaint primitive doll in Mrs. Dimick's collection is a 19-inch woman, fully jointed; the face carved and painted, the hair carved in ridges with a "bun" at the top of the head. Her wooden feet are painted green.

Among the several interesting wooden dolls owned by Miss Alma Robeck, of Annapolis, Md., is a Negro boy with pearl buttons set in for eyes and set-in teeth. He is made of chestnut wood and is jointed at shoulders, hips and knees. Although made in America and said to have been loaned to the Salem Museum for some years, this doll considerably resembles an ebony group of two contending figures on a single base—probably primitive gods or fetishes—

which have white stones set in for eyes and mouths. These figures were brought from Africa to Fort Ethan Allen by an American army officer and were purchased by the present owner, Mrs. Rose Parro of Waterbury, Vt., at an auction of effects when the officer left the Fort for other duty.

The bearded wooden figure whose picture was sent by Mrs. William F. Harvey, Cortland, N. Y., represents Abraham Lincoln and is one of a pair of "Lincoln" dolls carved for two little sisters in Rochester, N. Y., in 1863. Mrs. Harvey sold this doll for $150 several years ago and its present owner is unknown.

In every country of the Old World, the wooden doll has an honorable history from the flat, gaily painted wooden dolls from the tombs of the Egyptians, now in the British Museum, to the small wooden "Dutch" dolls, beloved of Queen Victoria, which grace the Albert and Victoria Museum.

The lonely little Princess Victoria played with dolls until, at fourteen, she had to put away childish things to prepare for the heavy responsibilities of her future state. Wax dolls were made in England, and papier mâché dolls were plentiful so she must have preferred wooden dolls as almost every one of her 132 dolls was of this same type, differing only in size—from 3 to 9 inches tall.

The book, *Queen Victoria's Dolls,* thus describes them: "There is the queerest mixture of infancy and matronliness in their little wooden faces due to the combination of small sharp nose and bright vermilion cheeks (consisting of a dab of paint in one spot), with broad placid brows, over which, neatly parted at each temple, are painted elaborate, elderly, grayish curls. The remainder of the hair is coal black and is relieved by a tiny yellow comb perched upon the back of the head."

Thirty-two of the dolls were dressed by the Princess herself, the remainder by her governess, Baroness Lehzen. Their costumes copy, with minute attention to detail, the gowns of ladies of the court or theatrical persons of the day. It is probably the most famous collection of costume dolls in the world.

The dolls from the collections of Mrs. Cyrus M. Beachy and of Mrs. Kenneth Colburn of California, serve to illustrate the type. Mrs. Colburn's doll was brought from Canada 125 years ago by her husband's grandmother.

Mrs. Nina Shepherd of Granville, Ohio, who has been collecting old dolls for years, has a special fondness for these small wooden dolls and has found ten of them varying from three to ten inches in height.

Mrs. Shepherd also has a very unusual wooden doll with a sort of plaster or composition hair in which is a comb with three red stones. There are red earrings that match the comb. The doll wears its original plaid dress. This doll is a bit of a puzzle since by its history and structure of its all-wood body, it dates back to the 1770's, yet the hair is arranged in the style worn in 1837–40 with braids coming from the front, looped *under* the exposed ears, and joining a knot in the back. One ventures a guess that the hair is a later addition. Be that as it may, the doll is an interesting and quaint little person.

Quite remarkable is Mrs. Blanche Watson's hollow wooden baby doll made by a Philadelphia cabinet-maker in 1840 and her 110-year-old "Brother Mo," whose body, hands and feet are whittled of wood and polished like glass. The parts are all hollow and strung with homespun linen tape. He has old blown-glass eyes, brown, set a little slanting, which gives him an Oriental look. He is completely bald. "Brother Mo," 28 inches tall, was born in Philadelphia and seems to represent a particular era.

DOLLS FROM THE FORESTS

"STORE" DOLLS do not come to the children of the remote settlement of the Kentucky mountains. In their place are "Poppets," primitive homemade dolls, whittled out by the mothers with a jackknife from the wood of the native buckeye tree. This is a soft, fine-grained wood of pale color. Rosy cheeks are added by rubbing the faces with the juice of cohosh or poke-berries. Hair is provided from the skins of small wild animals, such as squirrels or moles, or the wool of domestic sheep. Occasionally a bit of bear skin would be considered more realistic on the men poppets. The dolls are dressed in homespun or such materials as may be found in the mountain stores.

The mission schools and handicraft centers established in the Southern Appalachians made it possible for the mountain folk to sell their handiwork, weaving, basketry, etc., to the outside world and add to their meagre incomes.

Two sisters, Mrs. Anne Green Williams of Ary, Ky., and Mrs. Orlenia Ritchie of Viper, Ky., who had made these dolls for their own children, just as their mother and grandmother had made them so long as they could remember, began to make the Poppets for sale.

"These women, now quite old, live on farms, care for their gardens, a few chickens, cows and the general run of work farm women do in this

Pictures of dolls discussed in this chapter will be found following page 12.

section," writes Lula M. Hale, director of "Homeplace" of the E. O. Robinson Mountain Fund at Ary, Pretty County, Ky. "The making of the dolls for sale was not their aim originally—the first ones were made for the children to play with." (Now they are no longer being made. It took about ten hours to carve and dress a doll that sold for a dollar and when the Wage and Hour Law was passed in 1938 the sale of these dolls was no longer permitted as they did not comply with the restrictions of the law. It is an example of the hardship which a law, beneficial to many, may work upon the few.)

Up north in the shadow of Mt. Mansfield in the Green Mountains of Vermont, another farm housewife, seventy-three-year-old Mrs. H. A. Foster of Stowe, has created a truly American doll in her "Paul Revere," made from old yellow pine salvaged from the remodelling of the old First Congregational-Unitarian Church of Burlington for which, tradition says, Paul Revere cast the bell Mrs. Foster's doll is modelled on the china head type and painted to resemble them. "Paul's" black military boots are carved from wood as are his head and hands. The body is cotton stuffed with sawdust. His hair, painted reddish brown, is parted far to one side, as in the Atheneum portrait. His uniform, cleverly tailored by Mrs. Foster, consists of small clothes and vest of gray-blue and a greatcoat of darker blue with military brass buttons that are gilded shoe buttons. The lady dolls she makes are dressed in old materials with equal skill and ingenuity.

Let Mrs. Foster tell her own story:

"The way I began making dolls, I wanted to buy an old family doll from a cousin but he would not let me have it, so one day I thought I would try to carve out one of my own. My folks laughed at me but it made no difference. I went at it and they could not say anything when I got it made. I took it to an art and craft show and had an order for one from a friend. I made her one. She let someone see it and that one wanted a doll. That doll went to New Hampshire.

"I sold them in Massachusetts, New York, New Jersey, Washington, D. C., Florida, Burlington, Vt.; Barre, Vt., and Stowe, Vt. Three of my dolls were in Washington, D. C., for the month of April, 1940, at the Vermont Craft Show. One of them was sold.

25

"I have not had as much time to work at them as I wish I had. It takes quite a lot of time to put on the faces, carving them out and painting them. Sometimes I have to work all afternoon before it suits me, but I do enjoy making them. I tell folks that I have as good times as I used to have when I played with them. My girls say they wish I had made them when they were small—but I had something to do then.

"If more people would try doing things, see what they can do. You are never too *old* to learn to do something."

The hero of Mary Bryan Waller's *The Wood-carver of 'Lympus* (best seller of the early 1900's), a crippled lad in a lonely Vermont mountain home, learning the joys of self-expression and of useful work through the encouragement and guidance of a passing stranger, was the prototype of thirty-five-year-old Ila Fifield of East Calais, Vt. (Vermonters pronounce it "Calas"), who makes those fascinating plywood figures of the *Alice in Wonderland* characters.

Crippled by polio when a young child, Ila came under the supervision of Mrs. Eugene C. Rhodes, director of occupational therapy of the Vermont Department of Health, in 1925. A friend, returning from Europe, had given Mrs. Rhodes a set of English figures of the Alice characters—crude, cheap stencilled affairs. Ila was set to work copying these, but her native artistic ability led to her improving on the models, and, aided by her mother, a talented though untrained artist, added new figures, such as the White Rabbit and Fish Footman, until they are a completely different set of toys.

When her tubercular mother died, and, a year later, her father disappeared, Ila was left to shift for herself and has been a substitute operator in the small telephone office at East Calais, making the dolls in spare time.

Far across the continent in the Sierras, material for still other dolls has been furnished by the redwood trees of California. The bark of the full-grown redwood tree is from one to two feet thick, a rich purplish brown in color. From this bark, Mrs. Edith Groshong of Field's Landing, Calif., has made thousands of dolls: "Dollie Redwood" who wears a little hat trimmed with redwood cones; "Ramona Redwood" with hat and cape of bark; "Chief Big Tree" and "Princess Sequoia," quaint little ten-inch Indians. The dolls and their clothing are made of shredded bark. Mrs. Groshong shreds the bark with, she says, the help of an ordinary spring mousetrap, and she molds the quaint little faces of composition. These dolls are patented.

An interesting redwood doll, so typically American that it should be in every collection, is "The Padre" commemorating the old Spanish Missions of California founded by Father Junipero Serra and his fellow Franciscans for the Christianizing of the Indians.

The head, feet and arms of the doll are carved of redwood and the austere figure is clad in a habit and cowl of red-brown crêpe—the color of the wood. A rosary and a rope girdle completed the costume. Accompanying it is a bronze bell on a standard—replica of the markers of the *Camino Reale* (The King's Highway), the old road from San Diego to San Francisco by which the Franciscans travelled from mission to mission. The markers were designed by Mrs. G. F. C. Forbes, whose hobbies are California history and the making of bells. The dolls are carved by a handicapped man under the auspices of Good Will Industries of San Diego Co., Calif., Olin W. Gillespie, Manager.

Kimport Dolls of Independence, Mo., features many "State" dolls and quite a few of these are made of wood and are the work of native craftsmen. Among them are jointed dolls of cedar from the Tennessee mountains, spruce dolls from the Ozarks, and Katchinas made of cottonwood root. The Ozark spruce dolls are no longer being made, however, because the maker "got religion" and interprets literally the Biblical injunction against making any "graven image."

Avis Lee of Chicago has been carving dolls for the past six years and her dolls, featured by Marshall Field's, are to be found in collections throughout the country.

"I am self-taught so far as carving and costuming are concerned," says Miss Lee, "learning to carve by the simple expedient of having picked up a knife and finding a talent for whittling, which by continual practice has improved enough to be rated as 'carving.' I do everything myself from research on history and costume to printing small tags for each doll. I make use of any of the following woods: basswood, yellow poplar, gumwood, white pine and holly."

Her dolls are American types, ranging from "story book" dolls and child-types which she calls "Tykes" to various historical and regional characters called "Americanettes." Her doll-making is a full time job.

Such wooden dolls as those described in this chapter fit well into collections of either antique or modern dolls and would in themselves make an interesting collection.

THE SCHOENHUT DOLLS

FAMILY SURNAMES often have their origin in the occupation of the founder or some circumstance connected with his means of livelihood. According to family tradition, the Schoenhut family of Wurtemburg, Germany—wood-carvers and toy-makers for generations—derived their surname from the fact that the first wood-carving ancestor had made and hung above the entrance to his shop, as a sign, a large and finely carved wooden hat. The name means "beautiful hat."

About the time that the fertile mind of Joel Ellis was beginning to dream up his unbreakable wooden doll, Albert Schoenhut, a seventeen-year-old boy, left Wurtemburg for America. He settled in Philadelphia, firmly resolved to follow any other occupation than the one in which he had been so thoroughly schooled—the family trade of toy-making.

He did find other work, but, a stranger in a strange land, he occupied his lonely evenings by working in the cellar of his home constructing a toy piano for the little daughter of his landlord. A caller who saw the piano begged Albert to make one like it for his own little girl. When these two were finished, others who saw them also wanted pianos—and so a business was born.

Two of Albert's brothers, both skilled wood-carvers, followed him to America about this time, one settling in Philadelphia, the other in Buffalo.

Pictures of dolls discussed in this chapter will be found following page 12.

The Philadelphia brother went to work for Albert. The latter was naturally an organizer and executive, and this brother became, in effect, hands to carry out his ideas.

Experimenting with other toy musical instruments, Albert soon recognized the fact that there were limits to the possibilities in this type of thing and turned to making other toys: miniature shooting galleries, toy houses, etc. His ideas were considerably influenced by photographs that came from his old home, showing toys displayed at the annual toy fairs in Germany.

One of the most successful of his products was the Schoenhut Circus, parts of which ranged in price from $1 to $35 according to the number of figures. These figures—animals, ringmaster and clowns—were jointed with rubber cord and able to assume various realistic positions.

The cord with which they were jointed was purchased from the same man in Philadelphia for many years. This maker wove the covering of the rubber from threads of a different color each year so that by examining the cords one could tell by its color exactly the year in which the toy had been made.

What small boy could possibly resist a mule that could—and apparently did—kick the clown halfway across the ring? Even grownups were fascinated by the displays of the circus set up in stores at the Christmas seasons.

Members of the Schoenhut family do not recall the name of the man who conceived the original circus idea—perhaps they may never have known it, for it was a highly personal transaction between Albert and the inventor.

He was a stranger when he appeared in Albert's office with three wooden toys: a clown, a ladder and a chair. To judge by the few known facts of the transaction it may be supposed that their conversation ran something like this:

"I'll sell these to you for one hundred dollars cash."

Schoenhut studied the figures carefully: "But, man, you'd be foolish to sell this outright. It's a good idea—has great possibilities for development. It *can* be a moneymaker. I will give you a fair royalty, if you will sell it to me on that basis . . ."

The man shook his head. "I want $100 in cash—*now*" and he continued to insist stubbornly on the point.

THE SCHOENHUT DOLLS

"But why?"

"Well, Mr. Schoenhut, the truth is, I am having trouble with my wife and I want to leave her! A hundred dollars is all I need to take me far enough away so that I won't ever see her again. I am tired of quarrelling."

So, in the interests of the inventor's domestic peace, Albert Schoenhut paid him the sum he requested and never saw the man again.

It was thirty-eight years after the establishment of the business in Philadelphia that Albert Schoenhut invented the unbreakable all-wood doll that we know as the "Schoenhut doll." In Germany primitive wooden dolls had been made more than a hundred years before—in 1796—by Anton Wilhelm Schoenhut, Albert's grandfather; and from 1830 to 1860 less primitive ones were made by Albert's father, Frederick Wilhelm Schoenhut. It is hardly surprising that the son and grandson of these two men should see the possibilities of wood in doll-making.

The Schoenhut doll was put on the market in 1911. The head material was basswood on the end of the grain. In the process of manufacture, the heads were roughed out and then carved; later put under heavy pressure in hot molds which burned away the rough places, leaving the surface as smooth as glass.

The roughing out was done on a multiple carving machine. The number of heads that could be made at one time depended on their size. The mold in which the carving was done was 12 inches—or, at most, 14 inches long; into this were put various matrices according to what the maker desired to carve, whether an elephant's body or a doll head of any size. Only two of the largest size heads could be done at one time. The actual carving was done by a Weymouth lathe such as is used in making shoe lasts and similar to the one used on Joel Ellis dolls forty years earlier.

The most remarkable feature of the dolls was the way they were jointed, with what was described in the 1911 catalogue as "our new patent steel spring hinge, having double spring tension and swivel connection." This joint, patented in 1911, enabled the dolls to take and hold any pose that a human being could assume. Having no rubber cord used in the construction, there could never be any loose joints and the dolls would never need restringing.

The dolls were painted with enamel oil colors and could be washed.

When they first came out, they were made only in one size—16 inches, but later there were other sizes and models. The dolls with molded hair and those with mohair wigs were made in about equal numbers and came on the market simultaneously in 1911. Dolls came either undressed or dressed in "up-to-date" children's styles. The retail prices ranged from $2 to $5.

Albert Schoenhut had six sons. As they grew up, each one was specially trained for some part of the work and all of them took a turn on the road selling so that they might meet the customers and know all phases of the business.

The first heads, those of the 1911 dolls, were from models made by Graziano, a well-known sculptor of the day, who was a member of a noble Italian family. The features of the faces he modelled proved to be too old, as of children from eight to ten years old instead of those one to two years old.

During these first years of the doll business, Harry E. Schoenhut was attending a Philadelphia art school where his teacher in modelling and sculpture was Charles Graffly. Mr. Graffly it was who recommended a Mr. Leslie as a successor to Graziano. Leslie made the prettiest heads and faces, and his models were used in 1912 and until about 1916 when Harry Schoenhut, having finished his art training, took over the designing department and made the models used from then on.

In 1915, the company brought out an attractive line of infant dolls "with Nature Arms and Legs (curved)." These came in sizes 14 and 17 inches and could be had with either the molded hair or mohair wigs as desired.

Two special character types in infant dolls were "Schnickel-Fritz," a laughing, mischievous-looking baby, and "Tootsie Wootsie," a more sober-faced toddler. These dolls were 15 inches tall and had the molded hair. They had been registered with the U. S. Patent Office in 1911.

This year also came larger dolls, 19 and 21 inches tall, mostly with mohair wigs. The head of one of the boy dolls in this group is said to have been copied directly from a German doll head. This lad is dressed in the typical "Buster Brown" style: white linen suit, red reefer, and floppy cloth hat. The comic strip character, "Buster Brown," had as potent an influence on the clothes worn by small boys in the early 1900's as had Mrs. Frances Hodgson Burnett's Victorian hero, Little Lord Fauntleroy, in an earlier day.

The "Schoenhut Manikin," designed "For Students of Fine Art or as Dressed Figures for Window Displays," was presented in 1915. This is probably the rarest of all the Schoenhut dolls from the collector's standpoint. Only one thousand of them were ever made. A few of these were sold as artists' models; some of the dressed figures—basketball player, football player, baseball player, and farmer boy in overalls and straw hat—were sold for window displays and quite a number of them were junked and destroyed when the company went out of business. This Manikin was 19 inches tall and the list price of it was $42 per dozen undressed; the price of the dressed types being $66 per dozen for the baseball player or farmer boy and $72 a dozen for the football player and basketball player.

Up to 1919 all the Schoenhut dolls had "character faces." That year they issued four dolls with conventional "doll faces" to imitate bisque heads, in response to continuing demands for this type. The "imitation glass eyes" were not moveable; the wigs, mohair, and the sizes 15, 17, 19½ and 22 inches.

In 1919 also came the "Schoenhut Walkable Doll." It was not a mechanical doll but had a special arrangement of wires so that by holding it by the arm and proceeding slowly it actually walked. It was jointed at the shoulders so that the arms could move and at the hips so that it could sit, but all other joints were eliminated. The "Walkable Doll" was made in three infant sizes, 11, 14, and 17 inches.

The innovation that was introduced in 1921 was movable eyes that were put in some of the dolls with imitation bisque heads—"Movable eyes, Unbreakable Wooden Eyes, Imitation Glass Eyes," to quote the sales catalogue of that year. The mechanism of these wooden eyes is so interesting that the transcript of the patent application is reprinted here.

The business of the Schoenhut firm had its first great setback during the depression of 1921, which followed the close of the First World War. The causes of the trouble were various—the slump in sales caused by the depression; the competition from Germany's cheap labor; the fact that the all-wood doll was too heavy; and perhaps bad merchandising in relationships between the

UNITED STATES PATENT OFFICE.

HARRY E. SCHOENHUT, OF PHILADELPHIA, PENNSYLVANIA, ASSIGNOR TO THE A. SCHOENHUT COMPANY, OF PHILADELPHIA, PENNSYLVANIA, A CORPORATION OF PENNSYLVANIA.

DOLL.

1,390,820. Specification of Letters Patent. **Patented Sept. 13, 1921.**

Application filed March 22, 1920. Serial No. 367,960.

To all whom it may concern:

Be it known that I, HARRY E. SCHOENHUT, a citizen of the United States, residing in Philadelphia, Pennsylvania, have invented
5 certain Improvements in Dolls, of which the following is a specification.

One object of my invention is to improve the construction of the movable eyes of dolls so that they can be mounted to rotate freely
10 in sockets without pivot pins.

A further object of the invention is to provide an eye member for a doll, which can be readily assembled in a solid head.

This invention is especially adapted for
15 use in connection with heads made of a solid piece of wood in which a cavity is formed for the reception of the eye member, which is allowed to turn freely therein.

In the accompanying drawings:
20 Figure 1 is a sectional view of a portion of a doll's head illustrating my invention, the section being on the line 1—1, Fig. 3;

Fig. 2 is a sectional view on the line 2—2, Fig. 3;
25 Fig. 3 is a rear view with the back section of the head removed, and showing the eye member in place;

Fig. 4 is a view, similar to Fig. 3, showing the sockets for the eye member;
30 Fig. 5 is a perspective view of the eye member; and

Fig. 6 is a perspective view of the disk, which holds the eye member in the sockets.

Referring to the drawings, 1 is the head
35 of a doll made of a solid block of wood, in the present instance, having a recess 2 at the back, closed by a back section 1ᵃ of the head, as shown in Fig. 1. This recess extends well toward the front of the doll's head, and in
40 the recess are two sockets 4. The front walls of the sockets have openings 3, similar to the natural eye openings. Mounted in the sockets are the ball sections 5 of the eye member 6, made as shown in Fig. 5.
45 These two ball sections are connected together by a bar 7 to which is attached a wire 8 having a weight 9, forming a pendulum. Representations of eyes are formed on the ball sections 5 by painting, decalco-
50 mania, or other means. The sockets 4 are shaped to conform to the shape of the balls

of the eye member, as clearly shown in Fig. 1. The ball sections of the eye member are held in the sockets by a disk 10 of any suitable material, preferably flexible, and in the 55 present instance, this material is cardboard which is secured in place by tacks 11, or other suitable fastenings. The cardboard disk is slotted at 12 to allow free movement of the weighted wire or pendulum 8. 60

While the balls 5 of the eye member fit snugly in the sockets they are free to turn therein and the representations of eyes are so placed in relation to the pendulum that when the face of the doll is in an upright 65 position, the eyes are exposed, but when the doll is in a recumbent position the representation of the eyelids, which are above the eyes, are exposed, simulating sleep.

By this construction, all pivot pins are 70 dispensed with and the eye members can be readily assembled and secured in position without expert manipulation, and the eye section can be removed and repaired or replaced without difficulty. 75

I claim:—

1. The combination of a substantially solid doll's head having a recess at the back, eye sockets spaced apart and extending from said recess toward the front of the head, said 80 sockets having eye openings at their forward ends; an eye member consisting of a cross bar having a ball at each end; a representation of an eye on each ball member; a pendulum depending from the cross bar; 85 and a disk holding the balls in the sockets so that they will turn freely therein.

2. The combination of a doll's head having a recess at the back, two sockets connected to the recess; an eye member having 90 a cross bar; a ball at each end of the cross bar, the front portions of the sockets conforming to the shape of the ball members; a pendulum depending from the cross member; a weight at the end of the pendulum; 95 and a flexible disk secured to the head of the doll at the inner end of the recess and retaining the eye balls in their sockets, the disk being slotted for the free movement of the pendulum.

HARRY E. SCHOENHUT.

Patent papers and drawings for Schoenhut wooden sleeping eye with plastic lens.

1,390,820.

Patented Sept. 13, 1921.

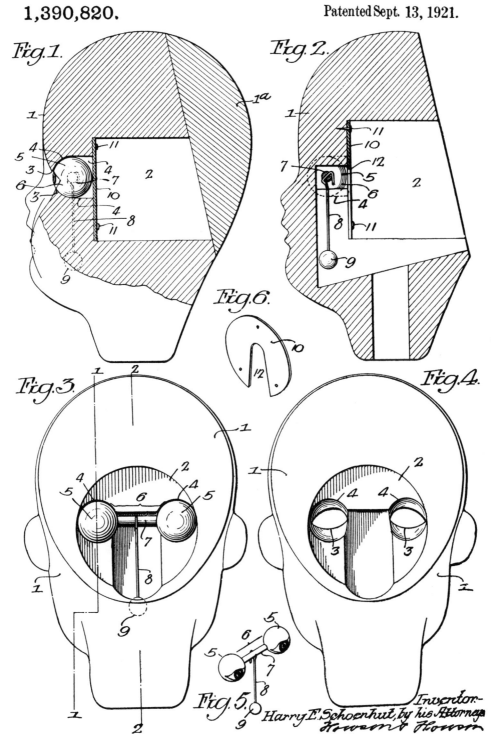

Fig.1.

Fig.2.

Fig.6.

Fig.3.

Fig.4.

Fig.5.

Inventor-
Harry E. Schoenhut, by his Attorney

company and department stores. Instead of reducing their prices when sales fell off, they raised their prices in some instances, cheapened their product in others. In consequence stock piled up on their shelves.

Their efforts to keep afloat and to save their basic idea—a doll with an unbreakable wooden head—can be traced in the descriptive catalogue of the period. It had been their boast in 1911 that no rubber was used in the joints and that therefore the joints would be indestructible—as they practically were. In their 1924 catalogue they were saying:

"In order to comply with a general demand for a cheaper, though good, fully jointed unbreakable doll, we have decided to make a condensed line of Wooden Dolls, jointed with *elastic cord* instead of *metal* springs, thereby *reducing* the *price*.

"This new line in appearance will be exactly the same as the All-Wood Doll, but will not pose and hold its position as perfectly as the metal-spring jointed doll; nevertheless, it will surpass all other similar jointed dolls.

"Metal stands *will not* be furnished with the new line!" Up to this time, every Schoenhut doll had been accompanied by an ingenious little metal stand, a round disk with a single upright peg. The shoes and feet of the dolls were equipped with two holes in the bottom of each foot to receive the post which helped in the doll taking various poses.

The Swan Song of the doll business of this company was in this catalogue of 1924—it was "Schoenhut Stuffed Dolls With Mama Voices. Hollow wooden heads, Strong and Durable. Fine Real Mohair Wigs. Very Prettily and Stylishly Dressed." This cheapened imitation of a really great doll was the end. No more of the dolls were made after 1924. The company was liquidated in 1935.

Mrs. Emma C. Clear, who introduced the dolls in Buffalo in 1911, writes interestingly on the subject of their passing:

"There was no interest in the dolls when they went off the market. Specialty shops like ours had no trouble in selling them but they did not go well in the big stores where most of the business was done during the holiday rush. Sold by clerks who were extra Christmas help, knowing nothing about dolls except the price tag, to customer who knew no more, they were smaller, relatively more expensive, and, to the casual buyer, looked no better than the big cheap glue and sawdust ones. I would class them as the best play dolls ever brought out.

"Collectors had not then become interested in them. Today perfect dolls of the best models are bringing from $25 to $35 and very ordinary ones $15 to $20. I have never known of a child making use of the cute little metal stands, but collectors always want them, so we now make a similar stand of wood for them."

There is yet one more doll made by Schoenhut. It was never catalogued; not many were made and only a few sold. This is the baby head with the sleeping glass eyes. It was not, as has been said, "the first doll designed by Harry E. Schoenhut" who began designing in 1916, for it was not made until 1924. It was designed, not by Harry E. Schoenhut, but by Grace Story Putnam! The head is nothing more or less than a wood copy of Mrs. Putnam's "Bye-Lo Baby."

When that little masterpiece came out in 1924, it took the whole doll-making industry "by storm," for they knew that it would—as it did—revolutionize the doll market and the buying public's ideas.

Immediately everybody tried to get in the new type. Every toy loft, almost, in New York City started infringing on the copyright.

Just why the Schoenhuts made a wooden copy of the Bye-Lo Baby is not clear. Perhaps they felt that they could do what everybody else in the business was doing. More probably it was a last frantic effort to save the all-wood doll head by demonstrating that it was adaptable to any design. It is hard to judge the motives after twenty-one years. At any rate, only a few were made, as said above, and very few sold by the Schoenhuts. Up to now, collectors have apparently never noted the similarity.

LIST OF PATENTS ISSUED TO A. SCHOENHUT

Patent No.	Title of Invention	Date of Issue
982,096	Jointed Figure	Jan. 17, 1911
1,326,790	Joint for Dolls	Dec. 30, 1919
1,358,470	Doll	Nov. 9, 1920

Patent No.	Title of Invention	Date of Issue
1,387,317	Doll	Aug. 9, 1921
1,390,820	Doll	Sept. 13, 1921
75,527	(Design) Push Toy	June 12, 1928

TRADEMARKS RECORDED IN U. S. PATENT OFFICE

No.	Date	Name	Address	Trademark
82,178	6–6–11	Schoenhut Co., The A.	Phila., Pa.	"Schnickel-Fritz"
82,179	6–6–11	Schoenhut Co., The A.	Phila., Pa.	"Tootsie-Wootsie"

PENNY DOLLS AND FROZEN CHARLOTTES

THE NAME "Frozen Charlotte" is applied to the unjointed china and stone bisque dolls, obviously made in Germany, that were so popular with little girls from forty to sixty years ago. It is generally used for the dolls that are four inches or over in height, but in strict logic should apply equally to the unjointed "penny" dolls of the same period which range from one-half inch up to about three inches. It seems to be a comparatively recent name.

Since doll collecting has become so popular, many doll legends have grown up which have no firmer basis than the fancies of some imaginative collector or the desire of some dealer to enhance the interest and value of his wares. Certainly, when this writer, in common with all the little girls of the neighborhood, played with these dolls and made extensive wardrobes for them, the tiny ones were called "penny dolls" and the larger ones were known simply as "twenty-five-cent dolls."

Perhaps it was because spending money loomed large in the child mind by reason of its scarcity, that one thought of them in terms of price. One had to forego many sweetmeats in the form of striped peppermint sticks or banana-flavored marshmallow in intriguing little crinkled tin pans, to be eaten with the tiny tin spoon accompanying each, if one would keep her standing as to

Pictures of dolls discussed in this chapter will be found following page 12.

who would have the largest family of these small dolls. There also were doll *collectors* in those days!

Part of their charm lay in the variety of costumes one could fashion for them out of incredibly small scraps of silks, ribbons and laces—veritable crumbs from the tables of the grown-ups. What a harvest time it was during the visits of the by-the-day dressmaker, who came every spring and fall for a week or a fortnight to refurbish the family wardrobes! How eagerly one watched for and how gleefully seized upon any sizable scraps that fell from her shining scissors. Looking back across the years, one marvels at the Job-like patience of the woman.

Not all penny dolls are Charlottes, for many of the tiny stone bisques had moveable arms and legs strung on thin wires at shoulders and hips. Penny dolls varied in color and race, though not in features; some had gold shoes, some had blue; many had tam-o-shanters, hats, or bonnets irrevocably fixed on their heads. A few even had wigs of flax. A certain pair of penny twins with thick "Sutherland Sisters" braids to their heels, owe their perfect state of preservation to their incarceration in a double tomato pincushion of turkey-red calico, with only heads and feet extending above and below—one of those decorative monstrosities which one finds only in *Godey's* and *Peterson's.*

Somewhat later, during the heyday of the Palmer Cox *Brownie* books children collected "Brownies" carved from date seeds. The writer still preserves one carved by a sixth-grade classmate behind his open geography during school hours. This classmate did not grow up to become either a doll-maker or a sculptor—he is Robert M. Chilton, the well-known newspaper man, sometime an editor of the old Pittsburgh *Chronicle Telegraph*—now the *Sun-Telegraph.*

The twenty-five-cent dolls—or, if you will, the Frozen Charlottes, are both china and stone bisques, blondes and brunettes. The chinas mostly have black painted hair, while the stone bisques are ordinarily blondes. Occasionally there is one that is different in type from the "run-of-mine" varieties. Mrs. Rose Parro of Waterbury, Vt., found a china Charlotte with a "page-boy bob," and Miss Alma Robeck of Annapolis, Md., has a little bisque, "Alice in Wonderland." Mrs. J. B. Lindsay of Spokane has a Charlotte that has been in her family for two generations and still wears its original costume.

While the name, Frozen Charlotte, is an apt one and will probably continue to be used, one may discount the name "Teacup dolls" and the story that goes with it, which says that the dolls were used to stir the sugar in ladies' afternoon tea and that the departing guest was given the doll and the teacup as souvenirs. It is a nice story until one chances upon an elephantine Charlotte 12 inches tall, with which not even the largest of great-grandfather's "mustache" cups could possibly have been stirred. Such a one is owned by Mrs. Velma F. Von Bruns of Bristol, Vt.

No one seems to be quite sure just how far back these dolls go, probably to about the end of the Civil War. Earlier than that there were the tiny wooden peg dolls of the 1850's. Miss Alma Robeck remembers her grandmother telling her of these wooden dolls and how she used to pay an old man a penny each for whittling them out for her.

Wax penny dolls are apparently much older and more rare than any of the other types. The only wax penny dolls that we have ever seen came from an old trunk belonging to the Goddard family of Massachusetts and according to the labels must date to about 1829. These dolls and two other dolls belonged to three little girls born in 1819, 1821 and 1823. The tiny dot eyes of two of the "pennies" are blue, the other two have brown eyes. On the back of one's head is a knot of wax suggesting a "hairdo."

The name, Frozen Charlotte, is derived from the more than century-old Vermont folk ballad "Fair Charlotte" which was composed by one William Lorenzo Carter, "the Bensontown Homer," whom Phillips Barry, in the *Journal of American Folklore*, calls: "A modern representative of the old-time wandering minstrel."

Carter was born in 1813 at Bensontown, Vt., on the side of what is locally called "Sherburne Mountain," near Rutland. He was the son of a Baptist minister, Rev. John S. Carter. Like the Greek Homer, William was blind from his birth, being only able to distinguish between light and darkness. At the age of twelve years, he began composing verses and singing them to amuse himself and while away the tedious hours that hung so heavily on his hands.

When he was sixteen, his mother died, and shortly thereafter his father embraced Mormonism and moved with his family to Kirtland, Ohio, the first Mormon colony. The father died a year later from cholera at a Mormon camp on the Missouri River. Left without means of support, the blind boy went back east; returned later to Ohio and spent a year and a half in the Columbus Institute for the Blind.

In 1860, he set out from his home in Kirtland, Ohio, to walk to Salt Lake City, got as far as Illinois—and disappeared. It may be that he was killed in some of the anti-Mormon demonstrations so frequent at the time.

Carter did a good deal of wandering about, thinking nothing of a walk of one hundred miles or more, which probably accounts for the fact that no less than nineteen versions of the ballad, "Fair Charlotte," have been found in many different states from Maine to the Dakotas and Oklahoma, and one even in Nova Scotia. The ballad was composed in 1833 before Carter left Vermont but was not written down for many years thereafter. The Vermont version, printed by Phillips Barry in the *Journal of American Folklore*, and reprinted in *Vermont Folksongs and Ballads*, edited by Helen Harkness Flanders of Springfield, Vt., is said to have been derived from a native of Vermont who "knew that the story was as related, taking place on New Year's Eve."

The Vermont version is here given for its interest to doll collectors.

FAIR CHARLOTTE

Fair Charlotte lived on a mountain side,
In a wild and lonely spot,
No dwelling was for three miles 'round
Except her father's cot.

On many a cold and wintry night,
Young swains were gathered there,
For her father kept a social board,
And she was very fair.

Her father loved to see her dress
Fine as a city belle—
She was the only child he had,
And he loved his daughter well.

42

On New Year's Eve when the sun was set,
She gazed with a wistful eye
Out of the frosty window forth,
To see the sleighs go by.

She restless was, and longing looked
Till a well-known voice she heard,
Came dashing up to her father's door,
Young Charlie's sleigh appeared.

Her mother said,—"My daughter dear,
This blanket round you fold,
For 'tis an awful night without,
And you'll be very cold."

"Oh nay, oh nay," young Charlotte cried,
And she laughed like a gypsy Queen,
"To ride in a blanket muffled up,
I never will be seen.

"My woolen cloak is quite enough,
You know it is lined throughout,
Besides I have my silken shawl,
To tie my neck about."

Her gloves and bonnet being on,
She jumped into the sleigh,
And off they went down the mountain side
And over the hills away.

With muffled faces, silently,
Five long cold miles were passed,
When Charles in few and broken words,
The silence broke at last.

"Oh! such a night I never saw,
My lines I scarce can hold,"—
Fair Charlotte said, in a feeble voice,
"I am exceeding cold."

He cracked his whip and they onward sped,
Much faster than before,
Until five other dreary miles,
In silence they passed o'er.

"How fast," said Charles, "the frozen ice,
Is gathering on my brow."
Said Charlotte in a weaker voice,
"I'm growing warmer now."

Thus on they went through the frosty air,
And in the cold starlight,
Until the village and bright ballroom,
They did appear in sight.

Charles drove to the door, and jumping out,
He held his hand to her,—
"Why sit you like a monument,
That has no power to stir?"

He asked her once, he asked her twice,
She answered never a word;
He asked her for her hand again,
But still she never stirred.

He took her hand into his own,
Oh God! it was cold as stone!
He tore her mantle from her brow,
On her face the cold stars shone.

Then quickly to the lighted hall,
Her lifeless form he bore,
Fair Charlotte was a frozen corpse.
And her lips spake never more.

He threw himself down by her side,
And bitter tears did flow,
And he said, "My own, my youthful bride,
I never more shall know!"

He bore her body to the sleigh,
And with it he drove home,
And when he reached her father's door,
Oh! how her parents mourned!

They mourned the loss of a daughter dear,
And Charles mourned o'er her doom,
Until at last his heart did break,
And they both lie in one tomb.

DOLLS IN STRANGE PLACES I

ESPIONAGE IN WARTIME resorts to many different cloaks. The outstanding spy story of World War II is one that deals with dolls and doll collectors.

Perhaps it was the knowledge of certain incidents in the Civil War when contraband and messages were smuggled across the Northern lines in the hollow interiors of dolls in the arms of little girls that caused the F.B.I. agents to look with special attention at a small flock of letters that began appearing with regularity from American doll collectors in different cities all addressed to one Señora Inez de Monanali in Argentina. The letters looked innocent enough on the surface, just friendly letters discussing their common hobby—doll collecting—but it did not take the alert gentlemen of the Bureau of Investigation long to realize that the "Irish dolls"—old women with packs on their backs—was a cryptic reference to modern airplane carriers, or that "the cute little doll shop" she had "happened to run across" in California where they did repair work so skillfully that they could make one good doll from two damaged ones, was not describing the famous Humpty Dumpty Doll Hospital at Redondo Beach, but the condition of the battleships damaged at Pearl Harbor.

If any of these letters had reached the South American addressee before the F.B.I. became suspicious of them, certainly none did from that time on. The letters were mailed in various cities and signed with the names of well-known doll collectors all of whom were members of highly respected, one hundred per cent American families with unsullied reputations for patriotism going back for generations.

The letters were all friendly, chatty affairs interspersed with bits of gossip about the collector's family and her personal comings and goings—gossip which, when investigated, tallied with known facts. Interwoven with this was doll talk, which, seemingly innocent, was a clever code relaying military and naval information which would have been valuable to the enemy had it reached them.

For a year the Federal agents shadowed these families and investigated their relatives, friends and all their contacts without much result. Finally, as a test, they marked several letters "Return to Sender" and dropped them in the post office. In due time they reached the supposed writers of them.

One of these was an Oregon collector, a physician's wife. The frail little woman, a semi-invalid opened the envelope wonderingly. It was a long type-written missive addressed to a woman of whom she had never heard, yet the signature was her own. Here were familiar incidents, *bona fide* family news, mention of members of the family by name. What did it all mean? "Am I going mad?" she thought as she read on. "Or is someone else crazy?" This sentence, for instance: "It is getting along towards the first of the month and I will be busy sending out my husband's monthly statements." Surely *she* had never said that to anyone.

For months this woman and her family had realized that they were being watched—were under suspicion—for what they did not know. Was this letter a part of all that mystery? She knew that she had never written this letter, yet it sounded so convincing and the signature was so like her own that anybody—even herself—would find it hard to believe that she had not. Here she was, inviting this supposed friend in South America to visit her in her home, "if you and your husband should decide to come to our city. Hotels are so crowded and we have a vacant bedroom since the marriage of our daughter."

She telephoned her husband at his office. Together they took the letter to the F.B.I. office. There they sat down with the Federal agents and the letter was taken apart sentence by sentence. . . . The clever questioning of the agents brought out many discrepancies between the letter and the facts. The name of one of her daughters was incorrect. Could she use a typewriter? Yes, better than the typing in this letter. Did she ever send out bills for her husband? No, never. Many doctors' wives did? Yes, but she never had. Her husband's office was downtown and his secretary attended to such matters. Had she been in Southern California recently? She had just returned. Now about this "cute little doll shop where they repaired dolls so skillfully"—had she "just happened" to find such a place—run into it accidentally? Certainly not. Nobody could just *happen* to find Humpty Dumpty Doll Hospital. It was twenty miles out in the country from Los Angeles and one had to hunt for it. Besides, Mr. and Mrs. Wallace C. Clear were personal friends and she always spent at least one night with them when she was in Southern California. She had done so on the recent trip.

The Federal men were fully aware of these facts for they had been in touch with the Clears for more than a year and questioned them minutely about this particular collector. The Clears were sure of her innocence but had been enjoined to strict secrecy by the agents.

Well, then, had she ever mentioned the vacant bedroom—ever invited anyone to occupy it? On the vacant bedroom, her mind clicked. Yes, she had told one person—and only one—*Velvalee Dickinson*. Mrs. Dickinson and her husband were travelling and had written that they might come to Oregon. The hotels were overcrowded and she had invited them to stay at her house while there.

Who was Velvalee Dickinson? She was the owner, since 1938, of a specialty shop on Madison Avenue, New York, dealing in rare antique dolls. Her name was known to every doll collector in the United States as an expert on the subject of dolls; she advertised in leading magazines; she belonged to doll clubs; her opinion was sought and respected on all doll subjects; she had customers all over the country; and her comings and goings, trips across the continent to California with her husband were news in the public prints.

This collector had bought dolls from Velvalee Dickinson—a few—in times past, and Mrs. Dickinson had continued to send her, all unsolicited, dolls on approval. She had wished that the over-zealous dealer would stop sending; she never bought any more of them but still they came—a doll a month—and being a friendly person, she had softened each rejection with a friendly note in which she occasionally made mention of some family news. Thus, all without realizing it, she had been carrying on a running correspondence with Mrs. Dickinson.

After this interview, the Federal agents notified the Clears that their Oregon friends had been freed of suspicion. It was only many months later that the two families were able to compare notes and each learn the whole story.

This incident of the vacant bedroom first pointed the finger of suspicion at the Dickinsons.

Meantime at least two other collectors and possibly more, had received the returned letters and turned them over to the F.B.I. or to the Postmaster, and had been questioned.

A woman in Spokane had received back a letter signed by herself in which she mentioned a trip to Seattle to spend a week with her son who was coming there on business. On questioning, she remembered that she had visited with this New York doll dealer in a Seattle hotel and told her of her son's coming which had brought her to Seattle. Here was a second clue leading to the Dickinsons.

To a collector in Springfield, Ohio, came a letter purporting to be written by her, discussing talk on dolls she had given before a club and telling of the "Irish dolls—old women with packs on their backs," which represented the airplane carriers. She had made the talk as described, she told the investigators, but she had no Irish dolls. She had no idea who had written about her talk and so was little help.

Too much credit could hardly be given the F.B.I. for their astuteness and energy in tracking down the spies from these two slender clues. They trailed every move the Dickinsons had made on their travels. The Clears have complete correspondence files and in them the Government men found post cards written by Mrs. Dickinson to Mrs. Clear from almost every city they had visited. These were handwritten but served to indicate the route they had travelled. The problem of identifying the typewriter on which the spy letters were written was finally solved—they were done on typewriters of the various hotels where the Dickinsons had stayed. Before the Federal agents had accumulated all their evidence Lee Dickinson died in their New York apartment from a heart ailment of long standing.

In due time Velvalee Dickinson was arrested as she came from the Safe Deposit Vaults of a New York bank where she had cached large sums in cash.

The first charge was of sending a letter in code—"confiding in writing information regarding the movement, numbers, descriptions and conditions of our warships." Later the Grand Jury indicted her on three additional charges of violating the censorship act; of having acted as a Japanese agent since 1937 without registering with the State Department; and of "conspiring with officers, agents and subjects of the Imperial Japanese Government, persons whose names are to the Jurors unknown, to violate the espionage act." The penalty for the espionage count might be death.

In the end, for reasons of public safety, she was not tried on this charge but allowed to plead guilty to the lesser charge of violating the censorship law and sentenced to ten years imprisonment and the payment of a tenthousand-dollar fine.

Velvalee Blucher Dickinson, California born and university educated, came of good American stock on her mother's side; was half German on her father's. In 1926, she married Lee Dickinson, a former Philadelphian, who died of heart disease seventeen years later. At the time of their marriage, he was connected with a California fruit firm which had headquarters in the same building as the German and Japanese consulates in San Francisco. The thirty-three-year-old wife worked in a bank which had many Japanese accounts. Later she spent seven years in the employ of a brokerage firm which dealt largely with Japanese clients. She thus made many friends among the yellow race and was a member of a Japanese-American supposedly cultural society. After she came to New York in 1937, she is known to have handled many Japanese commissions in buying and selling stocks.

Whether it was the husband or the wife who made the treasonable bargain with the Japs is a question. After her arrest, Mrs. Dickinson claimed that her dead husband had received $25,000 from Japanese agents to learn and betray his country's secrets. By that time Dickinson was practically a dying man with the heart disorder that ended his life.

In the light of subsequent happenings, it may well be that the doll shop on Madison Avenue was never anything more than a clever front for the real business of spying. Velvalee's only doll experience prior to the opening of her shop, appears to have been a few weeks as a saleswoman in Bloomingdale's doll department during the 1937 Christmas rush. For the rest—there were the clever publicity build-ups which gave her a nation-wide reputation as an expert, and the magnificent self-confidence that served her in living up to that reputation. Velvalee Dickinson was a smart business woman; she knew how to make the right contacts, but it is an open question whether she ever had anything more than a superficial knowledge of the merchandise which she featured.

In spite of the build-up, she did not deceive quite everybody. There were those who realized her limitations, and Mrs. Emma C. Clear, who is really an expert, has related this story which illustrates the *faux pas* Velvalee occasionally made:

"During one of the Dickinsons' California trips—it was August 10, 1941, to be exact—Mrs. Gustav Mox of Santa Monica, who has one of the broadest collections in the country, gave a garden party. We were to take the Dickinsons.

"The Mox collection fills a small cottage on the mountain side in the Santa Monica Canyon, back of their home. The most showy dolls are large French and German jointed dolls dressed as various queens. Costumes are of hand-embroidered satin with royal purple capes and real ermine tails and much jewelry.

" 'Do you collect *these*?' said Mrs. Dickinson superciliously. 'No one in the East would have them. We have a whole cellar full of them,' and turning to me said: 'You can have them for a song if you want them.'

"Little Bonnie Jean Mox, who was in her first long party dress, burst into tears and fled to her grandmother's arms to weep her heart out. She had built on the Dickinson story that the greatest doll judge in the country was their guest. Things went flat for a few minutes but Mrs. Dickinson did not sense that she had said anything wrong. Then she discovered a case of exquisitely costumed chinas, Parians, bisques and lusters.

"She was entranced. 'These,' she said, 'are the kind of dolls *we* love.'

" 'These,' said Mrs. Mox, 'are modern—the Clear dolls. We have them all.'

" 'Humph,' exclaimed Mrs. Dickinson and turned away, entirely missing the adjoining case with really rare old Parians, chinas and lusters.

"Mrs. Mox, trying to hold things, said, 'Perhaps you would be interested in these?' and opened a case of fine old Stieffs. Mrs. Dickinson did not know a Stieff. She asked: 'How do you tell them?'

"Mrs. Mox explained about the button in the ear, the trademark of these dolls. Mrs. Dickinson turned to her husband: 'Remember that—a button in the ear.'

"After the Mox party we took them to see another collection. There she looked around, walked up to a group of fine old ceramics, turned up her nose and remarked:

" 'Oh, some more Clear dolls!'

"The hostess, very proud of her antiques, blew up, and said in no uncertain tones that she did not have a Clear doll in her collection except the Washingtons—that all these were old and she'd paid plenty for each specimen.

"So things went pretty flat there too."

Such episodes tend to confirm the suspicion that she, or someone more clever than she, had deliberately planned her going into a business that would bring her into touch with people of irreproachable standing, whose confidence she could win and so make use of her knowledge of their affairs in her schemes.

Needless to say, the innocent Oregon collector who was unwittingly entangled in the affair, disposed of her collection and thinks now of dolls she loved only with bitterness and pain.

DOLLS IN STRANGE PLACES II

AMONG PRIMITIVE peoples dolls or images have always figured in charms and witchcraft. When the New Orleans voodoo doctors wish to work a charm to influence an indifferent sweetheart the properties used in the rites are said to be a bride doll, blue candles and apples. Uncle Remus' "Tar Baby" story has its origin in a belief in image magic, and the legend figures frequently in Negro folklore, probably going back to the heart of Africa.

Even among the more highly civilized peoples of antiquity—the Egyptians, Assyrians, Babylonians and Greeks—image magic was a common practice. Dolls or figures, supposedly resembling the victims were constructed of wax, clay or other substances, and when the figures were subjected to various mistreatments—thrusting pins or nails into their hands, burning or drowning them—the person against whom the charm was wrought, suffered, sickened and died, they believed.

Such things were done in England, too, until a comparatively late date and the influence of court favorites over some of the sovereigns were often ascribed by the populace to magic and witchcraft.

In 1944 a doll dealer offered this writer—for a considerable price—what the dealer called "a cemetery doll" and described as follows: "We also have a little Flanders baby in its original glass-topped case, with little old flowers, locks of hair, and all in a real graveyard setup. It has a very thin-looking wax coating, or maybe even just enamel over papier mâché . . . awfully cute dress of yellow tarleton-like weave, pin-sized beads and a small paper bouquet on her chest. The box itself is interesting and certainly looks extremely old. It has a brass hanger . . . really a most unusual old doll.''

The offer suggested tales one has read of over-enthusiastic china collectors who, finding a copper luster pitcher holding flowers on a grave in a lonely little cemetery, take the pitcher and leave a dollar in its place. Not a nice idea, to say the least.

Yet the term ''cemetery doll'' stirred vague memories in the realm of forgotten things. Dolls in cemeteries? Little glass houses? Somewhere, long ago, one had seen or heard of such practices. But where? The *Journal of American Folklore* seemed the likeliest source of information. It noted that Negroes in South Carolina and other parts of the South decorated graves with broken crockery, glass and empty bottles and that on children's were placed doll heads, toy animals, etc. It said the same custom existed in parts of the Congo and in Angola.

Query among the members of a Round Robin Garden Club with members in ten states brought the following from Mrs. Cornelia Pittinger of Gaston, Indiana:

''During the natural gas days in Indiana—about forty years ago—we had many glass factories everywhere. We had many Belgian people here working in the glass factories as blowers. They used to put dolls and toys on their children's graves under big glass globes. We still have some of the younger generation here but they do not do it now. I believe you will find that it is a foreign custom. These Indiana cemeteries were Catholic cemeteries.''

In response to a similar inquiry, a letter from Mrs. Anna McDermott of Carnegie, Pa., a suburb of Pittsburgh settled by Scotch-Irish Presbyterians, reported the same practice as having prevailed in the Chartiers Cemetery in that town a generation ago. Mrs. McDermott wrote:

''About the doll houses in Chartiers Cemetery, yes, Chartiers Cemetery had many, many doll houses containing dolls and toys of all sorts on the graves of

54

children. I remember, as a child, fifty-five years ago, I lived near Chartiers Cemetery. At that time, there weren't any playgrounds or places to amuse the children. We used to get tired looking at the dusty roads and Chartiers Creek wasn't anything very nice to wade in, so we would go to the cemetery and look at the little doll houses.

"Oh my, how we would frown and scold if we noticed a little mound that had no glass house or toys. Some of the little houses used to be real fancy; the windows were leaded in and the dolls and small toys looked so nice. Some of the graves had large glass globes with toys or fancy marbles.

"I had Mr. McDermott's grand-nephew inquire about the little doll houses this week, but the caretaker said they were gradually falling down. The parents are dead and there is no one to keep them repaired."

Thus it is clear that the custom, which may have prevailed in many other places, as well as in these two towns, belonged to a generation or two ago— to the sentimental Victorian era, when ladies drank their afternoon tea from Staffordshire tea sets printed with such melancholy pictures as "The Orphans" and "The Mother's Grave" and Messrs. Currier and Ives did a large business in Memorial certificates to be framed and hung in the parlor, depicting colored scenes in St. Paul's Churchyard, New York.

Still further back, of course, this use of dolls, has its origin in the funeral customs of the ancient Egyptians, the Greeks and the Romans.

S. Baring Gould in *Strange Survivals* tells of the finding of an ivory doll during the excavation of deposits some forty feet below the surface in La Langerie on the banks of the Yezere River in Dordogne, France. It was a relic of primitive man just after the glacial period, when the mammoth, the cave lion and the reindeer still walked the earth in that region. This early race had few tools and knew nothing of the art of making pottery. The workman who uncovered the ivory doll, being greedy and dishonest, secreted his find and sold it. Betrayed by a fellow workman, and forced to give back the money he had received and restore the doll to its rightful owner, the man who owned the land, vengefully knocked off the head, which was lost. The arms, if it had ever had arms, had been broken off before the doll was found. It seems to have been a child's toy.

THE DOLLS OF YESTERDAY

The Witte Memorial Museum in San Antonio, Texas, has what are probably the oldest American made dolls. They were presented by George C. Martin, an attorney of San Antonio who bought them in Mexico when searching for specimens for his coin collection. The dolls or figurines—and nobody is quite sure which they are—were found near the pyramids of Tectihuacan in the jungles of Central America where the wonders of the Aztec race have been uncovered by archaeologists in recent years. The arms and legs of the figures are attached so as to be moveable at shoulders and hips like some of the bisque penny dolls.

PRE-GREINER AND GREINER

THERE HAS BEEN a long-standing argument among collectors as to whether the papier mâché dolls of our first American doll-maker, Ludwig Greiner, which were patented in 1858, predated the papier mâché dolls made in Germany. The answer to the question has been provided by a large papier mâché with blown-glass eyes in the collection of Mrs. Ronald Burrows of St. Johnsbury, Vt. The Germans were the first in the field.

Several years ago, during the housecleaning season, this doll came to light in the attic of a neighbor of Mrs. Burrows' mother, Mrs. Fred Alexander of Whitefield, N. H., and the neighbor offered the doll to Mrs. Burrows who was visiting her mother at the time. The head of the doll was broken and bound together with cloth bandage. Because she feared to lose some fragments, the bandage was not undone before the doll was shipped to the Humpty Dumpty Doll Hospital in California for repairs. When Mrs. Clear examined the head, she found stuffed inside it a newspaper, the *Boston Daily Times*, dated August 27, 1845. It had evidently been put inside the head when it was new, for it was unyellowed by exposure to light, as it would otherwise have been. The importance of this find lies in the fact that this was the first authentic date on papier mâché dolls prior to the Greiner

Pictures of dolls discussed in this chapter will be found following page 60.

patent in 1858. It clearly proved that the German doll-makers had been making these heads at least twelve years before Greiner, and, judging by their quality, doubtless much longer than that. These German dolls have blown-glass eyes and are much thinner and finer in texture than the Greiner heads. The faces are more expressive and vary somewhat from each other. There is very fine workmanship in them.

The paper found inside the doll's head is an interesting item in itself. A four page sheet, 20½ by 15½, it contains among the items an announcement of the sale of Public Lands in "the Territory of Wisconsin" and "the State of Louisiana by the President of the United States, James K. Polk," and an item stating that "There is an Alderman in Philadelphia who marries parties for two cents a couple."

Quite similar to Mrs. Burrows' doll is one owned by Mrs. William Walker of Louisville, Ky. This doll was bought from an Ohio collector. We know, in the light of recent discoveries and research, that these dolls with blown-glass eyes are of German make. They were apparently imported as heads and given bodies by the mothers of their small owners. All of these dolls have leather arms.

Of special interest because of its unusual hairdress of long, molded curls is a similar doll of about the same size which is owned by Mrs. Rose Parro of Waterbury, Vt. It was found in Burlington, Vt., by Mrs. Genivra Wilder, a dealer, from whom Mrs. Parro purchased it.

Identical with Mrs. Parro's doll except that it has short curls instead of long ones, is a doll of Vermont interest because it belonged to the family of General Stark. It is now in the collection of Mrs. Winifred Harding of Woodstock.

A dignified and matronly figure as she stands in the open doorway, in her black dress and mosaic brooch is the old papier mâché of similar type from the collection of Mrs. Huntington Brown of Minneapolis.

Our own "Ridiklis," named for the rag doll in "Racketty Racketty House," is a solemn-faced child—so grave and serious that one fancies that she is filled with the conviction of original sin, and meditates on the judgment to come. Her head is 9 inches high and 9 inches across the shoulders. Her underwear *is* all handmade and the ruffles of her pantelettes are of fine handmade eyelet embroidery of exquisite workmanship. Her dress, thriftily cut down from an old child's frock, of a thin mustard-yellow silk plaided with red and green lines, has corded seams, "laid gathers," a deep pocket in the skirt, and is buttoned up the back with white shoe buttons. The old Vermont high chair, slat-backed and rush-seated, in which she sits must have sheltered some small pioneer of the settlement of that part of the New Hampshire grants which is now Vermont. Ridiklis' greatest friend and most devoted admirer is "Aunt Jennie," the three-colored Persian cat, who seems convinced that Ridiklis is a real child and never passes her without rubbing herself against the chair and lovingly caressing the doll's feet.

These German dolls with glass eyes come in several smaller sizes as well.

At the time Queen Victoria came to the throne—in 1837—the fashionable type of hairdress showed the hair braided on each side of the front and brought back under the ears, leaving the ears exposed, to join a braided coil in the back. This style may be seen in some of the *Godey* fashion plates, on some of the little "Milliners' Model" dolls, and in old prints. Papier mâché dolls with this type of hairdo are definitely dated as of 1837–1840. Probably they were intended to compliment the young English Queen, though hardly portraits of her. They were made in Germany and are of unusually fine workmanship. The two dolls shown here are rare and unusual. "Samantha Sue" from the collection of Mrs. Blanche Watson of Geneva, Ill., has the braids brought *above* the ear. "A portrait on china of Queen Victoria exhibited at the Crystal Palace Exposition in 1851 by the Sevrés factories, France, shows the identical hairdo of this doll which seems to date the doll as of 1850 and perhaps indicate that it is intended as a portrait of the Queen as of that period. At any rate it follows her fashions as did all the ladies of the day. On "Queen Victoria" from the St. George collection, the braids are looped *under* the ear. "Victoria" is almost identical with the early N. Currier print, *Matilda*. N. Currier, you will recall, predated Currier and Ives as a print-maker, beginning in New York about 1835. "Victoria" has painted eyes.

There is a sad little story connected with this doll. She was found in a Massachusetts antique shop by a well-known Massachusetts collector and was christened by her owner "Mona Lisa" from a fancied resemblance to that famous painting. Back of this antique shop, her story cannot be traced. Subsequently mental illness afflicted the owner who was taken to a hospital. Her collections were disposed of at public auction and the doll was purchased at the sale by Mrs. Grace Garland, a collector-dealer, of Worcester, Mass., from whom she came to Vermont. Her likeness to Queen Victoria (her dated hairdo) being recognized she was dressed in the character of Victoria and may well be a portrait doll of her Majesty. Miss Helen Hayes sent the doll an autographed picture of herself as "Victoria Regina."

Hearing that her former owner had partially recovered and was in a nursing home, the present owner wrote her and sent a picture of the doll, thinking that she might get some happiness from knowing that her beloved doll was safe and cherished, but the poor clouded and bewildered mind did not respond. Her reply was: "I never saw your doll—I once had a doll—we called her Mona Lisa—but she is gone—gone somewhere."

Ludwig Greiner of Philadelphia to whom was issued the first patent for doll-making ever issued in the United States, No. 10,770, dated March 30, 1858, was a German immigrant. We know little about him except what is recorded in the city directories of Philadelphia where his factory was located. He is first listed in the 1840 directory as a "Toy Man." He seems to have had more than one factory in his later years.

Greiner's method of making doll heads is clearly set forth in his patent application:

"The manner of preparation is as follows: one pound of white paper, when cooked, is beat fine, and then the water is pressed out, so as to leave it moist. To this is added one pound of dry Spanish whiting, one pound of rye flour and one ounce of glue. This is worked until it is well mixed. Then it is rolled out with a roller to the required thinness. After it is cut into pieces required for the mold, it is molded. Wherever there is a part projecting out—for instance the nose—it must be filled with linen or muslin. This linen or muslin must be well saturated with a paste which consists of rye flour, Spanish whiting and glue. After the heads are molded, each head consisting of two parts, they are left to get about half dry. Then they are put into the mold

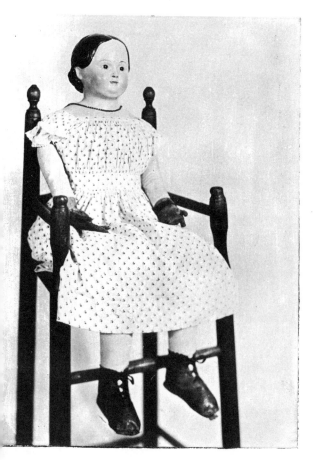

Left, Large papier mâché with blown-glass eyes. Pre-Greiner, German. *Collection of Mrs. Winifred Harding, Woodstock, Vermont. Right,* "Ridiklis"—large papier mâché with blown-glass eyes. Pre-Greiner. *St. George Collection.*

"Samantha Sue," 28-inch papier mâché with blown-glass eyes, 1840. German, all original. *Collection of Mrs. Blanche Watson, Geneva, Illinois.*

Left, Large papier mâché with painted eyes, 1837, 28 inches tall. Variously called "Queen Victoria" and "Mona Lisa." Probably a compliment to the young Queen. *St. George Collection. Right,* China doll with similar hairdo. 16 inches tall. *Collection of Mrs. Catherine Richards Howard, Hope, Arkansas.*

Left, Large papier mâché doll. *Collection of Mrs. Huntington Brown, Minneapolis, Minnesota. Center,* Large papier mâché with blown-glass eyes, found in New Hampshire. *Collection of Mrs. Ronald Burrows, St. Johnsbury, Vermont. Right,* Large papier mâché with glass eyes all original. *Collection of Mrs. William Walker, Louisville, Kentucky.*

Left, Print by N. Currier, about 1837–40. Note hairdo. *Right,* Portrait of Queen Victoria exhibited by Sèvres china factory at Crystal Palace Exposition, 1851. Painted earlier for the King of France to give to Victoria.

Helen Hayes as "Victoria Regina." Autographed photographs sent to the doll "Queen Victoria."

Left, Large papier mâché with unusual hairdo, found in Burlington, Vermont. *Collection of Mrs. Rose Parro, Waterbury, Vermont. Right,* Greiner doll, 1858—dressed to represent "Miss Vassar," 1865—the First Woman's College Freshman. *Courtesy of Miss Cynthia Carey, Worcester, Massachusetts.*

Left, Greiner doll, 1858. *Right,* Greiner? doll found in Burlington, Vermont. Bears traces of Greiner label and wears a second label "Unbreakable—without linen."

THREE MYSTERY DOLLS

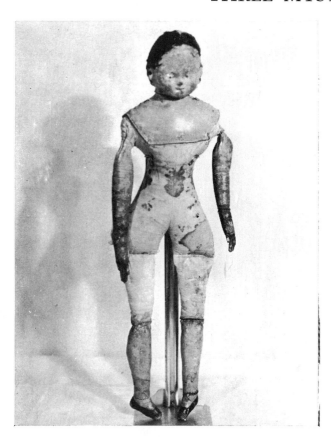

Left, "Sarah Swan Miles," showing wire around chest and commercial body. *Right,* Sarah Swan Miles, at nineteen years, 1861; later Mrs. John Apthorpe Sweetser.

Left, "Sarah Swan Miles," 1841 or earlier. *Right,* "Sarah Swan Miles" showing three-piece head.

THREE MYSTERY DOLLS

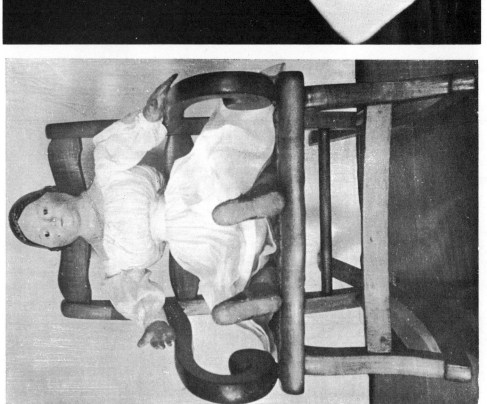

Left, Large "Mystery Doll" on homemade body. Collection of *Mrs. Henry Hepple, Fredonia, New York. Center,* Unusual Superior head sent from England in 1860's. Numbered 4515. It is 15 inches in circumference, 11 inches high, 11 inches across chest. Inherited by Mrs. Thomas Blunk, Kansas. *Right,* Very old body. Head is marked *Holtz-Masse. Courtesy of Mrs. Gurth Ritter.*

THREE MYSTERY DOLLS

Left, Usual type M. and S. Superior doll, *2015*. *Center*, Blonde M. and S. Superior doll, *2015*. Right, Wax doll, on body marked *Holtz-Masse* with maker's name above. Enamelled eyes.

Group of Milliners' Models, showing styles of hairdo which vary with period. "Miss Amanda Bandy," upper right, in hat.

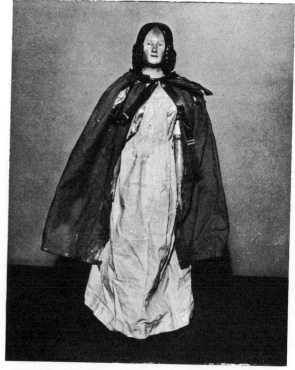

Left, Milliners' Model with coronet braid on hair. *Right*, Milliners' Model with curls, 1840. *Both, Collection of Mrs. Otis Carl Williams, Worcester, Massachusetts.*

Left, "Satira Severy"—comparison of size. *Collection of Mrs. J. J. Flynn, Williams Bay, Wisconsin. Right,* "Pin-cush-la," Milliners' Model of oldest type about 1820—made into pincushion in the 1860's.

Left, 20-inch Milliners' Model—marked: "Sarah Trombly Van Gorden Doll, 1863." *Right*, French Poupards used as fashion models. 13 inches without pedestals. About 125 years old. Found in Lancashire, England, **during** World War II.

Left, "Sethany Ann," 1850, china head doll by Mlle. Calixto Huret, Paris. Inherited by Mrs. T. L. McCready, Jr. (Tasha Tudor.) All original except wig. Present wig is made of Mrs. McCready's own hair. Doll's head is open at top and glazed inside. *Water color by Tasha Tudor. Right,* M. and S. doll models second-best dress of Martha Victoria, French fashion doll of 1869. *Collection of the author.*

French fashion doll. *Collection of Mrs. Edmund H. Poetter, Reading, Vermont.*

FRENCH DOLL CLOTHES

"Adeline Houghton," Parian "Countess Dagmar" doll brought from Paris in 1860 by the then American ambassador to a friend's little daughter. The doll is all original, the body is marked, the arms and legs of Parian. Red painted shoes. *Collection of Mrs. H. C. Ettinger, Laguna Beach, California.*

French fashion doll with sixteen costumes and accessories. Belonged to Anna Jamison, Albany, New York, 1869. *Collection of Mrs. C. L. Mitchell, San Antonio, Texas.*

French fashion doll with clothes, trunk, and accessories. *Collection of Mrs. J. J. Flynn, Williams Bay, Wisconsin.*

French fashion doll's costumes said to copy dresses worn by Empress Eugénie. *Collection of Mrs. Edmond H. Poetter, Reading, Vermont.*

Left, French fashion doll. *Right,* French fashion doll. *Both from collection of Mrs. Catherine Richards Howard, Hope, Arkansas.*

Left, American doll clothes. In Vermont, Worth's creation of 1876 for Princess Alexandra of Wales, the "Princess Dress" was made of plaid gingham and cotton-backed velvet ribbon for a Joel Ellis doll. *Right,* "Ida Mae Russ," named for her first owner who lived in Quechee, Vermont. A Parian "Countess Dagmar" about 80 years old, wearing dress of that period of dark-brown challis, figured with bright rosebuds and trimmed in a fancy red braid. *Collection of Miss Maris Ransom, Woodstock, Vermont.*

Left, Bright blue silk basque trimmed in black, over skirt of black taffeta. 1880 period. *Right*, Bustle dress of yellow brocaded satin trimmed with ribbon and brass buttons. 1870's period.

Left, "Miss Madge" ready for Vermont Town Meeting. Bordered cotton print. 1880 period. *Right*, 1880 dress of taupe figured brilliantine trimmed with blue and white plaid gingham. Flat silver buttons.

WAX DOLLS

Early English wax dolls. Hair set in slit in head. *St. George Collection*.

Early English wax over wood. Dolls given to Mary Dance, English actress, 1808. From the cover of *Hobbies* magazine, through whose courtesy it is reproduced.

AMERICAN DOLL CLOTHES

Left, "Laura Merrill" of Saxton's River, Vermont, wax doll, wears a red cloth polonaise elaborately hand-braided in white soutache braid, over a blue skirt. Early 1870's. *Center,* Bright blue cashmere overskirt dress trimmed with fringe, 1870's. Doll is much older than dress, being a German papier mâché with blown-glass eyes. *Right,* "Zazu," an 1870 ball-head composition doll from Vermont models "Laura Merrill's" house clothes, buttoned all the way down the front with white pearl buttons bordered in brown, and an ample apron.

again and the parts well saturated with the paste. At the same time linen or muslin is cut up into pieces to match the parts, and is also saturated with this paste and pressed on the inside of the parts. Then they are left to dry again as before. Then these parts are put together with the same composition as the head is made from. After this, when they are perfectly dry a strip of the linen or muslin saturated with paste is laid inside of the head where the parts were put together, and a piece is also put over each shoulder and extending over the breast outside. Then they are painted with oiled paint so that children may not suck off the paint.

"What I claim as my invention, and desire to secure by Letter Patent, is—

"Strengthening the seams and projecting or exposed parts of doll heads by cementing or pasting on those parts, muslin, linen, silk, or other equivalent material, in the manner and for the purpose set forth."

The cloth reinforcements are so distinctive that there is no difficulty in recognizing the Greiner doll by simply looking inside the head. Generally they bear the label, gold and black; but even when it is absent the types of faces and expressions are much alike and easily recognized. Of all dolls, the two dolls that are most frequently found wearing labels are the two that are most easily identified for what they are regardless of labels, namely, the Greiner dolls, and the M & S Superior. One really needs no label to identify either one.

Although the Greiner dolls vary in size, color of eyes and hair, they have the same placid well-fed expression, and rather dumb, stolid look. They have painted eyes, sometimes brown, sometimes blue. The hair, dark or blonde, is in rather massive curls, sometimes it covers the ears and often leaves the ears exposed. The heads are thicker than the German-made heads of papier mâché.

Formerly some of these German heads with blown-glass eyes had been attributed to Greiner, but there is considerable difference in quality of workmanship and texture between them. Greiner did not use glass eyes.

Greiner's composition was a durable one, particularly as to the glaze, and most of his dolls have come down to us in remarkably good condition after years of service. The weak spots in the Greiner dolls are the cloth-stuffed noses and chins. The end of the nose in particular is apt to be scuffed and flattened.

Greiner made only doll heads, the bodies were made at home and they usually have leather arms and hands.

Greiner's patent was extended in 1872—the labels on the later dolls read *Patent Ext. 1872.*

An interesting variation of Greiner doll comes from Burlington, Vt. It is unmistakably Greiner in appearance, has all the characteristics and shows the spot on the shoulder where the label has been—exactly the size and shape of a Greiner label. In addition there is a label beside it of white paper printed in black which reads, "Unbreakable *without* linen." A similar doll was advertised for sale in *Hobbies* not so long ago. The Burlington doll was in original clothes, which were of the style of about 1872—a "wrapper" of a brown cotton print of the period with a border such as was popular in the early 1870's. Would this doll have been a late development of the Greiner doll—or might Greiner's molds have been used by someone else after he went out of business?

A Greiner doll whose picture is well known to collectors because it has stood at the left of the caption of the Dollogy department of *Hobbies* magazine for several years is "Miss Vassar 1865," owned by Miss Cynthia Carey of Worcester, Mass. She is an old family doll and was redressed as "Miss Vassar 1865——The first woman's college freshman in the wide world," as Sarah Josepha Hale quaintly expressed it in *Godey's*, to represent the Worcester College Club in a doll show.

"Miss Vassar" has an 1858 label with the size, number 13, marked inside the head in ink, which seems to be the largest size of Greiner head.

THREE MYSTERY DOLLS

THERE IS SO very much that we do not know about the history of old dolls and their makers, and which we have little means of discovering, that many types may remain subjects of conjecture only. To make positive statements about such dolls is only to give rise to further confusion. For instance, there is the doll that bears the mark *Holtz-Masse*. (Some call it *"Boltz"* but on the ones we have seen, the word is *Holtz*.) The natural conclusion would be that this is the maker's name, but no one, so far, has been able to locate the history of any such maker. A good many heads with this mark found here in the East are of composition or papier mâché with molded hair and look to be of the era around 1870. The mark is generally printed directly on the back of the shoulder with ink, but one recently came to light in New Hampshire that had this mark impressed in the composition inside the shoulder.

Mrs. Emma C. Clear says that she has frequently had several different types, wax, papier mâché, etc., in for repairs at one time, all of which bore the Holtz-Masse mark. She believes that the dolls were made by several small makers and marketed through a jobber, who put his own mark on them all. She interprets the mark as meaning "Holtz-Wholesaler."

The New Hampshire doll with the impressed mark has a homemade body,

Pictures of dolls discussed in this chapter will be found following page 60 but many dolls marked *Holtz-Masse* have a commercial body stuffed with hair waste, with leather arms and leather shoes made on the feet.

The "M & S Superior" doll, though labelled, is still an unknown quantity. They are usually found in the sizes 20, 25, 30–32 inches tall and are both blondes and brunettes. The bodies that are original are mostly a commercial type, stuffed with hair waste and, like many of the Holtz-Masse bodies, have leather arms and leather shoes made on the feet. Many of these have the old sitting-type body with a broad sitting base in the rear.

The heads all have about the same type of molded hair in the so-called "Civil War" style—parted in front and with vertical curls around the head in the back. The painted eyes are usually blue on the blondes and brown on the brunettes. There are no blown-glass eyes in any of them. The appearance of these dolls, in whatever size, is so characteristic and consistently similar, that even when the label has been lost one can recognize the dolls as "Superiors."

Some collectors believe that the Superiors may have been made by Greiner but proof either for or against this theory is lacking. There is no patent or trademark for these dolls registered with the U. S. Patent Office. Greiner patented his doll head.

When discovered in pristine condition, the faces of the Superior dolls have a fine glaze and high luster, but dolls that have been in use, particularly in the case of blondes, this glaze is shown to have marred badly and the faces generally in a pretty dilapidated condition. The Greiner dolls on the other hand, except for a tendency to snubbed noses, have come through the years with their complexions in remarkably good condition. It is hardly reasonable to suppose that when Ludwig Greiner knew how to make doll heads with a good glaze that stood up under wear, he should have made heads—and continued to make them—with a glaze which, like the glaze on the Superiors, was certainly inferior in wearing qualities.

Greiner's labelled doll heads were all sold as *heads* and the bodies are homemade. Most of the Superior dolls have a uniform type of body which must have been commercially made.

Miss Jennie L. Abbott, librarian of Doll Collectors of America, says on this subject: "I wish someone would make a chemical analysis and comparison of the composition in the Greiner, Superior, and the Nonpareil W. A. H. heads." It would be interesting, but then again, it might not prove much either.

The label on the average Superior doll, printed in black on a gold background, reads *M & S Superior 2015* but there are variations. Mrs. Irene M. Lowe of Kirkwood, N. Y., had a Superior doll with the label reading *G.L. 2015 Superior—This Composition is Perfectly Harmless.* This head was 6 inches high, 11 inches in circumference and the complete doll 20 inches tall. It had blue eyes and dark hair. The body was the same type as others, differing only in the color of the shoes which were tan kid stitched with red, and the stockings were white muslin striped with blue. Most Superiors have red shoes and white stockings striped with red.

Fairly common in Vermont and New Hampshire is a 3½ inch Superior head that we have not seen mentioned in other discussions of this type. The writer has three of these small heads, two of which are blondes and without labels—the third, a brunette, has the usual label. One of the blonde heads came with a very crude homemade body stuffed with lamb's wool—evidently a farm child's doll. The second blonde has the commercial body, and shoes are brown leather.

In the summer of 1944 a columnist in a Wichita, Kansas, newspaper commented on a very large doll head in the possession of Mrs. Tom Blunk of that city which had an unusual history. Mrs. Cyrus M. Beachy and her daughter, the late Mrs. John D. McEwen of Wichita, enthusiastic doll collectors, investigated the story and put us in touch with Mrs. Blunk. It proved to be the largest Superior head of which we have any knowledge—11 inches high, 15 inches in circumference and 11 inches across the chest. It is blonde with a slightly different hairdo. The label has a different number, reading *M & S Superior 4515.*

The doll, of which only this head survives, came from England about 1860–1865. The story as told by Mrs. Blunk is as follows:

"My grandmother was Mary Ann Camp. She met and married George Young at Mason City, Ill. He was the youngest son of an English Lord, a member of the House of Lords in London. He came to America after graduating from Cambridge University and began the practice of law in Mason City where he later became a judge. He and my grandmother had six children, two of whom died in infancy.

"When Kansas was opened for settlement, my grandfather came here and took up a claim about twelve miles south of Parsons, near the little town of Labette. He died of smallpox soon after, and my grandmother was left with four small children. After my grandfather's death, my great grandfather in England helped my grandmother. She had many things from England, including this large doll.

"My mother married Harry Mills of Oswego, Kansas. She died at the age of thirty-two leaving an eighteen-month-old baby and three other small children. My grandmother raised us. She often told us of our English relatives —many names I've forgotten.

"The doll was sent to America during or just before the Civil War. My sister and I played with the old doll until we got the head off. Then my grandmother put the head on the piano where it remained. Years after she was dead we divided the relics, so I chose the doll head and my sister took the stamp with the coat of arms on it. It was wings, something like the English wear on their soldier suits now."

Checking on Mrs. Blunk's story, through Mr. George D. Martin of San Antonio, Texas, a specialist in genealogy and heraldry, we found that Mrs. Blunk's grandfather was not a member of the House of Lords but an Irish peer. John Young was created Baron Lisgar in 1870, and died in 1876 when the peerage became extinct because of the prior death of his two sons. The seal which Mrs. Blunk had supposed to be the family crest proved to be just a commercial seal. Mr. Martin said of it: "During the period from 1750–1850 seals were much used. Envelopes were just coming into use at the end of that period, and to the time of the latter, letters were folded and sealed with wax to keep them closed. Seals of the type depicted with birds, ships and other devices were for sale at stationers. . . . The device shown in the drawing is not a crest, merely a bird, probably a gull.

In a later letter, Mrs. Blunk recalled that the doll originally had elaborate clothes, including a plaid dress, and that it had "red shoes."

The story of this head is given in detail for two reasons: its authenticated history gives an early date for the Superior doll and suggests the possibility of a European origin. It seems rather unlikely that a doll made in America would have been purchased in England to be returned to the United States.

The date of this Kansas head is supported by a blonde Superior doll purchased in Keene, N. H., in 1944 from a very old lady who was living on an old age pension and was later removed to the Town Farm. She said the doll had been her sister's and it was accompanied by a card with this inscription:

" 'I know I had my doll in 1861. I do not know how long she had then been mine. I do not know when Georgia had this doll; she herself is three years and eight months younger than I am.

'See writing in my papers! Hold fast to this doll!'

Carrie E. Biglow, March 22, 1933 (Anniversary of Mother's death)"

That M & S Superior dolls were still being made in the early 1870's is evidenced by a doll 32 inches tall with a Massachusetts background that is in original condition and clothing. The dress is made Princess style and is of black silk—much worn. The Princess dress was designed by Worth of Paris in 1876 for the Princess of Wales (Alexandra), and worn by her. The red Morocco high shoes made on the feet of the doll are also of the style worn in the early 1870's, with high heels and very high insteps. The doll wears a cylindrical bustle of white muslin stuffed with sawdust, which is clearly of factory construction. We have seen the same bustle on a Superior doll from Kentucky whose known history would date her in the early 1870's and that, of course, was when the bustle first became a "must-have" for the fashionable lady.

Of even deeper mystery is a cloth doll found at Fairlee, Vt.—a type of which, in spite of rather wide inquiry, only three, possibly four, examples have been located. The history of this Fairlee doll is known and authenticated. It belonged to Sarah Swan Miles who was born in Shrewsbury, Mass., in 1841. In 1861, Sarah Swan Miles married John Apthrop Sweetser of Worcester, Mass., son of the Rev. Seth Sweetser who preached in Worcester for many years. The couple lived in Grafton, Mass., at Elmwood Farm, Brigham Hill, for forty years and then moved to Lexington, Mass. There they lived in a house on Massachusetts Avenue previously occupied by the Rev. A. A. Meredith, a preacher of some note. Sarah died in 1917 and the doll descended to her niece, Mrs. Sarah Smith of West Fairlee, Vt.

The doll, "Sarah Swan Miles"—called for her former owner—is therefore close to a century old. She wears her original clothing. Evidently a commercial doll, the head, hands and feet are painted, on cloth. The head is made in three pieces instead of the usual two and there is a seam down the back of the head. The hair is both molded and painted and the head is stuffed with sawdust. A distinctive feature is the reinforcing wire, about the size and weight of hay-baling wire that goes around the edge of the bust. The body has the legs attached about two inches below the crotch which is in one with the body. The doll stands on her toes like a ballet dancer. Her flat slippers, painted on the feet look like ballet shoes or the slippers called "Mary Janes" that children wore a few years ago.

The same doll, a size larger than Sarah, was found by Mrs. Rupert Jaques of Marblehead, in a Massachusetts antique shop. Mrs. Henry Heppel of Fredonia, N. Y., has a 23-inch doll with this head and a homemade cloth body, which came from a western New York town. Mrs. William F. Briggs of Auburn, Maine, thinks she saw a similar doll six years ago in the sales room of the Good Will Industries at Louisville, Ky.

"Sarah, Lady of Mystery," is minus an eye and looks as if she had been literally "loved to death." She is cherished for her quaint personality rather than for her beauty.

"Certainly not for her *beauty*," remarks the Man of the House, who calls her and an equally battered Joel Ellis doll, "Arsenic" and "Old Lace," adding, "The worse they look the better *you* like them."

To which the obvious answer is Othello's:

"She loved me for the dangers I had passed."

"MILLINERS' MODELS"

"**A**ND SAID LANDS** shall be subject to a pious rent for the support of the Kimball Union Academy so long as grass grows and water flows" reads the deed to a portion of the land on which these words are being written. When the early "proprieters" who came north from Massachusetts and Connecticut to settle on the land of the New Hampshire Grants—part of which are now Vermont—apportioned their lands and organized their towns, they set aside certain parcels of lands for the support of the clergy, for maintenance of education and for the propagation of the Gospel in foreign parts. Those who used those lands had to pay a yearly fee or tax which was known as a "pious rent." The old Kimball Union Academy in New Hampshire is one of the beneficiaries of these rents.

When Miss Mary Jane Dewey of Hanover, N. H., died on June 18, 1942, at the age of one hundred and five years, she was the oldest living resident of Hanover and the oldest living graduate of the Kimball Union Academy. A third cousin to Admiral George Dewey and daughter of the late George W. and Laura Chedal Dewey, she was born on the spot where Dartmouth's Wheeler Hall now stands, and she left her estate to Dartmouth College. From the sale of the personal property of the estate there came to us two small dolls of Mary Jane Dewey's childhood, and possibly they had even belonged to her

Pictures of dolls discussed in this chapter will be found following page 60.

mother before her. Seemingly a mother and daughter pair, they have been named (we think appropriately) "Laura Chedal Dewey" and "Mary Jane Dewey." With them came a homemade wooden treasure box which bears Mary Jane Dewey's initials and the date "1840."

Around these two dolls cling many memories—memories of five of our country's wars which they and their mistress lived to see: the Civil, Mexican, Spanish-American, and the First and Second World Wars; of United States presidents from Martin Van Buren to Franklin D. Roosevelt; of Dartmouth College from Nathan Lord to Ernest Hopkins; of Daniel Webster, whom Mary Jane Dewey knew in her childhood; and of men who had known Eleazer Wheelock, the founder of Dartmouth. There are more personal memories also, such as those of the young lover of Mary Jane Dewey's early twenties whose courtship suffered shipwreck through her obedience to the religious prejudices of her parents—a lover whom she never forgot and to whose memory she was faithful to the end of her days.

In the little papier mâché heads of these dolls may linger still other and older memories of the days before *Godey's, Peterson's, Demorest's, Delineator* or *Vogue*; of Paris salons where their stiff little unjointed kid bodies and carved wooden limbs were clothed in the *dernier cri* of fashion to carry the message of the mode in dress and coiffeur across the Channel to England and across the Atlantic to the United States, for these little ladies were once "milliners' models."

They may even remember—but they do not tell us—which was the country of their birth. Was it England? Was it France? Was it Holland, as some have guessed? Were they the "Flanders babies" which some writers mention? Of which it was said:

"What the children of Holland take pleasure in making
The children of England take pleasure in breaking."

We do not think this verse refers to this particular type of model but to some earlier doll. Papier mâché was invented in the eighteenth century. Its invention is attributed variously to Italy and to France. During that century it found many uses in many countries' architectural moldings, furniture, trays, boxes and other small objects, but Max von Boehn says it was first used for doll heads in Germany in 1810. Judging by their styles of hair dress, the oldest of such little dolls is not earlier than that date and none seem to be any later than our own Civil War period.

When they had served their fashion purpose, many of them found their way into nurseries as play dolls. Perhaps this may be the reason that so many of them have come down to us—and not the reverse, as many writers have suggested. Children in those long ago days had fewer toys and were consequently inclined to be more careful of those they had. This is evidenced by the fact that after Mary Jane Dewey had had her dolls for what must have been a minimum of ninety-five years—perhaps nearer a century—there was, in the year 1942, still pinned to the skirt of one of them, a tiny inch-square lace-edged handkerchief.

These little milliners' models range in size from 6 inches to 20 inches and the variety of their hair dressing, reflecting the times in which they came into being, the styles of coiffeur which it was one of their missions to demonstrate, may be judged from a statement of Mrs. Clear: "We have had as many as twenty-four of these little dolls come to Humpty Dumpty Doll Hospital for repairs in a single day and no two of them would have the same style of hairdo."

The high styles of coiffeur are the oldest (1810–1820), such are those of "Pauline"—who was found in Burlington, Vt., along with an assortment of child-made clothes in a variety of the quaintest and oldest of cotton prints we have ever seen, and 6-inch "Pin-cush-la"—from eastern Pennsylvania— so-named because she was imprisoned in a pincushion by some lady of the 1860's. The tall, severe-looking lady with hair braids looped under her exposed ears is clearly 1837—as will be seen in *Godey's* fashion plates of that year. Of two dolls owned by Mrs. Otis Carl Williams of Worcester, Mass., one is 20 inches tall with 1840 curls, the other 15 inches tall with a coronet braid well back on her head, and her original dress of faded pink tarleton. Mrs. Williams has a considerable number of these dolls collected by her mother.

The book against which "Satira Severy" (from the collection of Mrs. J. J. Flynn of Williams Bay, Wis.) is posed, and the evening slipper, placed in the foreground, indicate the size of the doll. The large placid lady in satin has written across her chest in an old-fashioned chirography and fading ink "The Sarah Trombly Van Gorden Doll, 1863." She came from the Finger Lakes region of New York state. Who was Sarah Trombly Van Gorden? Considerable research has not yet revealed the answer.

Of somewhat different type, yet obviously belonging to the same group, is little "Miss Amanda Bandy," the doll with the hat. She might have been a spy, for she came in disguise—a shirtwaist girl of the Gay Nineties—but her "waterfall" hairdo and her stout little leather "Balmoral boots" with soles just an inch and a half long dated her as a Civil War lady.

Stripped of her disguise, she might even have been the original of Charles Kingsley's *The Lost Doll,* for "Amanda" too had lain long in the meadow— or some equally damp spot—for the color was all gone from her shoulders and from her papier mâché back hair on which the net of the chignon still stood out in relief. Most of the color had flaked off the red-brown plumed hat that was molded to her head. The hands were missing from her incredibly dirty little arms. Her disproportionately long homemade cloth body, replacing, no doubt, the original, that ended in a pair of such absurdly short legs that they reminded one of a certain little sawed-off table that Grandmother always called her "bandy-legged stand," and she was christened "Miss Amanda Bandy."

Sent to California for a beauty treatment, Mrs. Clear restored the brown to her hair, the black hair net and the original reddish brown to her hat, contrasting it with nile-green plumes and a navy-blue bow.

When she returned she was given the appropriate garments of the 1860's including a hoop petticoat and a dress fashioned from a bit of striped challis as old and as quaint as Amanda herself.

Mrs. Clear called her "a fascinating little thing—the cutest doll of that type we have seen."

Amanda is just 11 inches tall from the sole of her shoe to the top of her hat.

Her hairdo, popularly known as the "chignon" or "waterfall" was much fancied during the decade 1860–1870. Empress Eugenie stamped it with her approval and wore it with her riding costumes. A frame of horsehair was attached to the back of the head with an elastic; the back hair was brushed over it and the ends turned up underneath. A net was worn over this chignon to keep it in place. Sometimes the whole structure was made of false hair and pinned on with hairpins. Thus the Empress wore it with riding dress.

Any doll with this style of hairdo, be it china, Parian, or papier mâché, may be safely dated within the decade of 1860–1870.

Many doll collectors are referring to this style and the net that covers it, as a *"snood."* This is a misnomer. *Brewer's Dictionary of Phrase and Fable,* a standard authority, says:

"A *snood* was a ribbon with which the Scotch lassie braided her hair and was the emblem of her maiden character. When she married, she changed it for the curch or coiff; but if she lost the name of virgin before she obtained that of wife, she 'lost her silken snood' and was not privileged to assume the curch or coiff."

The *snood,* therefore, was *the badge of maidenhood* and was not worn after marriage. The *chignon* or *waterfall* was something quite different in both style and purpose, and was worn by women of all ages from school girls to grandmothers.

Balmoral boots were introduced by Queen Victoria in 1863 for outdoor wear at Balmoral Castle. They were high shoes of stout leather, laced up in front and were very fashionable for seaside wear and for croquet (a game introduced in 1863).

In the spring of 1944 from "somewhere in England," an old Vermont friend and neighbor, Staff Sergeant Charles Mears, a radio operator of the U. S. Troop Carrier Command, wrote us:

"I am sending you for your birthday a pair of old dolls that I dragged down from the top shelf in the back of an antique shop. The shop-keeper called them 'pre-Victorian fashion plate dolls' but I call them 'The Two Dirty Gerties' and am sending them to you as is."

They were well named. In nothing less than a hundred and twenty-five years could they have acquired so much grime. It took a whole afternoon and much Vermont spring water and soap flakes to remove it all. When the house-keeper was instructed to empty the first basin of inky black water out-of-doors, she replied:

"Yes, I'd better. If I was to pour that much English soil on your house-plants, like as not Winston Churchill would come up and bloom!"

By their clothing these figures were of the date 1825. The dresses are quaint prints, one light and the other dark, with its leg o' mutton sleeves and neck kerchiefs in the vogue of the era, and red cotton aprons which were obviously part of the dresses since the print does not extend under the aprons—only lining. Aprons were much worn in that day as part of the costume. The dresses are three inches longer than the dolls which apparently had stood on pedestals in the milliner's or dressmaking shop. The heads are papier mâché, with painted hair and features, but the bodies are bottleshaped affairs, of papier mâché though unfinished, and without legs—flat on the base. There seemed to be some small stones inside that rattled about when the dolls were moved. The arms were stiff wire and the flat wooden hands, like glove-counter forms were fastened on the wires by being wound with cord. The figures are 11 inches high and the heads about 9½ inches in circumference.

They were subjects of much speculation for nothing like them appeared in any available books. Where had they been made? Finally a picture came to light in Leo Claretie's *Les Jouets, Histoire et Fabrication*, Paris, 1894 (out of print).

In a chapter on cheap French toys, it appeared in the reproduction of a news-paper cartoon showing a group of such toys selling for less than a *franc*. Claretie wrote of it:

"Much the drollest figure in the lot is the big, good-natured, agreeable-looking damsel who occupies the center of the picture. One can almost hear her say:

" 'Lady! What would you have? One can hardly give you more for a *sous* than a Venus de Milo!' She is like a babe in swaddling clothes, without legs or arms, painted head, hair in shining curls, eyebrows arched, mouth like a Cupid's bow, rosy cheeks, blue eyes and with three pebbles to rattle in the interior. Their birthplace is Villers-Cotteret from whence they are sent in huge paper cartons to Paris where they receive the brilliant varnish which is their only education."

These figures have evidently been made over a long period of years and, of course, were never intended for fashion dolls. Probably some enterprising Lancashire shopkeeper, visiting Paris, saw such possibilities in them that she invested a few sous, put the wire arms and flat wooden hands on them and set them on pedestals in her shop to display the miniature models of her wares. It may very well be that these are the only pair of such models in existence.

HISTORIC FASHION DOLLS

MAX VON BOEHN in his *Dolls and Puppets* has the best discussion of the subject of fashion dolls prior to the nineteenth century that we have found. It is a pity that the English translation of this book is out of print and so not available to the average collector of dolls.

Fashion dolls or "fashion babies" as they were called, preceded fashion books by many decades, before the invention of the processes of making copper plates.

Queen Isabeau of Bavaria made the first recorded use of dolls for this purpose when she sent several to the Queen of England (wife of Henry IV) to give her an idea of the fashions of the French Court. These dolls may be presumed to have been life size and made to the measurements of the recipient because the account books show that in 1396, Robert of Varennes, the court tailor of Charles VI, was paid for a doll's wardrobe the rather substantial sum—for that day—of 439 francs.

Isabella, Queen of Spain and patronness of Christopher Columbus, received a life-size fashion doll as a gift from Anne of Brittany, Queen of France, in 1496. The then middle-aged Isabella was a smart dresser and meticulous in sartorial details, and when the doll was dressed the French Court deemed it not sufficiently elegant, and ordered it redressed in a costlier ensemble.

To his fiancée, Marie de Medici, Henry IV of France wrote: "Frontenac tells me that you wish to have samples of our fashions; I am therefore sending you several model dolls."

We have all heard of the fashion figures that stood in the salon of the famous Mlle. de Scudéry and were known as "La Grande Pandore," and "La Petite Pandore," the one in the latest costume mode, the other, featuring the styles in lingerie.

As early as 1645, German women were being satirized by their native writers for sending to France for fashion dolls that they might copy French styles of dress and hair dressing; spending as much for these dolls, says a censorious writer of the latter in the same century, "as would serve them to emulate the fripperies of the devil."

Vienna and Venice were both patrons of the French Mode sent them in the form of dolls. Venice displayed a French fashion doll, at the annual Fourteen Day Fair, and the doll remained throughout the following year as a guide to fashions.

Marie Antoinette sent dolls to her mother and sisters. The names "Grande Pandore" and "Petite Pandore" for the dolls gave place to the titles "Dolls of the Rue St. Honore" which was in that day the street of *couturièrs* as the Rue de la Paix is in the present, and they were also called *"Les Grandes couriers des Modes."*

England took a leaf out of the French book, *The Gentlemen's Magazine,* for September, 1731, and reports:

"Several dolls, with different dresses made in St. James' Street have been sent to the Czarina to show the manner of dressing at present in fashion among English ladies."

In addition to these fashion dolls, equally elegant and expensive dolls were sent as gifts to royal children by other royal personages or fawning courtiers. A few such dolls were preserved in Paris in the Georges Seville Seligman and the Henry d'Allemagne collections. Are they there now? Did they perish in the ravages of war and the German occupation?

While such magnificent creatures served the uses of royalty and diplomatic intrigue, other smaller and less expensive dolls were going to less important folks.

The New York and Boston papers of the eighteenth century bear testimony in such items as this in the *New-England Weekly Journal*, July 2, 1733.

"At Mrs. Hannah Teatts, dressmaker at the top of Summer Street, Boston, is to be seen a mannequin, in the latest fashion, with articles of dress, night dresses and everything appertaining to women's attire. It has been brought from London by Captain White. Ladies who choose to see it may come or send for it. It is always ready to serve you. If you come, it will cost you two shillings, but if you send for it, seven shillings."

All this is interesting from a purely historical standpoint, but it has little practical value to the average present-day collector since it is unlikely that she can acquire any specimens of fashion dolls other than those of the nineteenth century, the milliners' models of the preceding chapter, or the richly dressed French bisques of the years 1860–90 which was the golden age of the "fashion doll."

Now once again, as a result of post-war conditions when civilian travel is restricted, the fashion doll is serving the dressmakers of Paris.

From the April 5th issue of the French language newspaper of Montreal, *La Presse,* the following is translated:

"PARIS.—A joyous bustle and an air of festivity, colorful and animated, marked the opening of a novel exposition entitled, *'Le Theatre de la Mode'* at the Museum of Decorative Arts in the palace of the Louvre, last Tuesday. It is a show of a new kind, not only in its form but in its purpose.

"Dressed by the leading dressmakers of Paris more than 200 dolls, presented in miniature settings, demonstrate the very last word in fashions in all its aspects. The creations which they wear were designed by French artists such as Christian Berard and Jean Cocteau. Measuring 18 inches in height, these dolls are entirely made of cloth except the heads which are most realistic and are crowned with wigs dressed in the latest styles of coiffeur.

"The purpose of the exposition, held under the auspices of the *Chambre syndicale de la couture Parisienne* (the League of Dressmakers) is to raise funds for the French Mutual Aide, an official charitable organization for helping the French poor.

"All these lovely dolls are the expression of the creative power of the French dressmakers who being unable to bring the world to their fashion salons, wish to send out these 'ambassadors' over the seven seas of the globe to demonstrate the vitality and the incontestable value of one of the most important industries of France. The Exposition will last a month in Paris, will go to Barcelona, to London and has been invited to America and Australia.

"Each *couturière* has dressed five dolls in the appropriate costumes for morning, afternoon, the cocktail hour, for dinner, and the fifth in a sumptuous evening gown.

"It goes without saying that exceptional care has been taken with the most minute details of these ensembles and dresses.

"In all fourteen scenes of about nine by four feet in size with decorations, lighting and accessories of the theatre have been provided as backgrounds for the dolls. Each of these backgrounds represents a different picture; one can see, for example, these 'ladies' in afternoon dresses on La Place Vendome, or if you please you may see them in morning dress on one of the bridges of the Seine. . . .

"The hats, gloves, shoes, jewelry and ornaments, executed by specialists—past masters in their art—happily complete the ensembles, and add to the charm of the 'spectacle,' unique of its kind and truly magnificent."

THE GLASS OF FASHION

A COLLECTION OF OLD DOLL CLOTHES, either on or off of their original wearers, can tell us almost as much about the fashions, the materials, the methods of construction, the social customs and the taste of the period in which they came into being as a whole run of *Godey's* or *Peterson's* magazines. Coupled with the style of hairdress, they go far towards fixing the date of the doll itself. Family traditions on this point may be wrong—and often are; antique dealers may be uninformed on the subject of types and dates; but the hairdo and the clothing, if original, are generally a pretty reliable guide.

Doll clothes were nearly always made from the materials at hand—leftovers from gowns of mother or aunt, and quite naturally they were apt to copy the styles of those gowns. Dolls in those early days were always ladies. There were no child dolls until 1851.

The sewing machine was invented by Elias Howe in 1846, but did not become a household fixture until well after the Civil War.

Women took much pride in their needlework, and with few interests outside the home they had time to do their work well. The woman of today must marvel at the tiny stitches, the "laid" gathers, the corded-in sleeves, the

Pictures of dolls discussed in this chapter will be found following page 60.

whale bones, the neatly bound seams, and the perfect buttonholes one finds in old doll clothes.

Nowhere except in an old log-cabin quilt, is there such an array of charming old prints, with patterns so neat, colorings so clear, as are found in these miniature dresses made in the American homes of the fifties, sixties, seventies and eighties. Other materials there are also—silks, satins, in plain, plaids or stripes; delaines, bombazines, brilliantines, mohairs, challis in a variety of colors and patterns—the history of textiles in miniature.

Godey's Lady's Book, the forerunner of a host of women's magazines, was founded in 1831. China doll heads were first made about 1820. Ludwig Greiner took out the first American doll-making patent in 1858, though dolls with papier mâché heads were made in Germany perhaps thirty years before that, and English wax dolls considerably earlier. These dates will suggest the time limits within which the average old doll dress may be likely to fall.

The clothes of American dolls were usually homemade but with the imported French dolls it was otherwise. Not only the clothes of the so-called "fashion dolls," but those of play dolls were professionally made in Paris. In this connection, it is interesting to note that according to the *Statistique d'Industrie à Paris,* Paris had in 1847 no less than 371 manufacturers of children's toys employing 2099 people.

About 1850 one could obtain a fully dressed doll for 4 francs and 50 centimes. A trousseau consisted of sixteen pieces: three dresses, shoes, stockings, hats, sacks and gloves.

M. Henry d'Allemagne in *Histoire des Jouets,* speaking of the period of the Exposition of 1849, says:

"There were several *modistes* who worked exclusively for these miniature people. The trade was lucrative; women earned three and four francs a day. The center of this business was in the streets around *le passage Choiseul* where there were many houses specializing in articles of dress for dolls, that made a fortune."

Not only were there modistes but shoemakers, wig-makers, and artificial flower-makers for dolls.

M. d'Allemagne, who is the best authority on this period says further: "The hair on these dolls was at first painted on papier mâché heads; but after, it was made of flax, and, for the finest dolls, of astrakan fur, which, not wearing well, was supplanted by the hair of the Tibetan goat."

In Tallis's *History and Description of the Crystal Palace Exposition of the World's Industry in 1851 in London,* we find:

"M. P. Jumeau of Paris received a prize medal for doll's dresses. The dolls on which these dresses were displayed presented no point worthy of commendation, but the dresses themselves were very beautiful productions. Not only were the outer robes accurate representations of the prevailing fashions in ladies' dresses but the undergarments were also in many cases complete facsimiles of those articles of wearing apparel. They might serve as excellent patterns for children to imitate and thus acquire the use of the needle, with knowledge of the arrangement of colors and material; in the latter respect they might indeed, afford valuable instruction to adults."

"Up attic," Tasha Tudor, the well-known illustrator of children's books (in private life Mrs. T. L. McCready Jr. of Contacook, N. H.), found "Sethany Ann," a doll of the period that had belonged to her grand-aunt. "Sethany Ann" is unusual because she has a German china head that calls for a wig. At this period France got its wax heads from England and its porcelain heads from Coburg, Sonnenburg and Nuremberg in Germany. The back of these heads was hollowed out, according to M. Natalis Rondot, a contemporary writer on commercial topics, "because this type of porcelain has to pay custom dues of 3 francs 80 centimes per kilogramme, so we are obliged to reduce the weight of these objects as much as possible."

This type of head in china is quite rare today. It is interesting to note that such china heads are often glazed inside as well as outside.

"Sethany Ann's" wig was missing when she was found and has been replaced by one made from Mrs. McCready's own hair. Her body is cloth, her arms, kid. She is 16 inches tall. When found, she was fully dressed with hand-made underwear, red silk garters with buckles, and a lovely striped pink taffeta dress with a dainty muslin guimpe. Everything is made with the most exquisitely fine stitches. She has eight pairs of shoes: five of them are boots, one of blue kid, trimmed with white kid and blue silk tassels; two pairs of bronze kid; one pair of blue silk with white kid toes; one pair, all blue silk; and three pairs of slippers, one bronze kid, one red kid, and one white taffeta. She had three pairs of kid gloves: one white with green stitching, two brown pairs, three pairs of half kid gloves and a long pair of black lace mitts. These are in a little red kid box 2½ inches long, marked "GANTES DE MA POUPÉE." She also has a vanity case of red kid, slightly larger and higher than the glove box in which there is a nail brush, a tooth brush, a mirror, a small pair of scissors and a tiny ivory-handled pen knife. In addition she has a sandalwood fan, delicately carved, and an ivory card case ¾ inch by ½ inch, that is lined with blue silk and contains tiny calling cards.

On the bottom of each tiny shoe and on the band of the skirt is marked *Huret à Paris,* and that would be Mlle. Calixto Huret, a Parisian doll-maker of 1850, who is noted for having invented a doll with gutta percha body and German china head—an innovation in dolls at the time.

Typical of the more elaborate and extensive wardrobes of some French dolls is that of a doll belonging to Mrs. C. L. Mitchell of San Antonio, Texas, which came to her mother, Anna V. A. Jamison of Albany, N. Y. about 1868. There are twelve dresses suitable for many occasions, nine hats, several cloaks or jackets, a silk apron, muff, ivory fan, numerous shoes and gloves; jewelry, a pocketbook, toilet case, and other accessories too numerous to mention. The doll wears a lorgnette on a chain and her hair is done in the waterfall style of the period.

Some idea of the luxury of the well-dressed Parisian doll may be gained from an enumeration of the dresses, which are all crinoline-lined, and each has an overskirt fastened on with a button. They are: black and white cotton with black taffeta ruching; tan organdie with red and white cotton braid trim; cerise taffeta trimmed with black velvet ribbon and black lace butterflies; black satin apron with paisley ribbon trim and sash; lavender taffeta with white silk lace and white chenille braid; black taffeta with fringed plaited ruching trim and a paisley shawl; grey and white brocaded satin trimmed with Alice-blue taffeta with black velvet ribbon and black and white silk lace; black brocaded taffeta with bunches of flowers, black velvet ribbon—and the finest workmanship; a blue and white striped wool, trimmed with a wider blue and white striped material, and an evening wrap of white cashmere and long silk chenille fringe, lined with pale-blue silk. The hats in various colors are trimmed with ostrich feathers and jet ornaments and one has a long real lace veil hanging down in the back to below the shoulders.

From Paris also comes "Adeline Houghton," belonging to Mrs. H. C. Ettinger, Laguna Beach, Calif. Like all Parians, Adeline was born in Germany, and is one of the few that have a commercial body. The body is marked on the chest in ink, now so faded that only a few of the letters are legible. She was given to Mrs. Ettinger in 1920 by a friend then about seventy-five years old who was the first owner of the doll. It had been brought to this woman from Paris when she was a small child, by a friend of her parents who was the American Ambassador to France.

Adeline still wears her original costume: the finest of underwear trimmed in tatting and thread lace; a dress in the style of the 1860's—plaid silk of red and dark blue, much ruffled, black jet buttons down the front of the waist, a val lace collar and an old coral brooch. The skirt of the dress is very full and lined with crinoline. Adeline has Parian hands and feet with shoes painted an odd shade of dark red.

"Ida Mae Russ," a smaller Parian, of the same Dagmar type as Adeline, belongs to Miss Maris Ransom of Woodstock, Vt., who is the third generation of the family to possess her. Her first owner was Ida Russ of Quechee, Vt., born about 1860, and who died when she was only ten years old. "Ida Mae's" old dress is a quaint brown challis figured with bright rosebuds and trimmed with a fancy red wool edging braid and red buttons.

"Laura Merrill" from Saxton's River, Vt., a wax doll—wax over papier mâché—of the early 1870's, in her red wool polonaise over a contrasting skirt of bright blue wool is the very "glass of fashion" of that particular period. Suggested by the Polish national costume, the polonaise came into favor in America just before the Centennial Exposition in 1876. It was generally worn with a skirt of a different color. The braiding on Laura's polonaise is intricate in pattern and hand-sewn with meticulously fine stitches. Her wardrobe is extensive and was not "made in Paris"—it is a product of Vermont mother-love.

"Zazu," a "ball-head" composition doll of the seventies, from Fairlee, Vt., models Laura's house-dress and apron. The dress, a wrapper made of an interesting bordered print in Persian coloring and design is buttoned all the way down the front with brown and white pearl buttons. Note the amplitude of the print apron. A similar apron, to be worn with the best dress, is of white figured Madras edged with blue plaid gingham.

The polonaise was soon superseded in popular favor by the Princess style created by Worth of Paris for the beautiful Princess of Wales, afterwards Queen Alexandra. In England and Paris it was made of rich materials, but for the Joel Ellis wooden doll of Chelsea, Vt., it was a creation of plaid gingham and cotton-back black velvet ribbon. Here is an example of how closely one may date a doll by its clothing. The Joel Ellis doll, as we have seen, was made in the later half of 1873, the Princess dress came out about 1876.

"Miss Madge" is a 12-inch wax doll whose determined mouth and piercing black glass eyes make her look like a spinster from some back hill Vermont farm on her way to Town Meeting, bent on speaking her mind on civic questions. She wears a neat print dress—"brown is so serviceable"—made in a style popular in the year 1880.

From Ludlow, Vt., comes the blue and white dimity dress buttoned with tiny three-holed buttons that is worn by the rare wooden "Martin" doll which was patented in 1879 and was an early product of the Mason and Taylor doll factory in Springfield.

The two dresses of the bustle period are worth notice. The model on the old blonde Superior doll is of brocaded brilliantine in taupe shade. The waist is buttoned down the back with silver buttons and the trimmings are blue and white plaid gingham. The second dress is figured yellow satin.

Of the overskirt period is the medium blue cashmere, made with a much ruffled underskirt and a basque. Fringe trims the pointed overskirt. The doll is much older than the dress, a German papier mâché with blown-glass eyes.

85

All these American doll clothes may be presumed to have been copied from gowns designed for and worn by women. Paradoxically, it is altogether probable that the gowns of some of the elegantly clad French dolls—even those that were not classed as "fashion dolls" were copied for and worn by women in England and America.

Godey's Lady's Book * became slightly doll conscious in 1868 and in July of that year published an illustration of "A FASHIONABLY DRESSED DOLL," and a page of doll clothes with the following comment:

"We present our juvenile readers with a complete outfit for a doll, a very desirable selection, as doll outfits are now made so complete as to frequently cost one hundred dollars. The Fashion Editress can supply the paper patterns for the underclothing."

This is probably the first time that paper patterns for doll clothes were ever offered for sale. The article also gives knitting directions for a doll's stockings and boots and for a muff and Victorine (a sort of neckpiece or tippet) to be "worked in fur knitting" in white and black Angora wool to simulate ermine.

Considerable difference of opinion exists among collectors as to whether old dolls should be restored to pristine beauty of paint and wig and given new wardrobes (frequently made of old silks and laces) or kept in original clothing "as is" with their honorable scars of time and much loving, and given only such restoration as may be necessary to keep them from being classed as "Lame Lizzies" and "Dirty Doras."

There is something to be said for both schools of thought.

For those who like to dress their own dolls, the following list of books will be found helpful:

Barton, Lucy, *Historic Costume for the Stage,* Walter H. Baker Co., Boston, 1938.

Edson, Doris, and Barton, Lucy, *Period Patterns,* Walter H. Baker Co., Boston, 1942.

* While dogs and cats frequently appear with children in the *Godey* colored fashion plates, dolls are extremely rare. A child with a doll on the frontispiece of the 1851 volume and a child with doll and doll carriage on an 1873 plate are almost the only instances.

Hall, Carrie A., *From Hoopskirts to Nudity,* The Caxton Printers, Ltd., Caldwell, Idaho, 1938.

McClellan, Elizabeth, *Historic Dress in America*, 2 volumes, J. W. Jacobson, Philadelphia, 1904.

These four books together with such volumes as may be available of *Godey's Lady's Book* (1831–1898), and *Peterson's Magazine* (1840–1898), will answer practically any costume question on any period in which the doll collector is likely to be interested.

Lucy Barton's *Historic Costume for the Stage* is extremely valuable because it covers not only clothes, but hair-dressing, jewelry, shoes and accessories, worn by both men and women at each period. There is also a valuable bibliography of costume books and fashion magazines at the end of the book.

Carrie Hall's *From Hoopskirts to Nudity* covers the years 1866–1936. It is useful because the majority of costume books end with 1879. Mrs. Hall speaks with authority on these later years of American dress during which she was the leading modiste of the Southwest. It is said that over 200,000 gowns were made in her Kansas City shop.

WAX DOLLS

JOHN ASHTON in *Social Life in the Reign of Queen Anne,* a book based on original sources, newspapers, pamphlets, letters, broadsides, handbills, etc. from 1702–1714, says:

"We know how, from earliest ages, dolls have been the favorite toy with girls, and the reign of 'Good Queen Anne' was no exception to the general rule—but they were not then called dolls, but 'babies.' . . . Some were of wax, but these, of course, were the expensive sort as must have been those in Widow Smith's raffle—'large joynted dressed Babies.' Probably dolls were the girls' only playthings."

In the same volume, we read of a maker of wax figures, a Mrs. Salmon, who, according to her handbills, had an exhibition "of famous persons and incidents, all richly dressed and composed with so much variety of invention that it is wonderfully diverting to all lovers of Art and Ingenuity. All made by Mrs. Salmon and to be seen at the Horn Tavern in Fleet Street."

There was a similar show of "effigies of famous persons, to be seen every day at Mr. Goldsmith's, in Green Court in the Old Jury." A contemporary newspaper paragraph from the *Daily Courant,* August 6, 1702, speaks of this artist as "Mrs. Goldsmith, the famous Woman of Waxwork," on the occasion of her bringing "to Westminster Abbey the funeral effigy of that celebrated beauty,

Pictures of dolls discussed in this chapter will be found following page 92.

the late Duchess of Richmond, which is said to be the richest figure that ever was set up in King Henry's Chapel."

Did either of these "famous women of waxwork" make wax dolls? We do not know—but they may well have done so. Just how much earlier than this wax dolls were made in England we probably will never know.

Max von Boehn in *Dolls and Puppets* says that wax dolls appeared in Germany in the seventeenth century and that the products of one Daniel Neuberger of Augsberg were praised by Joachim von Sandaart as being as hard as stone and "so marvellously colored that they seemed alive."

In Italy, it is said, wax was used for making religious figures very early. Dolls for this purpose were made and sold outside the Church of the Annunciation in Florence, the walls of which were covered with such offerings. These—if they can be classed as *dolls*—were probably the earliest made in Italy.

It was in England, however, that wax dolls, as such, were developed, and that country continued to lead in their manufacture until the very last years of the nineteenth century at least.

A few years ago Howard F. Porter, of the Old Print Exchange, New York City, when purchasing a group of old prints from the descendants of the famous British actress, Mary Dance, discovered—and purchased—four early wax dolls made about 1770 and presented to Mary Dance in 1808. The dolls, which represent a clergyman and wife, and a soldier and wife, are made of yellow and pink wax over wood. Their picture, taken from a cover of *Hobbies*, shows that the English doll-makers were using glass eyes at least as early as the end of the eighteenth century. These dolls were sold to Mrs. Velvalee Dickinson, and their present whereabouts is unknown. (Shown following page 60.)

The glass eyes in the early English wax dolls were without pupils and very dark—violet-blue and brown, almost black. Mrs. Clear thinks she has found traces of cobalt blue in the making of these eyes. Such eyes were used down to about 1840–50.

An early type of French wax doll—wax over papier mâché—is sometimes found. The head is about the size of a pullet's egg, with oval glass eyes and real hair wigs. Some heads are "ball-head" type with a slit cut into the top into which the hair is thrust. Mrs. Ralph E. Wakeman of Claremont, N. H., found that the hair was firmly glued between half moons of stiff paper, thrust into the slit and then slightly turned to prevent slipping out. Another type has open heads with wigs, similar to modern dolls.

The dolls are about 15 inches tall with cloth bodies and arms of leather or white kid. Those with the brown leather arms have only three fingers on their hands, a fact pointed out to us by Mrs. Katherine Frye of Claremont, N. H. Those having arms of white kid have the usual five fingers, and sometimes have three rows of stitching up the back of each hand, simulating long white gloves.

The clothing is always beautifully hand-sewn and obviously French.

These dolls are definitely dated as about 1838 by one which B. H. Leffingwell of Rochester, N. Y., bought from a Massachusetts "picker." It had evidently been in an antique show or Historical Society exhibit for it bears a tag reading:

"Brought to Abbie Foster from Paris in 1838."

This doll, which has the open type of head, is shown in the group of illustrations following page 92.

Moving eyes in dolls were first used in England and the date is about 1825. The eyes were opened and shut by means of a wire coming out of the body at the waist line.

About this time France made two further advances in the art of doll-making. Walking dolls appeared in Paris in 1826, and a children's periodical, *Le Bon Genie,* reported that in the Exposition of French Industry, in 1823, there were dolls which said "Mamma" when their right hands were touched, and "Papa" when their left hands were touched. This mechanism was patented in 1824 by Johann Maelzel (1772–1838) whose invention, the metronome, is familiar to all students of the piano.

About 1850 M. Natalie Rondot of Paris wrote: "We get our papier mâché (doll) heads from Germany and our wax heads from England."

In 1861, there were 23 wholesale doll-makers in London and about this time a glass manufacturer in Birmingham gave testimony before the House of Commons that he had received a single order for 500 pounds ($2500) worth of doll eyes. In 1877 we find that London is importing glass doll eyes from Germany:

"Hundreds of gross of them, assorted in size and packed in large cases, are sent over to England annually." (*Harper's Bazaar,* Aug., 1877.)

In spite of these facts, which indicate the considerable extent of the doll-making industry in England, we know almost nothing of the history or the personality of the men who were responsible for it. The names of only two firms are familiar, the Montanari family and Charles Marsh.

Certain late wax dolls—wax over papier mâché—are marked *Charles Marsh, London.*

Marsh's name first appears in the Post Office London Directory and in the "Trades Directory" section of the same, in the year 1878 as:

"Charles Mash, Doll manufacturer, 114 Fulham road SW."

This misprint of the name is corrected in the Directory of 1879 and there reads:

"Charles Marsh, Doll Manufacturer, 114 Fulham Road SW."

In this form the entry continues down to 1891. Directories between 1891 and 1895 are not available in the Library of Congress. In the edition of 1895, the name of Charles Marsh no longer appears and he may be presumed to have died in the intervening years but his successor—apparently his widow—was carrying on the business at the same address. From 1895–1900 (which is the last issue of the London P. O. Directory in the Library of Congress) the entry appears as:

"Mary Ann Marsh (Mrs.), Doll Manufacturer, 114 Fulham Road SW."

Mary Ann Marsh may conceivably have continued the marking used by her husband so that any doll marked "Charles Marsh, London," can be dated as made anywhere between 1878 and 1900.

From Tallis's *History and Description of the Crystal Palace Exposition of the World's Industry in 1851 in London,* we learn of the Montanari:

"The only exhibition of wax dolls that was deserving was one by Augusta Montanari, of Upper Charlotte St., to which a prize medal was awarded. The display of this exhibitor was the most remarkable and beautiful collection of toys in the Great Exhibition. It consisted of a series of dolls representing all ages, from infancy to womanhood, arranged in several family groups, with suitable and elegant model furniture. These dolls had the hair, eyelashes, and eyelids separately inserted in the wax, and were, in other respects, modelled with life-like truthfulness. Much skill was also evinced in the variety of expression which was given to these figures in regard of the ages and stations which they were intended to represent. From the prices of these dolls, however, they were adapted rather for the children of the wealthy than for general sale; since the prices of the undressed dolls were from 10*s.* to 105*s.* each; the dressed dolls which were attired with much taste, were much more expensive, and varied in price according to the richness of the material of which the robes were made. In a small case adjoining that which contained the toys just enumerated were displayed several rag dolls, which were very remarkable considering the materials of which they were made. They consisted entirely of textile fabrics, and the dolls which were intended and very well adapted for the nursery, were reasonable in price, varying from 6*s. 6d.,* to 30*s.* per doll.

Of the Paris World Exposition, 1852, M. Henry d'Allemagne wrote—

"In this same Exposition the wax dolls were of beautiful workmanship, but their prices were prohibitive for general trade.

"Mme. Montanari of London showed wax dolls of large size and of great variety executed with care and a remarkable perfection; M. Napoleon Montanari of London exhibited some groups of statuettes and figurines in wax of a perfect execution; and M. Richard Montanari of London exhibited heads of dolls in wax covered with fine muslin. This invention, which seems to be good, has not yet the sanction of use or time.

These two paragraphs regarding their exhibits in two expositions seem to be the source literature on the subject of the Montanari family and everything that has been written about them since is derived from these two paragraphs.

This may be supplemented somewhat by reference to the Post Office London Directory. In available volumes—1856, 1857, 1858, 1860—the following listing appears:

Left, Early sleeping-eyed doll. England, 1825. Eyes work by wire at the waist line. *Right,* Early English wax dolls. About 1845. *Collection of Mrs. Otis Carl Williams, Worcester, Massachusetts.*

Left, "Victoria," Montanari doll by Richard Montanari. About 1880. Marked inside with incised "M." *Collection of Mrs. William Walker, Louisville, Kentucky. Right,* Old French wax doll. Card reads "Brought from Paris to Abbie Foster, 1838." Head probably made in England. *Courtesy of B. H. Leffingwell, Rochester, New York.*

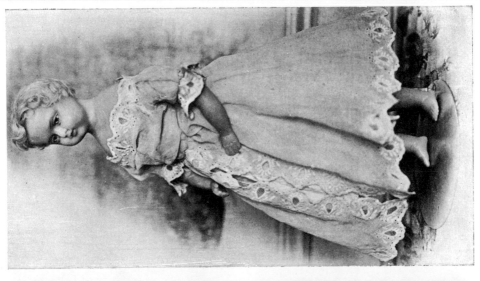

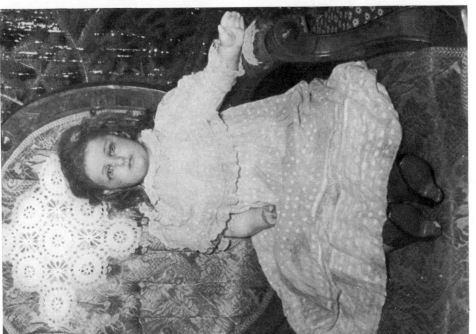

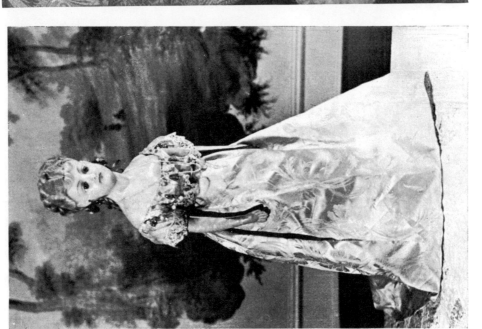

Left, Montanari doll loaned to Joslyn Memorial Museum, Omaha, Omaha, Nebraska. About 1851. Collection of Mrs. John T. Buchanan, Omaha, Nebraska. Center, 41-inch wax doll. Hair set in the wax. Original clothes. About 1850, probably Montanari. Collection of Miss Grace Woodworth, Colorado Springs, Colorado. Right, Original Montanari child doll, exhibited at Crystal Palace Exposition, London, 1851. On loan to Joslyn Memorial Museum, Omaha, Nebraska. Collection of Mrs. John T. Buchanan, Omaha, Nebraska.

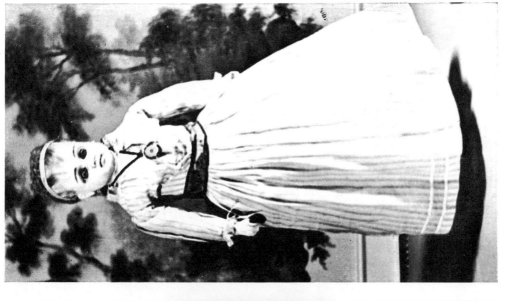

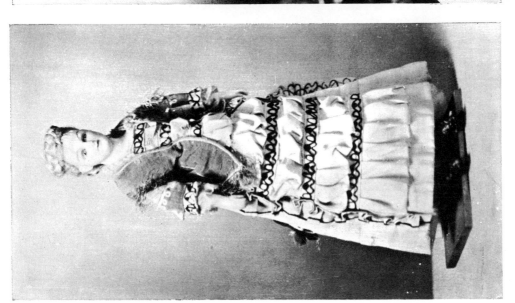

Left, Montanari doll by Richard Montanari, 1873. Represents Princess Alexandra of Wales. All original. *Center*, "Janet"—wax doll about 1850. *Collection of Mrs. William Walker, Louisville, Kentucky. Right*, "Amelia Earhart" old wax doll, all original. *Collection of Mrs. John T. Buchanan, Omaha, Nebraska.*

Collection of wax dolls. Note the rare boy doll. *Collection of Miss Marie Ketterman, York, Pennsylvania.*

Left, "Gussie"—wax doll with lamb's wool wig. *Collection of Mrs. H. C. Ettinger, Laguna Beach, California.*
Right, Wax child doll about 1885. *St. George Collection.*

Types of china dolls. *Back row, left to right*—"Jenny Lind," "Countess Dagmar," Pink Luster, Flat Top. *Front row*—Brown-eyed, 1880 type, "Ball Head."

Comparison of old dolls with Staffordshire figurine. *St. George Collection.*

Super-rare china doll with sleeping eyes. Probably the only one of her type. Pink Luster china. *Collection of Miss Grace Bennet, Oregon.*

Left, 10-inch ball head or Biedermeier china doll, presumably about 1830. *Right,* Types of china doll—Blonde "Curly Top" or "Godey" doll; 7-inch "Jenny Lind"; small Pink Luster.

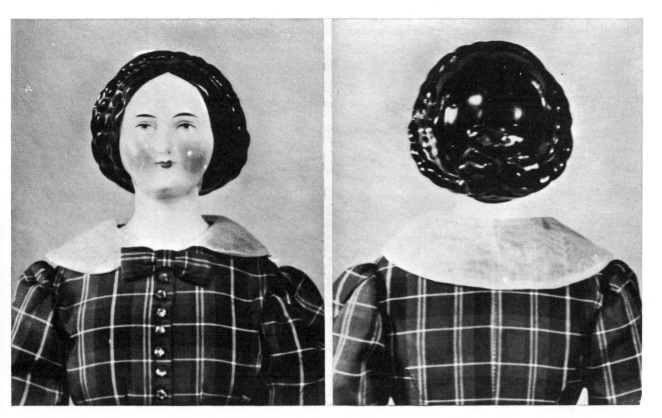

"Victoria," a rare type of china head doll. May be intended for a portrait of Queen Victoria. *Collection of Mrs. Webster Sugg, Jr., Morganfield, Kentucky.*

Left, Red-haired china doll. *Collection of Mrs. George De Sylva, Los Angeles, California. Right,* Doll with blown-glass eyes. *Collection of Mrs. John M. Pierce, Springfield, Vermont.*

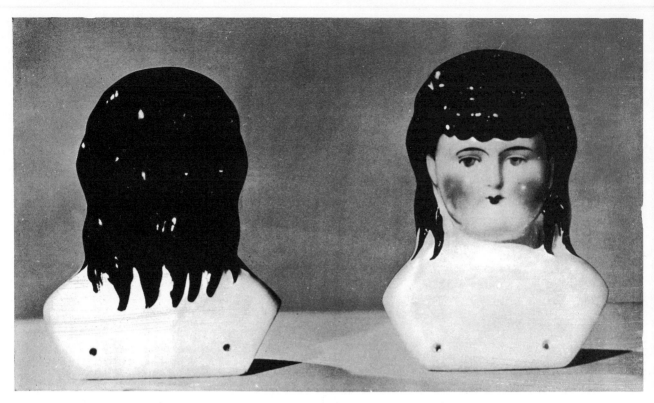

China head with long curls. *Collection of Mrs. Edmund Poetter, Reading, Vermont.*

Left, Brown-eyed china doll with molded eyeballs. *Collection of Mrs. E. A. Heiss, Washington, D. C. Right,* Brown-haired china doll. *Collection of Mrs. Nina Shepherd, Granville, Ohio.*

Left, Unusual china doll with head definitely turned to one side. Ribbon molded on head confining regularly placed curls. *Collection of Mrs. Leo F. Lamb, Santa Ana, California. Right,* China doll with swivel neck and turning head, 10 inches tall. *Collection of Mrs. Cyrus M. Beachy, Wichita, Kansas.*

Left, "Frieda von Schall," rare early Meissen doll. *Collection of Mrs. John T. Buchanan, Omaha, Nebraska Right,* "Alice in Wonderland" china doll. About 1865. *Collection of Mrs. Cyrus M. Beachy, Wichita, Kansas.*

Caterina Conaro Lusignan, rare Capo di Monte doll (or figurine?). *Collection of Mrs. Grace Perlberg, New York.*

Left, "Cecile," rare pink luster Meissen doll. *Collection of Mrs. H. C. Ettinger, Laguna Beach, California.*
Right, "Francis Dee," china doll with unusual hairdo, all original. 1850's. *Collection of Mrs. John T. Buchanan, Omaha, Nebraska.*

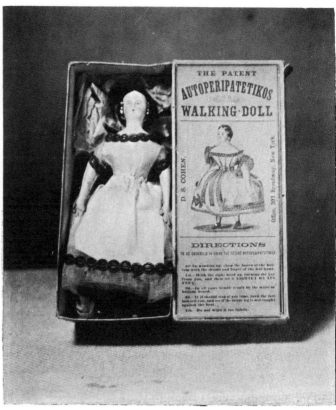

Left, "Mrs. General"—unusual china head doll. *Collection of Mrs. John M. Pierce, Springfield, Vermont. Right,* 10-inch china walking doll in original box. *Courtesy of Mrs. Lily M. Toth, Vineyard Haven, Massachusetts.*

Left, "Marie Marseilles" of Woodstock, Vermont. About 1850. *Right,* "Rosaleen" of Fairlee, Vermont. An unusual type with china hands and leather arms. All original. 1873.

Dresden or Parian head imported by Alma Robeck's grandfather, an Annapolis, Maryland, baker and confectioner, about 1860. Found in original wrappings. *Collection of Miss Alma Robeck, Annapolis, Maryland.*

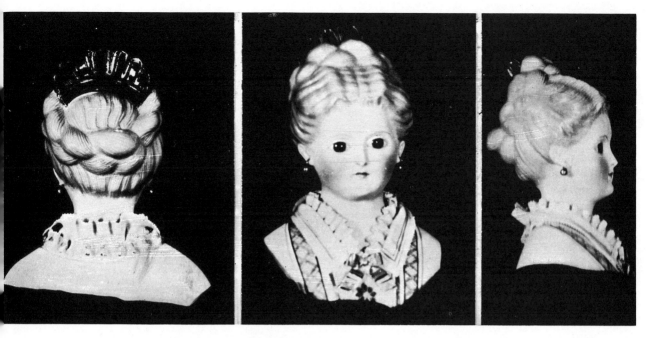

Rare Dresden or Parian head with triple luster ruff and blown-glass eye. *Collection of Mrs. Gurth Ritter, Torrence, California.*

Left, Rare Parian sometimes called "Toinette" or "Mary Antoinette." Found in Woodstock, Vermont, by Mrs. Winifred Harding. Present owner is unknown. *Right,* Parian head with flowers. *Courtesy of Mrs. William F. Harvey, Cortland, New York.*

Left, Parian doll said to represent the Empress Eugénie. *St. George Collection. Right,* Parian doll with blown-glass eyes. *Collection of Mrs. A. E. Heiss, Washington, D. C.*

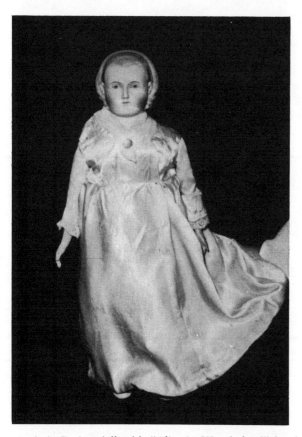

Left, Parian doll with "Alice in Wonderland" head, 1865. Head is a replacement on a much earlier heirloom doll which has belonged to four generations of one family. Owned by Mrs. Charlotte Sizemore, Keene, New Hampshire. *Right,* Parian doll. *Collection of Mrs. William Walker, Louisville, Kentucky.*

Parian dolls. *Collection of Mrs. Glen Bartshe, Cleveland, Ohio.*

Left, Modern Parians made by the Clears. Designed by Martha Oathout Ayres. Called the finest portrait dolls of all time. *Right,* "Carrie Ordway," Parian doll, found in Vermont. *Collection of Mrs. Chester Dimick, Gales Ferry, Connecticut.*

Two Jumeau dolls representing different periods. **Large** doll has stationary head. Small doll has swivel neck. Dolls have been redressed. *Collection of Mrs. Leo F. Lamb, Santa Ana, California.*

WAX DOLLS

Montanari, Augusta (Madame), Model wax doll manufacturer.
13 Charles St., Soho Square W.
Montanari, Napoleon, Modeller, 13 Charles St., Soho Square W.

In the Trades Directory section of these volumes, under the heading: "DOLLS" only the name of Mme. Augusta Montanari appears—*not* Napoleon. Under the title "MODELLERS" in the Trades Directory is the note: *"See also* SCULPTORS."

In the next available volume of the Directories, 1870, the names of the elder Montanari, Augusta and Napoleon, do not appear, but among the twenty-three names listed under DOLL-MAKERS is:

Montanari, Richard (wax), 70 Warren St., Fitzroy Square, W.

and the name is marked with a dagger indicating a wholesale Doll-Maker.

In the 1873 volume on page 1116, Commercial section, the listing is:

Montanari, Richard, prize wax and rag dolls manufacturer, artist
and modeller in wax, 12 Oxford Street W.

Here in 1878, Richard Montanari has changed his address to "3 Rathbone Street W." and this continues to be his address in 1879 and through 1884. In 1884 he is designated as a "Wax and Rag Doll-maker" and still carries beside his name the dagger indicating a wholesale doll manufacturer.

In the only available volume of the Post Office London Directory, between 1884 and 1891, 1887, Richard Montanari appears as above but in the volume of 1891 his name is not listed.

The name of no other Montanari appears in any of the directories so we can assume that the doll-making Montanari were Mme. Augusta Montanari, the mother, and Richard Montanari, her son. Evidently the husband and father, Napoleon Montanari, was a modeller and sculptor in wax, but not a doll-maker. The Montanari wax dolls, then, appear to cover a period of approximately thirty-seven years—from 1850 to about 1887.

For the rest, we must turn to the study of the dolls themselves, as with other dolls. Prior to 1850 dolls were conceived as being "ladies" and it was Mme. Montanari in her exhibit at the Crystal Palace Exposition that year who introduced and popularized the "child" doll and the "baby" doll. An example of the child doll, which came from the hand of Augusta Montanari, herself, and was exhibited by her at the Crystal Palace is the charming "Amy May Hockaday" from the collection of Mrs. John T. Buchanan of Omaha, Nebr., which, with others of Mrs. Buchanan's fine collection, is on exhibit at the Joslyn Memorial Museum in Omaha. There are several lovely wax dolls in this collection, one other at least that may be considered to be a Montanari doll, "Mrs. White," 1863.

Not too many of the Montanari dolls have come down to us because, being of thick wax, they were much more subject to vicissitudes of climate—the extremes of heat and cold—than the cheaper and stronger heads of papier mâché, simply coated with wax. The Montanari wax dolls are characterized by great beauty, exquisite modelling and workmanship, and fine eyes. They do not have wigs. The hairs are set individually in the wax. This process is described in an article on "The Manufacture of Dolls" in *Harper's Bazaar,* August 18,1877.

"When the eyes are inserted in the head, the next point is the putting on of the hair. This is an important consideration of the manufacturer, being the most costly part of the whole toy. . . . This work is all done by women. The head to be adorned is placed on a block, and the operator holding in her left hand the hair, carefully combed and cut in a uniform length; in her right hand a dull knife, with which she lifts a small piece of wax, and pushes the hair underneath. When she has finished this process by inserting only two or three hairs at a time, she takes an iron roller and gently but firmly rubs it over the surface, thus fastening the hair securely on the head This is a very tedious process and only used on the more expensive dolls. In the less expensive or composition ones, a deep groove is cut completely through the skull along the top of the head where the parting is to be and the uncurled ends of the ringlets are pushed in with a blunt knife and then fastened down with paster."

Montanari dolls are not supposed to have been marked, but the very English-looking Montanari baby doll, "Victoria," which Mrs. William Walker, a Louisville, Kentucky collector, bought from a toy shop window in Knightsbridge, London, was found to have an incised "M" on the inside of her shoulders, when her head accidentally came off. Judging by the style of her dress which has the panel front that was fashionable for infants in the year 1880, "Victoria" is probably among the last dolls of Richard Montanari. Mrs. Walker carried "Victoria" all over Europe and across the ocean carefully packed in cotton batten. Some time after she was home she remembered that there had been two other Montanari wax dolls in the shop and wrote the United States Ambassador and Mrs. Robert Bingham, who were friends, asking them to procure these two dolls for her. When they visited the place, they found that the owner had died, the stock had been dispersed and the shop closed.

Also by Richard Montanari would be the dainty 20-inch little lady who is the only Montanari doll in the writer's collection. Her date would be about 1876 as she is clearly a portrait of the lovely Princess of Wales, afterwards Queen Alexandra. In original condition down to the tiniest button, she wears a cream white wool dress in the "Princess" style, designed by Worth for Alexandra in 1876. This doll, discovered in the attic of a Maine sea captain's home, evidently considered too fine to be played with, had been stored away in the attic, and forgotten for years.

A wax lady of unusual individuality, who might well be a Montanari, but is not, is "Janet" (1848), owned by Mrs. William Walker.

Mrs. Walker's collection is especially interesting because many of the dolls have been given to Mrs. Walker by descendants of their original owners (well-known Kentuckians). Nearly all are dressed in materials from wedding gowns or party dresses of earlier generations—people well-known locally—which make the dolls of special interest to Louisville. Mrs. Walker, who is a florist, displays her dolls in connection with the flowers in her shop, so that others may share her enjoyment. Occasionally they have been exhibited at the Art Museum and she has given talks before the Filson Club, an historical society, co-operating in the displays with Mrs. Charles W. Allen whose collection of doll furniture, much of which has local interest, is also notable.

"Janet's" head was given Mrs. Walker by an old friend, Miss Lillie Keller, about eighty years old, along with a beautiful Jumeau doll that had belonged to Miss Keller's aunt, Anna Dorothea Vohler, who was born in Louisville in 1845, and died at the age of sixteen in 1861. The wax head had belonged to a sister of Dorothea, which would make the head about ninety-two years old.

The face was almost black. The hair was in a net and there was a little Roman striped ribbon around the hair. Mrs. Walker washed the face with a little butter and found underneath all the grime a little beauty with classic features and glass eyes. Sent to Mrs. Clear at Humpty Dumpty Doll Hospital to make a body, she came back perfect and with lovely wax hands. Says Mrs. Valker: "Miss Alice Jones gave me an old striped French mull that was originally a child's dress which made a lovely gown for this beautiful lady. The material was 125 years old so I had to line it throughout with net."

After the Montanari dolls were exhibited in Paris, the French doll-makers also undertook the manufacture of thick wax dolls. These French dolls are very lovely but not many of them have survived for the same reasons that we have so few Montanari dolls. The French dolls generally have wigs. In the Joslyn Museum, Omaha, in the collection of Mrs. John T. Buchanan, is a lovely French wax doll, exquisitely dressed in Paris in pale blue brocade, real lace and pearl trimming. Less elegant, but also French, is a later example from the author's doll family, in her original 1880 overskirt dress of white cotton.

Max von Boehn seems to imply that after the English put glass eyes in wax dolls, the Germans, with their cheaper labor, were able to practically take the market for these dolls. This is hardly borne out by the facts; the high quality of the English wax dolls and the number of doll-makers which P. O. London Directory lists during the 1870's and 1880's—the period during which wax dolls were most favored.

Germany did make wax dolls, generally of the cheaper kind. In the 1870's, a popular style of hairdo showed the hair parted in the middle with high rolls, like the pompadour—at right angles to the forehead on either side of the part. Sometimes on cheaper wax and composition dolls, these rolls had a foundation of matted hair similar to the "rats" worn in the nineties. Quite often, on the cheapest dolls, the foundation of the rolls were just raised places in the composition—"bumps" on the doll's head, as it were. We are inclined to think that these are German made dolls. We have seen few fine wax dolls to compare with the English or French dolls that can be definitely traced to Germany, though such may exist, of course.

Mexico has some fine wax dolls as will be seen by two examples: the figurine, "The Water Carrier" owned by Miss Grace Woodworth of Denver, Colo., and "Areza," the very Spanish Senorita from the collection of Mr. John D. McEwen of Wichita, Kansas. She was found in a shop in Dallas, Texas, in 1939, but is clearly of Mexican or Spanish origin. The head is wax with brown molded wax hair; the hands and feet are wax with high button boots molded on. The body is cloth.

About 1840–45 wax dolls with molded hair, the so-called "pumpkin" or "squash" head dolls were fairly numerous. Examples of these are the two dolls in the Boston rocker belonging to Mrs. Otis Carl Williams of Worcester, Mass., collected by Mrs. Williams' mother, a generation ago, and the 10-inch doll which Miss Alma Robeck of Annapolis, Md., found in Gettysburg, Pa., in a house on the site of the battleground. Its former owner said it had come from France.

Lambs' wool wigs were used to some degree on wax dolls and occasionally on bisque dolls in the 1880 period. A charming example of this is the wax doll "Gussie" which belongs to Mrs. H. C. Ettinger, Laguna Beach, Calif.

One sometimes sees a wax head with the hat molded on the head, a sort of "walking" hat shape, with three plumes. Mrs. Cyrus M. Beachy, the well-known doll collector, of Wichita, Kansas, who is past eighty years old, remembers having worn identically this type of hat when she was a child. Yet most owners of such dolls dress them as "ladies" and call them "Empress Eugenie." We wonder.

There are many interesting types of small wax dolls to be found such as Mrs. P. C. Beatty's little beauty with violet eyes that came from Philadelphia, or the quaint little 1880 school girl—9 inches tall—and the 1870 housewife with wooden arms and legs, from the author's collection. A group of small wax dolls owned by Miss Marie Ketterman of York, Pa., all of which were obtained from first owners, includes a boy doll, not often seen in wax.

Wax dolls, after being somewhat neglected by collectors until a few years ago, are coming into their own. The prices are still within reason, however, and it is possible for a collector with a modest budget to assemble a very interesting group of wax dolls without her conscience reproaching her for extravagance.

CHINA HEAD DOLLS

IN RESPONSE to an inquiry, the Victoria and Albert Museum, London, wrote under date of December 19, 1944:

"There is no record of the making of dolls' heads in any of the foremost English potteries. It would perhaps be surprising if the numerous Staffordshire potters did not turn their attention to this minor phase of their craft in the second half of the nineteenth century when the china head was so popular, but there is no record whatever of their having done so."

This statement from so good an authority would seem to dispose of the earlier classifications of china doll heads as "Staffordshire," "Chelsea," etc., and the talk about "moon spots" in the china as identifying the heads as "Chelsea." If any doll heads had been made commercially in any of the English potteries, the evidence of the fact would still exist in the waste piles and rubble dumped from any ceramic factory, for the fragments are practically indestructible. These piles have been turned over again and again and since remains of doll heads have never been found, it can only mean that none ever existed there.

This does not, however, preclude the possibility that individual workers may not have tried their hands at making an occasional doll for their own children or as an experiment. Such a thought is suggested by a comparison of

Pictures of dolls discussed in this chapter will be found following page 92.

the small old china doll heads with the figures on the Staffordshire inkwell in the same picture. The taller of the two dolls is very early. She is all original: body of homespun linen; dress and petticoats of old hand block-printed cotton. She was "my dear dolly" who comforted her little girl owner, well over a hundred years ago, through the tedious days of the long sea voyage from England in a sailing ship.

Possibly the rarest of all china head dolls are those with inset glass eyes. These too may have been workmen's experiments, for Mrs. Clear says they have had a few of these dolls in for repair that seem to suggest an English origin in the fact that the eyes are similar to those used in the early English wax dolls—dark blurred eyes with the pupils not clearly defined and separated from the iris as they are in the Continental-made eyes.

The Humpty Dumpty Doll Hospital is a wonderful clearing house for doll information because thousands of dolls of all types pass through their hands in the course of each year. Mrs. Clear's generosity and unselfish willingness to share this information with others puts the whole doll collecting world deeply in her debt.

A super-rare china doll head with *sleeping* glass eyes, possibly the only one of its kind in existence, was recently in the hospital for repairs.

Almost as rare is the type with swivel neck similar to the Jumeau doll patent. There are only two of these known to us. One is "Thelma Todd" owned by Mrs. Cyrus M. Beachy of Wichita, Kansas; the other was found some years ago in an estate auction in New England by Mrs. Ralph E. Wakeman of Claremont, New Hampshire, and later on found its way into the collection of Mrs. Charles Allen of Glenview, Kentucky.

China doll heads were made in continental Europe—chiefly in Germany and the industry has centered around the cities of Sonnenberg and Nuremberg. All over Europe there are deposits of clay suitable for making of porcelain and china. The quality of the china depends—in addition to the quality of the clay —upon the fineness with which it has been ground. China is always glazed.

The number and variety of facial types and hair dress in china head dolls, indicate the probability that most of them were made in small back-yard kilns— a family industry, as toy making has largely been in Germany. Their beauty and detail depend on the taste and skill of the individual workman. Quite often they have been cast in the same molds as Parian or other types of material. An instance of this is the so-called "Countess Dagmar" head which is found in china as well as Parian; blonde in the Parian, it has black hair in china. It is much more rare in the latter medium. The picture of the china Countess Dagmar belonging to Mrs. Ruby Selby is shown following page 12 through the courtesy of the Charles W. Bowers Memorial Museum, Santa Ana, California. The daguerreotype setting was designed—and is patented—by Mrs. F. E. Coulter, who is Curator of the Museum, for the artistic display of dolls at the National Doll Exhibit in the Museum.

In the matter of complexion, black-haired dolls outnumber blondes about ten to one in the china heads and blue eyes far outnumber brown eyes. Considering that the Germans are blonde blue-eyed people, it is probably because the contrast between whiteness of the china and the black hair seems more striking to the doll-artist. There are a few china dolls with brown hair—such as the brown-haired china doll belonging to Mrs. Nina Shepherd of Granville, Ohio. Occasionally there is even a red-haired doll like the little girl with curls and a blue china hat in the collection of Mrs. George De Sylva, Los Angeles. This is a most unusual head. Brown-eyed china-head dolls are very attractive. Occasionally these eyes are luster. A point worth noting about the painted eyes of china heads is that a red line indicating the eyelid is usually found on the old dolls but this is missing on more recent and cheaper heads.

The style of hair dress is a pretty good indication of the period in which the doll was made; the waterfall or chignon, mistakenly called snood, for example, may be dated as 1860 1870—the period when this style was fashionable. Bangs would naturally indicate the early 1890's when this style was worn.

One type of china head is without any molded hair at all. This is the so-called "ball-head" or "Biedermeier" type which has only a small tonsure-like spot of black at the crown of the head. This doll is supposed to have a hair wig attached to this spot with glue. To be correct the wig should be made of very fine hair—a child's hair.

There is some difference of opinion about the date of this doll but it is generally conceded to be of about 1830 or soon after—the Biedermeier period.

Certainly this doll, which comes in several sizes, is older than most china-head dolls. Such specimens as are found with original cloth bodies and china arms and legs have the flat heelless shoe of the Empire and Romantic periods. Flat slippers were worn during the First Empire, 1798–1815, and during the Romantic period, 1815–1840. In the latter years ankle boots without heels were worn as well as the slippers and this is the type of shoe found on these dolls. In Max von Boehn's *Dolls and Puppets* is pictured a similar doll without wig, labelled *Biedermeier*.

China is both "hard paste" and "soft paste" according to the elements in the clay, so doll heads are both hard and soft in texture. The white "soft paste" heads usually show more signs of wear than the others. Some of the white china heads are extremely hard. The pink heads, which are quite numerous in various sizes and types are of harder paste than most of the others and so are better preserved—often quite new looking. These are the heads that collectors formerly called "Chelsea." They are now generally known as "pink luster."

Very deep shoulders are characteristic of many of the older china heads—but not of all by any means.

One line of china heads, probably dating after 1880 have necklaces of gold paint adorned with colored glass "jewels" fused into the glaze. Comparatively late also, are the dolls with names such as "Bertha," "Dorothy," etc. marked on the chest or back with gold.

China heads after 1898 will, of course, be marked *Germany*. Occasionally china heads are marked with other letters and figures but there seems no way of finding out the meaning of these markings.

There are a number of china portrait dolls, most notable of which are the various "Jenny Linds" which were made during the Jenny Lind craze when the Swedish singer visited the United States in the 1850's. Some of the others may be only attributions by collectors because of fancied resemblances to noted women. The name of Mary Todd Lincoln, the wife of Abraham Lincoln, has been given to a whole group of dolls of a certain type for instance. Adelina Patti, Dollie Madison, Empress Eugenie, Queen Victoria, are among the supposed likenesses in china-head dolls.

Two "Queen Victoria" dolls are outstanding. One of these belongs to Mrs. Blanche Watson of Geneva, Ill. She has a very beautiful hairdo and is really much handsomer than the plain little Queen. The other "Victoria," owned by Mrs. Webster Sugg, Jr., Morganfield, Ky., really does look like the Queen, so much so, that Jan Struther, the English author, immediately recognized it as Victoria and begged to take it back to England with her. The hair is done in a coronet braid and is very plain in the top and back. This is evidently a rare type. The doll was found in a roadhouse in Illinois.

Dolls with the head turned to one side are fairly common in bisque, rare in china. One of these few is the lovely old china doll belonging to Mrs. Leo F. Lamb of Santa Ana, Calif.

"Frances Dee," of the collection of Mrs. John T. Buchanan in the Joslyn Memorial Museum of Omaha, Nebr., came from California. She was given to a little girl there in the early 1850's. She has an unusually beautiful hairdo, low on the neck. Her gown is of old figured taffeta in two tones of dark green with trimmings of green velvet.

Of three "different" Vermont china dolls, "Mrs. General," named for the Dickens character, was found by Mrs. John M. Pierce of Springfield, in a Westminster antique shop; "Rosaleen" who came from Fairlee, and has china hands on leather arms, and a rather unusual hairdo of stiff little vertical curls; and "Marie Marseilles," who although an immigrant from Canada, lived in Woodstock for many years. "Marie" was inherited by the late Miss Marie Marseilles of Woodstock, Vt., from her mother. The doll is well over a century old.

Of the "Alice in Wonderland," circular comb type of doll, inspired by the popularity of Lewis Carroll's book in 1865 is "Katy Oppelbaum," from the collection of Mrs. Cyrus M. Beachy, Wichita, Kansas. "Katy" came from the Pennsylvania Dutch region of Eastern Pennsylvania.

Quaint and very German-looking is Mrs. William Walker's little girl doll, "Anastasia." She is all original except her checked green taffeta dress with "pinked" ruffles and that is an exact reproduction in every detail of the original dress.

December 15, 1885, Philip Goldsmith of Covington, Ky., took out a patent for a doll body with corset made on the body. This firm made dolls for several years. Mrs. Dora Walker is authority for the statement that Goldsmith made some bisque heads for these dolls and she had one marked *G.* Very likely he had imported German workmen to make them, and these heads were experimental and few. At any rate, on most of his dolls Goldsmith used china heads imported from Germany, like the large blonde doll in the picture. This head is exceptionally heavy china.

The National Doll Exhibit, Charles M. Bowers Memorial Museum at Santa Ana., Calif., is by far the outstanding doll event in the country. It was held every year until the war and was resumed in 1946. The dolls are by invitation only. No prizes, just a ribbon of appreciation. No entry fees and no charge for admission to see the dolls. It lasts about two months and takes about the same length of time to prepare. The whole museum is given over to the dolls.

There is a reception at the opening and closing of the show, and some outstanding person in the doll world is the speaker. It is a get-together for doll lovers. Cards are on the dolls. Nothing is for sale and everything is under glass.

California collectors costume their dolls beautifully—real laces, fine furs, beautiful silks and materials are the rule. It is a real "fashion show" at the National Doll Exhibit. Yet at the show several years ago, the "Belle of the Ball," the outstanding china doll of the exhibit, was Mrs. H. C. Ettinger's "Cecile," a doll in a shabby, timeworn, old green silk dress. Other dolls were larger; all of the dolls in the case with her were elaborately dressed, beautifully coiffed; she was so simple yet she held herself proudly and seemed to say: "I am superior." She had something the other dolls did not have—and she knew it.

Mrs. Ettinger found the doll in an antique shop in Germany. All the dealer who sold her could or would say about Cecile was: *"Alte Hollandishe!*

Alte Hollandishe!" What he probably meant was that he had bought her from a Dutch family for she is clearly of German—not Dutch—manufacture.

Mrs. Clear writes of her:

"I classed her as a Meissen pink luster. The arms are typically Meissen models and the modelling of the head is similar to the Meissen figurines, not doll-like. Also, the texture and coloring is like the figurines.

"I have seen only one other head like this one. It belongs to Mrs. Olin Wellborn 3rd, Los Angeles. She bought it in New York some years ago. It was the head only."

The Clears copied "Cecile" and they call their copy "The Highborn Lady." The girls in the workshop call her "Snooty."

Another important Meissen (or Dresden) doll is "Frieda von Schall" in the collection of Mrs. John T. Buchanan, Omaha, Nebr. "Frieda" is named for the little girl who brought her to America in 1825. The doll had belonged to her mother. The family had lived in the same house in Dresden for one hundred and seventy-five years before coming to America in 1825. The doll is marked on the back of the shoulder with the crossed swords mark of the Dresden pottery in blue under the glaze. The date of this doll is 1770, which is confirmed by the form of the mark. The "crossed swords" mark varied at different periods.

Quite as different from the usual run of china dolls as Mrs. Ettinger's Meissen is the rare "Capo di Monte" doll owned by Mrs. Grace Perlberg, New York. This exquisite creature might almost be classed as a figurine. She sits on a Roman chair of china from which she can be detached much as a comport may be detached from its base. The head and upper part of the body, the arms and lower legs are china, as is the butterfly that rests on her hand. Her gown is old silk brocade in a dull brown with old gold lace panel and a trimming of simulated ermine.

The doll is a portrait of Caterina Cornaro Lusignan (1454–1451), mother of James III, last king of Cyprus, long held by the Lusignan family. James died at two years old and Caterina ruled Cyprus capably for some years. Being a Venetian lady, she was made a Daughter of the Republic at the time of her marriage to the King of Cyprus. Venice obtained from her a cession of the

Island of Cyprus in 1488. She was blonde and beautiful and was often painted by such noted artists as Paul Veronese, Titian, and others.

Also unique, but for another reason, is the china doll with a walking mechanism known as "Autoperipatetikos," patented in 1862, which is shown in her original box by the courtesy of Mrs. Lily Toth, Vineyard Haven, Mass. She has the hairdo of the 1860's with waterfall held in place with a gold net. She is 10 inches high.

PARIAN OR DRESDEN DOLL HEADS

THE TERM "PARIAN" used in connection with the fine unglazed doll heads so much sought by doll collectors is as much a misnomer as "Chelsea" or "Staffordshire" used in connection with the glazed china heads. We even hear some collectors refer to them as "Parian marble" when, of course, they are really neither from Paros nor are they marble.

Parian marble is the white, rather coarse-grained marble from the Isle of Paros quarries from which the masterpieces of ancient Greek sculpture like the Venus de Milo were carved, and it gets its beautiful finish from sanding and polishing. The most modern example of the use of Parian marble of which we are aware are the interior finish and pillars in the sculpture galleries in the Carnegie Institute at Pittsburgh, which were purchased for it by the late Andrew Carnegie at enormous cost. At the time of the building of the gallery it was said to be the largest quantity of the marble taken from the quarries since ancient times.

Vitreous clay from which all porcelain is made has within itself elements which fuse together when subjected to certain degrees of heat and is available in deposits in most parts of Europe. Marble, on the other hand, does not have this fusing element. It is akin to limestone which disintegrates and becomes

Pictures of dolls discussed in this chapter will be found following page 92.

a dry powder when subjected to heat in a kiln. This is how agricultural lime is obtained—by baking limestone in a kiln. Obviously, marble, which would behave in exactly the same manner under heat could not be used to make porcelain doll heads which are baked at high temperature in kilns.

All unglazed heads are properly called "bisque" which is a contraction of "biscuit," the technical name for the "mix" from which they are made which resembles biscuit dough in the same stage. Glazed china heads are made from similar mixes but are dipped in a glazing material and refired.

This is about as technical as we need to be here.

The name "Parian" doubtless arose from the fact that some of these heads were made pure white, without any coloring, and so bore some resemblance to marble statues. There was a white unglazed pottery used mostly for vases, etc., made in certain of the Staffordshire potteries that was called "Parian ware" for the same reason.

Those heads to which coloring was applied and fired in, were called "blonde bisque." The early Jumeau heads are examples of blonde bisque and later examples are the lovely George and Martha Washington dolls by the Clears.

The later and more highly colored heads, such as we find in modern play dolls are called simply "bisque."

The fine early "Parian" or "blonde bisque" heads which might be more properly called, perhaps, "Dresden," were made in the Dresden potteries and possibly, in other parts of Germany. The earlier heads, dating in the decade between 1850 and 1860, are generally the finest and most artistic. Many are decorated with flowers, ribbons, combs, scarfs and veils, molded separately and applied to the hair. Some have knots on the hair and luster decorations. Some have glazed china ruffs around the necks, decorated with colors and lusters; these are sometimes single, double and occasionally even triple. Some have yokes molded into the bisque.

Quite a few of the Dresden heads have blown-glass eyes inserted. These are the more rare types, usually. The majority have painted eyes. The color of the hair is almost universally golden. Only a few black-haired heads are found. This is very probably because the blonde hair works out better in the un-

107

glazed medium, just as the black hair works out best in the glazed china heads and is almost as universally used in them.

Evidently the Dresden heads were made as saleable novelties for exportation. In this country they were imported and sold by jewelers, confectioners, etc.

Parian heads were often made in the same molds as china and even wax heads. The so-called "Countess Dagmar" head comes in both china and Parian or blonde bisque and we have seen a late "Parian" that was identical with a wax (over papier mâché) doll that we have.

There are also the small, rather coarse doll heads and "bonnet dolls" that are called, for want of a better name "stone bisques." This is largely a matter of grinding and workmanship. The finer the clay is ground, the smoother and finer the resulting bisque or porcelain.

"Bennington Parian" doll heads simply don"t exist, for, according to John Spargo (and who should know better?), the Bennington, Vt., potteries never made doll heads. The rubble piles have been carefully gone through but reveal no evidence of any dolls—and it would be there if they had been made since the fragments would be practically indestructible. One nearby doll dealer has assured us that she once "saw an old receipted bill from the Bennington factory for a doll head"—but, *we* haven't seen such a bill and we are prepared to take John Spargo's judgment as the final authority on "matters Bennington."

In connection with the Dresden heads, it is interesting to note that we have been unable to find in any china collectors' manual or in any work on the subject of fine porcelains, available for examination, mention of the making of doll heads. This seems to indicate that they were regarded by the makers as mere commercial "hack-work," even though as we know, some of the finer heads are worthy of any potter's pride. The only marked porcelain doll head that has come to our attention is a doll belonging to Mrs. John T. Buchanan of Omaha, described in the chapter on china head dolls. This head as we have seen, is marked with the crossed swords in blue under the glaze.

It is interesting to note that Max von Boehn in his book *Dolls and Puppets* makes no mention of these Parian heads of which we think so highly. He does discuss Dresden china figurines, however

PARIAN OR DRESDEN DOLL HEADS

Two well-known doll collectors have thrown some light on the importation of the so-called Parian heads to this country. One of them is Mrs. Otis Carl Williams of Worcester, Mass., whose grandfather was a leading jeweler of Providence, R. I., during the 1860 decade. When a child, Mrs. Williams found stored in a box in a corner of her grandfather's barn, a number of these beautiful heads remaining unsold from an importation he had made years before. She was given permission to take the box, and these heads were the nucleus of the doll collection assembled by their mother which has been inherited by Mrs. Williams and her sister.

The other collector who has first-hand information on the history of a Dresden Parian doll head is Miss Alma Robeck of Annapolis, Md. Miss Robeck's great grandfather came from Germany in the 1850's and conducted a confectionary and bakery business in Annapolis. Every Christmas he sent to Germany for various novelties for his Christmas trade. Among these were a number of the Dresden Parian doll heads. One of these heads was bought by an Annapolis family and when the old lady who owned it died a few years ago, the head was found still in its original wrappings as it came from Miss Robeck's great grandfather's shop and was purchased from the woman's estate by Miss Robeck. This unusually lovely head has an elaborate hairdress decorated with flowers and a pink scarf drapery, as will be seen by the pictures of the head shown following page 92. The exact date is not known but it is one of the early heads, because the contents of the Robeck store was entirely destroyed by Union soldiers during the Civil War.

An example of the pure white heads which caused the name Parian to be applied to these German heads is shown herewith. It was sold by a Kentucky antique dealer and the name of its present owner is unknown to us.

Mrs. Winifred Harding bought the "Toinette" head shown after page 92 from a family in Woodstock, Vt. It is identical with the same doll, in original milkmaid dress, purchased in Switzerland years ago by Mrs. Cyrus M. Beachy of Wichita, Kansas. Marie Antoinette, you will recall, was fond of playing at being a "farmerette" and dairymaid, and the *"Petite Trainon"* at Versailles was built for her and her ladies in waiting to play at rustic "make believe." This doll is most probably intended as a portrait doll of the French Empress.

Another portrait doll presumably representing another French Empress, Eugenie, is in several collections. This doll has golden hair, like the Empress and wears the chignon or waterfall hairdo with a luster ribbon at the top and sides of the head. The net on the pictured example, shown following page 92, is green, but Mrs. Mary Lewis of Brooklyn has one with a black net. Such slight variations are found in many types of dolls.

The head of this doll pictured was purchased during the First World War in the antique shop of the old Quaker Negro dealer on Pine Street, Philadelphia, who was a quaint and familiar character in the antique business of that day. It was bought, not for its interest as a doll head, but as an addition to a luster collection—and the price paid, "believe it or not," was exactly twenty-five cents!

Dresden Parian dolls seem to have been favored by Vermonters and many very excellent examples in outstanding collections throughout the Eastern States have been purchased there. Such a doll is "Carrie Ordway" now owned by Mrs. Chester Dimick of Gales Ferry, Conn. "Carrie Ordway" was originally owned by the first wife of the husband of Mrs. Rosaleen Ordway, of the Corner Cupboard Shop, Fairlee, Vt. There are three different sizes of the so-called "Countess Dagmar" doll, owned by families in this immediate neighborhood, and we have heard of an example of the head popularly known as the "Caroline Channing" doll found in Vergennes by Mrs. Johanna Bristol.

Elaborate styles of hairdress are the rule in these Dresden dolls, examples of this are the two dolls belonging to Mrs. Glen E. Bartshe of Cleveland, Ohio. The one on the left of the picture has lines of gold beads between the separate puffs.

A super-rare Dresden doll head was recently acquired by Mrs. Gurth Ritter of Torrence, Calif. This doll has a triple luster-trimmed china ruff about the neck and has violet-blue blown-glass eyes. Mrs. Clear calls this "the most beautiful Dresden" she has ever seen.

Perhaps the most unusual Dresden of all is Mrs. Blanche Watson's "Senorita" which came from South America. It has no hair molded on its head—a true ball-head, and the only one of that type in the Dresden Parians which we ever had. She wears a cap of fine lace and over that, a typical

South American woven straw sombrero. Her little Parian bare feet are exquisitely modelled.

While the Dresden heads are very lovely—and of course in comparatively small supply, we do think the prices asked by dealers and paid by collectors today, not a little bit absurd. It puts them within the reach of wealthy collectors only—and perhaps that is what some collectors like, but it is not in the true collector spirit. For the comfort of those whose means are more modest, it is to be remembered that there are other and very interesting types of dolls to be collected which do not climb into such fantastic investments. A collector's hobby can still be a lot of fun without that. How much more interesting than the most expensive doll head, for instance, would be a genuine Montanari *rag doll*—if only one knew where to find it and how to identify it!

111

THE JUMEAU DOLL AND OTHER
FRENCH BISQUES

THE JUMEAU DOLL—which virtually means the French bisque doll—was an evolution. We have read in Tallis's *History of the Crystal Palace Exposition in London* (quoted in the chapter on "The Glass of Fashion") how the dolls exhibited by M. Jumeau at the Exposition were notable chiefly for their beautiful clothes and that as dolls they did not rate a prize. M. Jumeau began to be known to the doll world of Paris about 1844, importing his bisque and porcelain heads from Germany, as did all the French doll-makers of that day.

In 1855, of the three houses that became supreme in the manufacture of dolls in Paris, M. Jumeau stood first.

"This manufacturer," says M. Henri d'Allemagne, in his *Histoire des Jouets*, "exhibited dolls preserving the *cachet* of elegance and good taste which has always distinguished the productions of his house, in which are made not only dolls *de luxe* but also ordinary dolls, with or without *trousseaux*, and whose prices have increased the important sale of dolls in France and for import."

About 1862, M. Jumeau decided to free his industry from Germany by undertaking the manufacture of his own doll heads which should be more

Pictures of dolls discussed in this chapter will be found following pages 92 and 140.

beautiful and artistic than the German heads. He had a head modelled in biscuit and decorated by a skilled artist. These heads were superior in beauty to anything that had yet appeared. The hair was either Tibetan goat hair or real human hair. The eyes were made with enamel exactly like artificial eyes for humans. The eyes of Jumeau dolls have always been notable for beauty and were generally over-size, giving the faces unusual expressiveness. This departure of Jumeau's was the real beginning of the French doll as we know it—the doll *de luxe*.

The dolls came in fourteen sizes and were well proportioned—the largest being about 29 inches. They wore beautiful dresses, as we have seen, even as early as the days of the Crystal Palace.

At first the heads were in one piece with the bust, then M. Jumeau's eldest son patented a device by which the head could turn in all directions.

From 50,000 francs a year, the Jumeau business soared to a million francs a year.

The heads of the Jumeau dolls were open at the top, probably to facilitate the eye work and possibly only because the bisque heads from Germany they had formerly used had been open at the top to save weight and duty. The opening in the heads was fitted with a large piece of cork to which the wigs were nailed with small nails or tacks. With the passing years, these corks have sometimes dried out and become loose bringing the wig with them.

The Jumeau doll does not appear to have been marked until the advent of the composition body about 1880, then generally on the body—only very occasionally on the head. We have never seen any of the old ones that were marked. Of course, there may have been an occasional doll made for some special event, like the Centennial Exposition in Philadelphia, when the dolls would be marked for advertising purposes.

However, there is little chance of mistaking a Jumeau doll for any other, for the blonde bisque heads are so beautiful and the eyes so distinctive. As Mrs. Clear says, "One soon learns through handling, to recognize the work of the different doll artists even when little is known of the artist."

Especially is this true when one knows the evolution of the different types of body used by the Jumeau factory. The first body was all kid stuffed with sawdust and had kid feet and hands. The body was beautifully made and shapely. It had a small waist and large hips. The weakness of this type was, that with handling, the kid joints filled with sawdust and presently did not joint freely or stand erect.

To overcome this, apparently, they developed a new type with body and joints all inside a loose kid over-garment similar to a suit of long underwear. The joints functioned inside this kid. This is apparently the rarest of all Jumeau dolls. Mrs. Clear says they never had had but two in for repairs and no record had been kept of their ownership. We were unable to obtain any photograph of the type or discover any collector who had one.

Through the courtesy of Mrs. Elsie Clark Krug of Baltimore, Md., who generously gave us the doll for the book so that we might thoroughly investigate its interior structure, we are enabled to present another extremely rare type of Jumeau body, quite different from any we have ever seen. This may be the "walking Jumeau." At any rate she is truly "different." She came to a Baltimore family from Paris about 1875, and has been the property of this owner until the present day.

The doll is 18 inches tall with the usual Jumeau head. Inside the stockinet covering, which apparently never was covered with kid, the body, to the hips, consists of a flat block of wood about one-half inch thick to which the arms and legs are hinged with metal hinges. At the top of the block there are four round disks of wood fastened, on which the bisque shoulders and head rest. The body and limbs are evenly wrapped first with tow and then with lamb's wool. This is covered with the stockinet which comes to the wrists on the arms, the hands being bisque. On the legs the stockinet comes to the knees. From the knees down the legs are bisque and the feet are beautiful, slender and shapely with toenails defined. This seems to be the only Jumeau that has such bisque legs and feet. It is interesting to note that the leg swings from the hip both backwards and forwards and to the side. One bisque leg was missing and has been replaced by wood carved by Ralph E. Wakeman of Claremont, N. H. If the two legs had been of the same weight, there is little doubt the doll could be made to walk, although there is no mechanism.

The doll had no clothing and has been beautifully dressed by Mrs. Ralph E. Wakeman in a changeable green and gold taffeta dress and hat copied from another French fashion doll.

After this, or perhaps after the body with the suit of underwear-type of kid covering, came a body and limbs of all wood, covered with kid, the kid being shrunk on the joints before assembling.

This was followed by the beautiful all-wood body, jointed at the waist, wrists, elbows and ankles, as well as the usual places. Mrs. Robert G. Fiscus of Pittsburgh, has a lovely example of this type, all wood except the head which is a lovely blonde bisque. The joints are double-action hinge and swivel combined. All joints have this double action, even the beautifully carved hands and feet. It is all of exquisite workmanship.

This type of construction was obviously very costly. The son of Jumeau is credited with inventing the composition body strung with elastic cord, as we have it today. The shoulders of bisque were discarded and the head strung into the body.

These are the principal types of body used. Of course, there were often variations from these. For example, the writer has a beautiful Jumeau of the early kid-bodied type that has the upper third of the arms of wood, the lower two-thirds of bisque. The two are joined together with a small strip of kid about an inch wide. The bisque part is beautifully modelled and dimpled and curved at the elbow but has no joint at the elbow.

The reasons for such variations are probably two: 1. They were always experimenting for improvements; 2. They doubtless thriftily used up any parts that were useable from previous types remaining on hand.

Jumeau also made cheaper dolls with the beautiful bisque heads but with a simple stuffed cloth body having curved leather arms to the shoulder and leather shoes made on the feet somewhat similar to the body used by the M. and S. Superior dolls. The stocking on this Jumeau doll was plain with a colored band at the garter. Such of these dolls as we have seen have been of the larger sizes—from 23 to 29 inches. Evidently an attempt to give much for less money, for the clothes were less elaborate and expensive than those of the ordinary fashion doll.

Here too, it is profitable to study the actual dolls, particularly those with known histories and dates.

"Little Eva," named for the golden-haired heroine of *Uncle Tom's Cabin,* still a "best seller" in 1869, when the doll was brought from France, is a very beautiful 23-inch Jumeau. Her story as told by her first owner, Mrs. Rose Webb Davis of Maine, is given in the following letter:

"My father, Captain Webb, bought 'Eva' for me in Paris seventy-five years ago (1869). He sailed many years in the Clipper Ship, the *Rosie Webb* which my grandfather Augustus Webb of Waldeboro, Maine, built and named for me. On her first arrival in New York, she was reported as 'the magnificent new Clipper Ship for the California Line.' The papers said: 'Every modern improvement that experience can suggest has been lavished upon her.'

"I was three, a very young child, and I can just remember the crowds that came to see her. Later *The Rosie Webb* received the highest price ever paid for wheat freight from San Francisco to England.

Rose Webb Davis."

Mrs. Davis cherished "Little Eva" until her fiftieth wedding anniversary when she let her go to another owner.

The doll is a lovely blonde bisque with blue eyes and abundant golden hair—human hair. She has a kid body stuffed with sawdust but the upper arms are wood, covered with kid, and the shoulder and joints are similar to the Mason-Taylor joints as in Mrs. Fiscus' doll. The bisque hands and forearms are beautifully modelled. The head turns on the swivel neck. The face is very French in features and expression.

Her clothing is all original and she has been so carefully preserved that it is fresh and lovely still. The underwear is beautifully handmade and is trimmed with fine tatting. The waist is pale blue lansdown trimmed with narrow, white silk fringe. The skirt is a fancy-textured striped silk of blue and white. The picture hat is of pale blue velvet with lace and beads and small ostrich tips of pale blue and crushed strawberry.

Another Jumeau doll of known history and of similar type and about the same date, possibly a bit earlier, is in the collection of Mrs. William Walker, Louisville, Ky. It belonged to Anna Dorothea Kohler, born in Louisville in 1845. "Nothing has been done to her except to wash her clothes which were in very good condition. Dorothea was perfect from her little French hat to her shoes, her green taffeta dress, green and white striped taffeta skirt, ribbon around the neck, earrings, kid body and parasol."

A Jumeau doll with the all-kid body is "Martha Victoria," pictured with the illustrations following page 188. She was brought from Paris by the late Mrs. James M. Carnahan of Oil City, Pa., and inherited by her niece, Mrs. Sydney John Morse of Hartland, Vt. She has the swivel neck and lovely blonde bisque head with pierced ears and wig of Tibetan goat hair.

Two dolls owned by Mrs. Leo Lamb, Santa Ana, Calif., are examples of two stages of the Jumeau doll's evolution. The larger doll pictured has the fixed head in one with the bust; the exquisite smaller doll has the swivel head.

Miss Alma Robeck's group of Jumeaus are typical.

Very lovely is the Jumeau owned by Mrs. Velma Fuller Von Bruns of Bristol, Vt. It was formerly in another Vermont collection, that of the late Mrs. Edward S. Lane of Bristol.

Of the year 1882 is the little girl Jumeau which came to us as a gift from Mrs. Marshall Carroll of Hartland, Vt. The doll had been her mother's. This doll has the later jointed composition body—strung with rubber which is now generally used. The doll is marked. On the head the marking reads: *Deposé Tête Jumeau S.G.D. 4.* The body is marked: *Jumeau Mèdaille BMA Paris.*

She has a very complete little girl wardrobe of the 1880's. Her best dress is dark-green lansdown, featherstitched, and the hat is of dark-brown felt. The modern "Patsy" doll illustrated following page 140 wears one of her gingham dresses. The Jumeau doll has pierced ears and wears little blue earrings. One recalls that it was quite customary to pierce the ears of small girls in the early eighties as the process was supposed to be beneficial for the child's eyes. Earrings, of course, were worn.

The little bisque girl on the left of the group is probably French, by her expressive face, but is not by Jumeau. She has the same composition body as the

Jumeau, and her dark eyes are lovely, and she has the same closed lips. Her head is closed at the top, what is popularly called "ball-head." There are two small holes in the top of the head to which the wig is fastened with cord. Her clothing is commercial.

Many dolls in the 1870–1880 period in bisque, wax and papier mâché had this closed-top head combined with the closed lips. The writer has three composition-head dolls of this type that are very lovely and much finer than the workmanship of the average composition head. These dolls came from one home in Northern Vermont and are quite obviously from the same maker and shipment, by their quality. All three have cloth bodies stuffed with hay. Most probably they are of German manufacture.

The success of the Jumeau firm after they began to make their own bisque heads also benefited several other French doll firms that, encouraged by the improved markets, went into the same line, although few, if any, ever approached the Jumeau dolls in beauty and fine workmanship.

The next most important house to Jumeau was that of M. Bru whose business, according to M. Henri d'Allemagne, reached 200,000 francs at the time that the Jumeaus were grossing one million francs or more. The Bru head was more highly colored than the Jumeau and the faces heavier as to chin, much more like present day dolls. They could hardly be mistaken by even the merest amateur for the Jumeau.

Bru used kid bodies but he also used the all-wood body—in fact he may have used it before Jumeau—may even have invented it. But Jumeau certainly improved on it. The Jumeau all-wood body is more slender and delicate. It is also jointed at the waist which no Bru within my knowledge is.

Mrs. Venita Miller of Los Angeles, who has a number of rare dolls in her collection, has one Bru doll with the wooden body which is less slender, more of a child-type than the wooden bodies used in Jumeau dolls. The head is high in coloring with fine eyes, and it is marked.

$$B$$

Bru dolls are usually marked with the word R in vertical position at

$$U$$

the incised left rear side of the bust. The writer has a Bru with wooden body which is marked across the back on the bottom of the chest with an incised *B 2 S*. The face is also deeper in color than a Jumeau and has fine eyes.

Bru, like Jumeau, made a few dolls with brown bisque heads to represent Negroes.

A rather interesting type of Bru doll which is in the collection of Mrs. Grace Sawyer of Newton, Mass., is what is known as the "Whistling Bru." The lips of the doll are in whistling position and on its back are the remains of a rubber gadget which apparently produced a whistling sound.

Of smaller firms of doll-makers, several were eventually absorbed into the Jumeau company.

As the dolls of these smaller French firms were not marked, it is unprofitable to attempt to enumerate the houses or identify their dolls. French dolls are generally on kid bodies, some of very skilful workmanship. Some are white kid and others pink—M. d'Allemagne says that the pink was generally used on the cheaper dolls. This we doubt because of a French doll with pink kid body which we have that looks anything but "a cheaper" doll. She has a shoulder head of the early immovable type, brown eyes, her original Tibetan goat hair wig, closed lips. The upper arm is wood covered with kid and with the Mason and Taylor type of shoulder joint. The bisque forearms, beautiful and shapely, are fastened to the elbows with a metal pin on which they move freely.

German firms, looking at the profitable French doll industry, began to infiltrate it by buying into smaller houses, importing heads from Germany where they could be made for less cost, with the result that before the First World War, France had virtually ceased to have a doll industry of her own.

To the Jumeaus, father and son, must always belong the glory and the credit of inventing and giving to the world the lovely French bisque doll.

GERMAN BISQUE DOLLS

A S WE HAVE SEEN in the preceding chapter, all unglazed porcelain heads are classed as some form of bisque.

The Germans have been making the majority of bisque heads for many years as well as the glazed china heads. France got its bisque and china heads from Germany until the Jumeaus undertook to make their own doll heads and succeeded in producing the lovely French bisque heads that we know.

Collectors generally have been seeking only the French bisque heads in the dolls since 1862 but many German makers have turned out heads so fine that it is hard to tell them from the best of the French dolls. Mrs. C. H. Criley, a Los Angeles collector, writes of one of these:

"I have a doll in my collection which fools even the best of collectors. She is beautiful. She has that shiny, very fine bisque head—more the Viennese type —her head is solid—swivel neck on bisque shoulder piece—very Frenchy body, tiny waist, dangling legs of pink kid. By solid head, I mean no opening at top of head. She has the open-closed mouth so often seen on the Jumeaus. The bisque is closed over the mouth but the lips are slightly parted in a smile—no teeth showing." Almost at the top of her head, under her wig one finds *S 9 H.*

Pictures of dolls discussed in this chapter will be found following page 140.

This mark means, of course, Simon and Halbig—one of the best makers of German bisques. It is the mark—with variations of figures, found on some of the largest and finest modern dolls. It is often found in connection with the name "Heinrich Handwerck." An example of this combination of names is the marking of the large brown bisque doll owned by Mrs. Rose Parro of Waterbury, Vt., which is described in the chapter on Negro dolls. This is marked:

Heinrich

Handwerck

Simon & Halbig

7

The quality and workmanship on this doll is very fine. So also is a doll in the author's collection which is marked:

S 12 H 719

D.E.P

Miss Jennie L. Abbott of Doll Collectors of America suggests that the letters *D.E.P.* mean that a model of the head has been placed in the patent office.

There is a good deal of discussion of the various marks on bisque dolls and a great deal of research to be done before we will have much exact information on the subject. It offers a fascinating opportunity for a study by someone who knows German well.

Doll Collectors of America have collected and listed a number of the marks on both French and German bisque dolls and are making some attempt at interpretations of them in the third monograph to be issued by the Club. Generally speaking such marks are incised or molded in the bisque.

Many good bisque dolls—especially in small sizes, dating before 1880 or shortly after—which are apparently German are unmarked. Dolls of this period have the closed or semi-closed mouth such as Mrs. Criley's doll and show no teeth. They are also quite apt to have the ears pierced for earrings. (It will be remembered that it was customary to pierce the ear-lobes of little girls and insert small earrings during the early 1880's.) In this period, the dolls usually have swivel necks on wood or composition bodies and are strung with rubber.

THE DOLLS OF YESTERDAY

Not all of the dolls of this period or a decade earlier have this type of body however. There are many charming bisque shoulder heads on kid or cloth bodies. Some of these have the head definitely turned either to right or left. Many, but not all, of the lamb's wool wigs on both wax and bisque dolls date from the 1870's and 1880's.

In 1891 when Congress passed the law requiring that imported merchandise be marked plainly with the name of the country of origin, it simplified somewhat the problem of identifying and dating German bisques. Any dolls with the word *Germany* included in the marking is necessarily after 1891.

A group of lovely small heads of fine bisque with inserted eyelashes and beautiful mohair wigs, which turned up in an old store stock in the midwest last year, had no incised marks but bore an oval ink stamp with the maker's name, *Kammerer and Reinhart* and *Made in Germany*. The heads had evidently been made before 1891 and had been stamped in order to comply with the law.

The German bisque dolls vary greatly in quality and beauty but are almost always of the "doll-face" type, that is, except the attractive little "playhouse" dolls and special types like the "Bye-Lo Baby." The "playhouse" dolls are always dressed with meticulous attention to detail, as will be seen by the two pictured following page 140, which were bought in Germany in 1908.

An interesting variation of these small dolls is the pretty little floating "Bath doll" intended to amuse a small child while in its bath. This doll is owned by Mrs. John McDill of Woodstock, Vt., and was a childhood treasure of Mrs. McDill's mother, the late Laura Billings Lee, a member of the well-known Vermont Billings family.

An antique dealer opening a shop near Philadelphia stocked it by the simple expedient of taking his mother's furniture out of storage where it had been for forty years or more. Among the things he found an interesting family of cloth and bisque German peasant dolls—a man and woman 8 inches tall and a child 4 inches tall. The smiling faces are of unusual expressiveness with wrinkles of age, care and humor on them. These dolls were made after 1891 as they all bear the word *Germany* incised in the bisque, and are probably about fifty years old.

Their unique feature is that in addition to their interesting heads, the torsos and outer garments to the waist are cast in bisque, colored to match the cloth nether garments. The hands and feet are also bisque and the other parts of the bodies are cloth stuffed with sawdust. The woman's jacket is brown to match the polka-dotted-like skirt; the child is in light blue; the man's jacket is black to match his wool trousers; his cap is brown bisque and his hair is grey. Of these dolls, Louis Bossard of the George Borgfeldt Corporation said: "The dolls represent typical German peasants who work in the fields. No doubt they were made many years ago and from our observation were made by Hetwig and Co., Hatzshutte, Thuringia, Germany. The models were made by expert sculptors and painted by artists who work in these factories for wages about those of the average workman. . . . It no doubt sold for about twenty-five cents when the doll was put on the market. The value of the doll today is what a collector would pay for it."

A sweet-faced child doll with an unusually animated expression is the first doll remembered by Mrs. Nan Bregg, well-known Pittsburgh newspaper woman, Woman's Editor of the *Sun-Telegraph* for many years. This Christmas doll of 1898 has a fine bisque shoulder head, with no other marking but an incised *Germany* at the base of the shoulders. It has a lamb's wool wig, which Mrs. Bregg thinks her mother made from lamb's skin obtained from the neighborhood butcher. It has the effect of a "wind-blown bob" that is really charming. The body is home-made with almost life-size composition hands and feet. The sturdy leather baby shoes it wears, made by the neighborhood shoemaker, are worthy of notice.

Like the wax dolls, German bisques have of late been receiving more attention from collectors and those who have been neglecting them in favor of other types seem likely to find themselves regretting the fact in the not too distant future. This is particularly so in view of what the war seems to have done to the German doll industry. It is still possible to assemble a very good collection of these bisques at sensible prices and they offer an interesting field for both collecting and for research.

RAG DOLLS, RUBBER DOLLS
AND RAWHIDE DOLLS

OUR FIRST MOTHER, Eve, never made rag dolls, but Cain and Abel were probably the only children who never had any. Rag dolls are so satisfyingly soft and cuddly; so cheap; so easily made by mothers that it is no wonder they have been so universal. Children's toys have really changed little through the ages. In Leo Claritie's book *Les Jouets; Histoire et Fabrication* there is a reproduction of an old engraving—a very early one—depicting children playing in the open square of an old town in Holland. The games they are playing, and the equipment they are using are almost the same as children use today and they play the very same games that these mediaeval children seemed to be playing. Even the two little girls in one corner of the foreground sitting on the ground are evidently "playing house" with their doll and kitchen equipment, and might be your neighbor's children next door.

In the Royal Ontario Museum, Toronto, are a group of small toys of ancient times, including some little lead dishes that might almost have come from Woolworth's, so alike are they to modern toys of the same sort.

In this Museum, also, are two rag dolls, stuffed with papyrus that are Roman of the third century A.D. These were found in Egypt and probably owe

Pictures of dolls discussed in this chapter will be found following page 140.

124

their fine state of preservation to the dry sands of that country. These two dolls bear an almost startling resemblance in type to the American colonial rag doll "Mollie Brinkerhoff" described in the chapter devoted to Association Dolls.

Richard Montanari, son and successor of Mme. Montanari of English wax doll fame, is listed in the commercial section of the Post Office London Directory as "Maker of Wax and Rag Dolls" during several years. The last such listing is in 1884. This throws new light on the Montanari family and coupled with the following paragraph which immediately follows the paragraph describing the Montanari wax dolls in Tallis's *History of The Crystal Palace Exposition,* 1851, indicates that rag dolls were probably made by Mme. Augusta Montanari herself.

"In a small case adjoining that which contained the toys just enumerated, were displayed several rag dolls, which were very remarkable productions, considering the materials of which they were made. They consisted entirely of textile fabrics, and the dolls which were intended, and were well adapted for the nursery, were reasonable in price, varying from 6s. 6d. to 30s. per doll including dresses."

We have also seen that M. Richard Montanari exhibited wax doll heads covered with cloth at the Paris Exposition of 1855.

However, no rag dolls that can be identified as the work of the Montanari have come to light, so far as we know. It is interesting to note however that the rag dolls displayed at the Crystal Palace were "very remarkable productions considering the materials of which they were made" so we may infer that their rag dolls were executed with the same skill and care that went into the making of their wax dolls.

In 1855 at Central Falls, R. I., a woman named Izannah F. Walker was making rag dolls which are now much sought by collectors and nearly twenty years after, she received a patent on these dolls, November 4, 1873. The patent is numbered *144,373.*

Dear, quaint little "Thankful" found and dressed by Mrs. Ralph E. Wakeman of Claremont, N. H., and so charmingly photographed by her second owner, Mrs. Katherine Frye, also of Claremont, is a typical example.

125

Her present owner is Mrs. George Brinton Chandler of Columbus, Ohio. If you have access to a copy of Doll Collectors of America Inc.'s *American Made Dolls and Figurines* (1940), it will be interesting to compare this picture with the two Walker dolls on page two that are in the collection of Mrs. Earle E. Andrews. Note the same two little painted curls in front of the ears on each of the three dolls.

The bodies of the original Walker dolls appear to have been of heavy cream sateen, although many of them now show one or two additional coverings because of wear. Mrs. Earle E. Andrews' dolls show two additional coverings over the original sateen.

A Walker doll, which she had in her childhood and cherished for many years, was the inspiration that led Mrs. Martha Chase, born Martha Jenks, of Pawtucket, R. I., to create the delightful Chase doll still being made by her children in the Chase Doll Factory at Pawtucket.

The "Chase Stockinet dolls," which come in several sizes are very like real children. Mrs. Martha Chase began experimenting with an idea of making attractive rag dolls for her own family, then she made a few dolls to give to the children of neighbors and friends. While she was fitting one of these life-sized child dolls with shoes in a Boston store, it was seen by the store buyer who insisted on her making a few for the store. This was in 1891. The instant and enthusiastic response of the buying public led to her building a small factory in the rear of her own home. From this small beginning has grown up the present Chase Doll Factory in Pawtucket.

In 1910, at the request of a hospital superintendent, Mrs. Chase, who was the daughter of a physician, designed and brought out the Chase Hospital Doll as an aid to teaching and demonstration in nurses training schools, Home Nursing classes, etc. It is designed in the correct proportions both of the child and of the adult human female figure and has a water-tight interior of rubber to permit the teaching of the technique of giving douches, enemas and other treatments. These hospital dolls have been shipped all over the world.

The child Hospital Doll is made in five sizes: newborn infant, two-months-old baby, four-months-old baby, one-year-old baby and the four-year-old child.

Thus do "great oaks from little acorns grow."

RAG, RUBBER AND RAWHIDE DOLLS

Martha Jenks Chase died in 1925. She never patented her doll and did not need to do so, since it would be hard to imitate. The dolls all bear a label which reads: "The Chase Stockinet doll. Made of Stockinet and Cloth. Stuffed with cotton. Made by Hand. Painted by Hand. Made by Especially Trained Workers."

The Chase play-dolls are made in several sizes. One mother used to cause the doll to disappear just before Christmas and replace it on Christmas morning with a new, but exactly similar doll, a size larger, so that the doll grew with the child who thought of it as still the same doll and was thrilled with the idea of her doll growing, just as she herself grew older.

In the early 1890's there came on the market a variety of printed and painted commercial rag dolls on cloth to be cut out, sewed and stuffed. These included story book characters like the Palmer Cox "Brownies"; animals—cats, dogs, families of kittens, roosters and various other things; cartoon characters such as Buster Brown and his dog Tige, Foxy Grandpa and Boys, Abie the Agent and the like. Most of these were made by the Arnold Print Works at North Adams, Mass. The Foxy Grandpa dolls were sometimes made of pink stockinet and possibly did not come from this factory.

In addition to these were dolls given by commercial products companies as advertisements: "Aunt Jemima" of the Aunt Jemima Pancake Flour; and, for a while, an Aunt Jemima "family"; "Sunny Jim" who changed from being "Jim Dumps," a grouch, to being Sunny Jim by eating "Force" for breakfast; "Rastus," the Cream of Wheat Chef, among others. More recently one heard of a proposed "Elsie the Cow" doll but this does not seem to have materialized.

Much more interesting and individual than these commercial dolls, however, are the various home-made rag dolls. How intriguing is "Bridget" from the collection of Mrs. J. J. Flynn of Williams Bay, Wis.! Or "Julia" with her ravelled rope hair and checkered dress! Home-made rag dolls, conditioned by materials at hand, give much scope for the imagination.

Corn shucks were used in making dolls that are somewhat allied to rag dolls and are still being very skillfully made in the mission schools in the Southern Appalachians. The old corn shuck doll sent us by Mrs. Nina Shepherd

127

of Granville, Ohio, represents "The Village Seamstress," and shows how much character can be expressed in a simple material.

Charles Goodyear, an American inventor who was born in New Haven, Conn., in 1800, after much experimentation during the years following 1836, discovered in 1839 the process of vulcanizing rubber. The missing *factor* (for which he had been searching) was discovered to be heat. Success came more or less accidentally when he spilled a mixture of rubber and sulphur with which he was working on a hot stove. He took out his first patent in 1844. Many infringements on his patent were fought through the courts with his final victory coming in 1852. Articles of his vulcanized rubber—including rubber overshoes—were displayed at the Crystal Palace Exposition in London in 1851. They were enthusiastically praised in the land where Macintosh and Hancock were already applying caoutchouc to the waterproof coats for which the name "Macintosh" is still used.

Goodyear tried to establish a factory in England but was unsuccessful in doing so. He did establish one in Paris and when this failed, in bankruptcy, he was arrested in 1855 and thrown into a French prison for debt. He died in New York City in 1860.

Nelson Goodyear, brother of Charles, took out a patent for hard rubber, May 5, 1851. This type of rubber was used for doll heads, and there are many in existence bearing the legend, *Goodyear Pat. May 5, 1851,* which seems to refer to the material rather than the type of head.

Mrs. Otis Carl Williams, Worcester, Mass., has a very interesting rubber doll head (shown following page 140) that is in first-class condition, never having been used on a doll. Still attached to the base is a paper giving direction as to how it should be attached to a body. This base would have been cut away had the head been used. The unusual hairdo shows crossed braids in the back with a large lavender flower on each side of the back of the head.

As can be seen on the shoulders of this doll, the rubber heads cracked and became otherwise defaced with age.

In 1866 a patent was issued to Franklin J. Darrow of Bristol, Conn., for the manufacture of doll heads from rawhide. The process was simple. The rawhide, cut in disks of suitable size was subjected to steam of a solution of lye and water to soften them. The softened discs were then put in dies under a press to form the head.

The heads were unbreakable and quite pretty. The shoulders were deep, smooth and well rounded. Like the Greiner dolls, they were sold as heads only, the bodies being supplied by the home seamstress.

Not many of these dolls have survived, because rats have a fondness for rawhide. Those that remain clearly indicate the basic weakness of the doll which was that the paint was inclined to flake away from the rawhide. The original Darrow model head deposited in the U.S. Patent Office, which is now in the collection of Mrs. Imogene Anderson of Greenwich, Conn. shows this weakness.

The author has two of these dolls, a five and a half inch head that has been repainted, and a three-inch head in original condition. Neither are marked. The smaller one is interesting, the body being the obvious attempt of some mother to copy in cloth a French kid Jumeau body. Most of the heads carry the Darrow name in an oval trademark on the front of the bust.

Doll-making was only a side-line of the Darrow factory which made rawhide belts for machinery. It was opened on a small scale in 1863 and went into bankruptcy in 1877, so that all rawhide dolls must fall within this period.

AMERICAN DOLL ARTISTS

THE SMITH FAMILY—GRACE STORY PUTNAM—MARTHA OATHOUT AYRES, GRACE C. ROCKWELL, GERTRUDE FLORIAN, LEWIS SORENSON

ONLY A FEW FORTUNATE collectors, chiefly in California, where the dolls were made, possess examples of the charming infant dolls created by the Smith family of Santa Cruz in 1916 and 1917. The makers were Mr. and Mrs. Putnam David Smith, portrait artists, and their young daughter, Margaret, who, even before she had reached her teens, was showing remarkable skill in the modelling of figurines. The three figures shown following page 140, "Doughnut Girl," "Bathing Girl," and "Red Cross Nurse," created by her in 1914 and 1915, when she was but twelve years old, show the talent she had for expressive faces.

As the flow of dolls from Europe had been stopped by the First World War, there seemed to be an opportunity for real artists in the field of doll-making. Mrs. Mabel Smith, always loving babies and dolls, had never felt quite satisfied with any dolls that she had seen, feeling the lack in them of the qualities of life-likeness and reality. She and her husband decided to make dolls that would have such reality.

Pictures of dolls discussed in this chapter will be found following page 140.

They had little or no capital and less experience when they embarked on their doll-making enterprise. The venture was entirely, and, as it later proved, *expensively* experimental. Although a portrait painter, Mrs. Smith had never done any modelling, never handled clay or plaster of Paris, yet the very first doll heads she made were remarkably interesting and life-like. The dolls pictured in the baby carriage were among the first group she created. In the beginning Mrs. Smith modelled all the heads, and later, Margaret shared in the work.

The material used, an original composition, was not unbreakable, although they experimented for months trying to evolve a material that would have that quality. The bodies were cloth, and the legs and arms of composition like the heads.

Artistically, the dolls which Mrs. Smith made were a success. They looked like real babies, healthy, good-natured and full of mischief as a real baby should be, and they had the most enchanting dimples. People admired them. Mrs. Clear used some of the heads for replacements in her repair work. Nevertheless, handmade dolls at from five to eight dollars each proved over-expensive for play dolls, while the makers found that they could not make a profit at these prices nor turn out the dolls in sufficient quantities by their methods. After a few months they decided that it would be more profitable to make larger dolls for store display figures. Margaret designed a few lovely life-sized babies and tots which were absorbed by Los Angeles department stores, but the Smiths failed to charge enough for these to even make expenses. Before long they were forced to let a manikin company take over the making of their dolls and display figures, under their supervision, on a royalty basis. From lack of business experience they made wrong contacts and did not know how to protect their interests. The products of the factory were much inferior to the originals.

Neither the Smiths nor those who undertook the making of their dolls on a commercial basis seem to have had any advance knowledge of the financial problems involved or the difficulties that would be encountered. Ruinous competition from the cheap labor in Germany increased after the war as more and more foreign toys came on the market. Experienced workmen were not available. Inexperienced workers demanded the pay of skilled workers; expenses pyramided and the inevitable crash came.

It was heartbreaking to artistic souls to see their creations cheapened and discredited. Mr. and Mrs. Smith fell ill and Mr. Smith died.

Molds of the original dolls and of Margaret's lovely little figurines were stolen from storage. Patents were infringed on by unscrupulous makers of cheap plaster work, and the market was flooded with cheap reproductions.

Disheartened and discouraged, the Smith women, mother and daughter, turned to other work. Margaret later married and went with her husband as a missionary to the Indians in South America. She is now Mrs. Francesca Tapia. As the busy mother of six children, she has little time to devote to artistic pursuits though she occasionally does a plaque or figurine of the fascinating little native Indian babies and children for her own pleasure.

It was a loss to the American doll collectors that the Smiths could not have made better contacts for the manufacturing and marketing of their dolls. Had they been able to do so, there is little question that they might have rivalled in popular favor even Grace Story Putnam's "Bye-Lo Baby" (which holds the world's record for sales for three successive years), for they, too, were works of art.

The Bye-Lo Baby, Mrs. Putnam's masterpiece, which was cast in bisque in Germany, is now being made in composition in America, and will undoubtedly achieve a new popularity in this cheaper form. The story of the Bye-Lo Baby and its creator has been so ably told in Janet P. Johl's *The Fascinating Story of Dolls* that there is little to add to it here. The original model was in wax and Mrs. Clear, who saw it recently, says of it:

"So soft and warm and lifelike in texture and coloring that you would think you were holding a living breathing infant."

It was inevitable that some of this charm is lost in the harder medium of bisque, but it is still the outstanding baby doll that America has yet produced.

Three years ago, at the National Doll Exhibit at Santa Ana, California, Mrs. Putnam showed an exquisite group of doll-house dolls, an American family, from infant to grandparents. Because of the war and production difficulties, these are still in the model stage.

At the instance of the George Borgfeldt Co., Mrs. Putnam designed another almost forgotten doll called, "The Fly-Lo Baby." We are indebted to Mrs. C. H. Criley of Los Angeles for the picture of one of the very few of these little dolls that were made and for its history.

It was done about two years after the Bye-Lo Baby came on the market. Mrs. Putnam had had no intention of making another doll but the company was insistent. When she modelled the head, Grace Story Putnam had had in mind a fairy doll—an elfin doll. It was meant to be a novelty doll and the designer had plans for gorgeous wings. The Borgfeldt Company insisted that it be a baby. They were not interested in anything elfin. The body was similar to that of the Bye-Lo Baby except that it was designed so that the doll was always in sitting position. It had little wings and was dressed in a silk or satin all-over suit. It wore a little cap. An attractive little thing it lacked the appealing idea that was back of the Bye-Lo Baby. About the moment it was put out, bisques were being superseded by composition-head dolls and troubles about importing heads from Germany were increasing. Then the depression struck and that ended the doll altogether. Only a few had been put out.

Of the charming little head by Grace C. Rockwell, an American illustrator, which Mrs. Criley has, she writes: "I am quite sure that it was put out about the same time and by the same company as the Fly-Lo Baby, as the coloring of both heads is very much alike—more tan in the pink than the regular run of doll heads, also the eyes are the same, and put in a little different than so many of the bisques."

The best portrait dolls of recent years and probably the best of any period are the "George and Martha Washington" designed for the Clears by Martha Oathout Ayres. Historically correct, dignified and wholly artistic they have found a place in most of the finest collections. In blonde bisque or Parian, they are not surpassed by the finest products of Dresden in any period. Martha Washington is portrayed in her later years—a beautiful and gracious woman. She wears a mob cap which is adorned with a band of delicately handpainted flowers. Her hair is gray and her hands, for which Mrs. Emma C. Clear's own hands were the models, are beautifully veined and the hands of middle age.

While designing the George Washington doll, Mrs. Ayres visited the

133

Metropolitan Museum and studied the John Ward Dunnmore portrait of Washington. As in the case of the Martha Washington figure, the hands are particularly noteworthy—the fine strong hands of the statesman and country squire. There is an intriguing little bit of human interest in connection with these hands. Mrs. Ayres found in the hands of her own husband, exactly the right model, but like many another husband, he regarded the whole affair as nonsense and declined to pose. About that time he had a serious illness and his wife was his nurse. As he slept, she modelled the hands of George Washington from those of her reluctant husband.

Mrs. Ayres has done some other fine portrait dolls for the Clears. One of these is the lovely little boy, "Danny," modelled from her own small son, and "Modern Madonna," a portrait of her daughter. When war priorities and labor difficulties are ended, Mrs. Clear plans to combine these two figures with an infant—yet to be modelled—in a modern group of "The Madonna and Child with St. John."

Several American artists are making individual dolls—copies from old family portraits, from paintings, or have created ideal characters. Miss Gertrude Florian of Detroit has done some interesting types. Her "Widow Howland," portrait of an elderly woman, is outstanding and has won many prizes at doll shows. Until her death a few months ago, Miss Florian's mother worked with her and was particularly skillful in designing and creating the individual wigs.

Lewis Sorenson of Los Angeles, a young Dane, has been attracting considerable attention with his interesting types of bisque dolls. Among his subjects have been Will Rogers, a hobo, Ramona, "Mother Mormon," Marie Antoinette and others. Mr. Sorenson worked as a costume designer at one period of his life and his costuming of the dolls, all of which he does himself, is notable for perfection of detail and appropriateness. There is an impish, whimsical quality about the doll faces which Mr. Sorenson creates that makes them more interesting than the mere prettiness in which most of them are lacking.

Mr. Sorenson is a Mormon and his group of "Mormon Pioneers" which is in the State Capitol at Salt Lake City is his most notable work to date. The group suggests an old time tin-type or early photograph—which is probably what suggested its making to the artist. Only two of the figures in the group are actual portraits, Brigham Young and his youngest wife. The others are types, the best of which are the banker and his wife. When it became known that Mr. Sorenson was undertaking the project, old photographs, and costume materials were sent to him from all over Utah.

The group is selected for use in this book because of the fact that Joseph Smith, the founder of the Mormon church, was born in Vermont and the farm at South Royalton on which he was born is preserved by the church as a Memorial to him. Many of the pioneer Mormons came from Vermont.

ASSOCIATION DOLLS I

THERE ARE QUITE a few dolls which derive special interest from their history or their association with famous persons. Such a doll is "Molly Brinkerhoff," a heroine of the Revolutionary War, who is the oldest doll in Vermont and probably one of the oldest of American made dolls. Molly is mother-made of old homespun linen stuffed with flax. Her hair and features are embroidered. Poor little Molly! The years have taken toll of her—one arm is gone and her clothing has long since vanished—but who would not look the worse for having lived a century and three quarters, seen our country engaged in seven wars, and herself been buried for many months?

The colonial Brinkerhoff children loved their Mollie doll and when the British army was sweeping towards their Long Island home, they wept because they could not take her with them when the family fled from their home before the tide of war. Mollie, with other precious possessions, was put in a chest and buried in the sands of Long Island.

When the war ended and the family returned to their home and to the pursuits of peace, Mollie was dug up and restored to loving arms.

The Brinkerhoffs intermarried with the Kips. Both families had come from Holland with Peter Stuyvesant, Dutch Governor of New Netherlands (New

Pictures of dolls discussed in this chapter will be found following page 140.

York). Battered but brave little Mollie Brinkerhoff has come down to her present owner Mrs. Richard G. Miller of White River Junction, Vt., who is a direct descendant of this intermarriage of the two colonial families.

After her mother's death, Mrs. Miller found Mollie in her attic, together with a plaque, which had accompanied her to some money-raising fair, possibly in Civil War times. The plaque reads:

MOLLY BRINKERHOFF

"I am not made of dust or wax,
But homespun linen stuffed with flax.
No human being treads the earth—
That was alive at Molly's birth,
Many score years have I, old Molly,
Kept the Brinkerhoff children jolly.
During the war of '76—
The clothes I wore were in a fix—
In oaken chest deep in the sand—
I was buried on Long Island strand
There safe from the British and Tories I lay
Till the last of the Redcoats skedaddled away."

Mollie is twenty-five inches tall and is very firm and solid but repairs have almost covered the original homespun linen which is still visible only in places.

Also of historic interest is "Sally—the White House doll" who made her debut in the Executive Mansion in 1829 during the administration of President John Quincy Adams. President Adams' children were all grown up at the time and the "White House children" were his grandchildren.

The present owner of the doll, Miss Mary Louise Adams Clement of Edge Hill, Warrenton, Va., writes of Sally:

"Sally is still very much of a personage, although now she leads a quiet life in Virginia and rarely makes public appearances except at an occasional exhibition.

"She is a large rag doll with painted face and dark hair. Her eyes are still very bright. Her dress of white and cherry calico is somewhat faded but otherwise has come through the years well. She was made by Mrs. Thomas Boylston Adams for my grandmother, Mary Louisa Adams—the little granddaughter of John Quincy Adams (daughter of his son, John) who was born in the White House during her grandfather's administration."

One of the important figures in Washington, D. C. during President Lincoln's administration, was a famous newspaperman, Crosby Stewart Noyes (1825–1908) who was a friend of Lincoln and Stanton, war-time editor of the *Washington Star,* and, later, its owner. That Noyes, in the days of his successful career, did not forget the little town in Maine where he was born is evidenced by the "Jenny Lind" doll which he sent to Alice Brown, a little girl of Minot, Maine, in the early 1850's.

It was in Minot that Crosby Noyes had his first editorial experience when at fifteen he wrote and edited the four page weekly, *Minot Notion.* After his graduation from Bowdoin College, he went to Washington, D. C. as a reporter, contributing to the *Washington News, Evening Journal* (Lewiston, Maine), the *Yankee Blade* (Boston), *Spirit of the Times* (New York) and to the *Saturday Evening Post.* Editing the *Washington Star* during the Civil War years, he bought the paper in 1867 for a hundred thousand dollars upon a forty-eight hour option. He became a wealthy man, endowed a chair at Bowdoin College and gave his library and his collection of prints to the Library of Congress.

Jenny Lind, "the Swedish Nightingale" made her first American concert tour under the sponsorship of P. T. Barnum in 1850–51. The public went wild over her. When she arrived September 1, 1850, 30,000 people met the boat. P. T. Barnum was the greatest showman of his day—perhaps of all time— and this outpouring of popular enthusiasm was probably no more spontaneous than the fact that everything marketable was immediately named for the celebrity: articles of clothing, lamps, buttons, dolls, etc. The bed which we now know as the "Spool bed" was then known as the "Jenny Lind bed"; food was served "à la Jenny Lind"; old-fashioned pound cake was given a new name, "Jenny Lind Cake." The whole craze was ridiculed in a song published in the contemporary *Weekly Boston Museum:*

"My wife has a Jenny Lind bonnet,
And a Jenny Lind visite;
With Jenny's portrait on it
Her handkerchief looks quite neat.
My wife's a slave to fashion,
Against it never sinned,
Our baby and the kitten
Are called after Jenny Lind.
Yes, all is Jenny Lind, now,
In every shop she's found;
Jenny Lind you can get at retail
By the yard, quart, pint or pound."

Familiar with all this publicity, it was natural that the young reporter, Crosby Noyes, should have selected a Jenny Lind doll to send as a gift to Alice Brown, his young kinswoman, in Maine. Alice Brown never married nor did her sister with whom she lived, so "Jenny" was never subjected to many of the vicissitudes that have wrecked the beauty of some "dolls of other days." "She is wonderfully well preserved for a lady of more than ninety years old," says her present owner, Mrs. William E. Briggs of Auburn, Maine, who herself writes for Maine newspapers under the pseudonym "Aunt Hitty."

Mrs. Briggs was a connection by marriage of the family of Alice Brown, and has known and seen the doll which she now owns, for more than fifty years.

The Jenny Lind dolls were made in Germany, in various sizes and types of facial expression; but practically all have the same hair dress with thick masses of hair drawn over the ears and with a knot in the back. The hair is always black. Jenny Lind actually had light hair, but it is said that she wished it were black and often wore a dark wig on the stage.

Mrs. Briggs' "Jenny Lind" doll is of unusual beauty, the china is of a creamy tint, not white, and for a four-inch head, has exceptionally heavy hair.

While we are on the subject of historic dolls we might here lay to rest the myth of the so-called "Dixie Bride" doll, a doll dressed as a bride which is supposed to be "still treasured in the family of the Union soldier" to whom it was presented by the Southern belle he sought to wed. It was given, the story says, with a note saying: "This is the only Dixie bride you will ever claim." The story has been repeated so often that many collectors have believed it true.

We checked on the legend with Mrs. Frances Parkinson Keyes of New Hampshire. Mrs. Keyes replied:

"I once wrote a short story which *was* founded on fact, entitled 'The Dixie Doll' and which was published in the *Home Magazine,* but if the original doll is still preserved, I do not know where or by whom.

"However, there is a very interesting angle to this story; it was read by Miss Helen Walter of Staunton, Va., and she created a Dixie Doll for my collection, inspired by the one I had described. This was so much admired that she was asked to make replicas of it, and she has been doing so ever since."

So the fact is that the real Dixie Bride doll is not an antique doll "cherished by the family of the jilted soldier," but a doll created by Miss Helen Walter of "Just Folks" originally for and with our fellow doll collector, Mrs. Frances Parkinson Keyes. It is an old china head doll but not *the* old doll of the story.

An interesting Vermont association doll, now owned by Mrs. Elizabeth Fitts of Keene, N. H., was found in Brandon, Vt. It is said to have belonged to Sarah, the sister of Stephen A. Douglas. Certain it is that "The Little Giant" was born in Brandon and lived there during his earlier years. After the death of his father, the family saw hard times and Stephen was apprenticed to a Brandon cabinet-maker. Later the family moved to Canandaigua, New York.

"Felicia" is a wooden doll about ten inches long of the "Dutch doll" type so much loved by the little future Queen Victoria of England.

Among eugenists it is almost axiomatic that girls are apt to inherit the tastes and character traits of their fathers. It is almost equally axiomatic that the man of action, the outdoor man, wants his women folk to be soft and feminine—as little girls, to love dolls—as young ladies, to love dainty gowns and furbelows. Colonel William E. Cody (Buffalo Bill), pony express rider,

Left to right, Ball-head French bisque doll, 1882, original clothing. Jumeau doll, marked "Composition body," 1882, original clothes. Modern "Patsy" doll models one of Jumeau's extra dresses. *St. George Collection.*

Group of Jumeau dolls. *Collection of Miss Alma Robeck, Annapolis, Maryland.*

SIX TYPES OF BODY USED BY JUMEAU

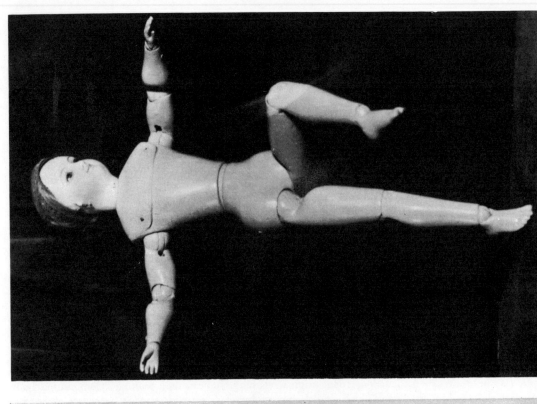

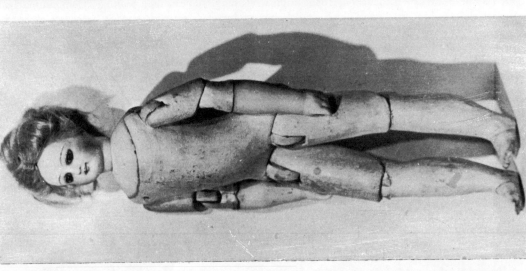

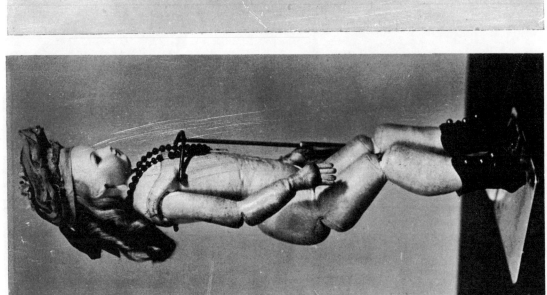

Left, 1st type, 1869. All-kid body stuffed with sawdust. With use, the joints filled with sawdust and would not straighten. *St. George Collection. Center,* Wooden members separately covered with kid. *Collection of Mrs. Edmund H. Poetter, Reading, Vermont. Right,* 4th type. Rare all-wood jointed body. *Collection of Mrs. Robert G. Fiscus, Pittsburgh, Pennsylvania.*

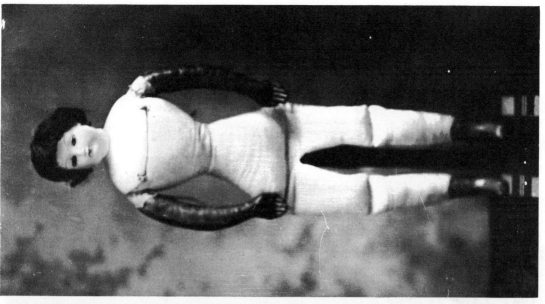

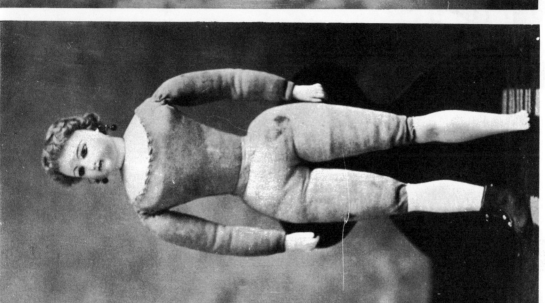

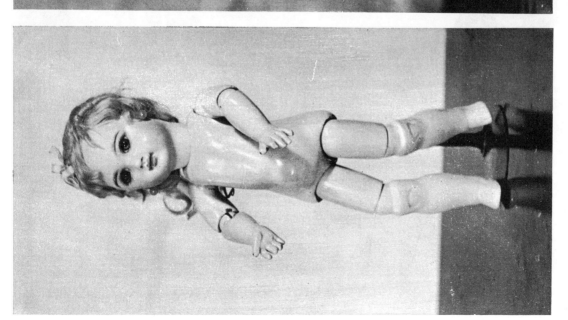

Left, 5th type. Composition body jointed with rubber cord. Head fits into body. Used entirely after 1880. *St. George Collection. Center,* Very rare type of Jumeau doll. Body of stockinet. Bisque foot and leg. Probably "Jumeau walking doll." Only type with bisque feet. *Courtesy of Mrs. Elsie Clark Krug, Baltimore, Maryland. Right,* Jumeau doll with cotton body. Leather arms and shoes made on feet. Cheaper type of body. Doll 23 inches tall. *Courtesy of Mrs. Ralph E. Wakeman.*

Left, Jumeau doll—original clothes. *Collection of Mrs. William Walker, Louisville, Kentucky. Right*, "Little "Eva"—29-inch Jumeau, 1869. Brought from Paris on the Clipper Ship *Rosie Webb*. All original.

Left, Jumeau doll. *Collection of Mrs. Velma Fuller Von Bruns, Bristol, Vermont. Right*, Bru doll—28 inches —marked on head: *"Bru Jerr 12." Collection of Mrs. Margaret Bohacker, Lynn, Massachusetts.*

Group of German bisque dolls. *Collection of Mrs. Rose Parro, Waterbury, Vermont.*

Left, Bisque playhouse dolls. Brought from Germany in 1908. *Right,* German peasant dolls—bisque and cloth
—about 60 years old. Made by the Hetwig Co., Germany.

Left, Bisque twins. *Collection of Mrs. William J. Connors, Dorchester, Massachusetts. Center*, Crying boy— German bisque head. About 50 years old. *Collection of Mrs. William J. Connors, Dorchester, Massachusetts. Right*, "Rosebud," a charming brown bisque doll. *Collection of Mrs. Louis E. Lahn, Amarillo, Texas.*

Left, German bisque doll of unusual expression. Marked simply *Made in Germany*, 1898. Belonged to Mrs. Nan Bregg, Woman's Editor of Pittsburgh *Sun Telegraph*. Lamb's wool wig was made by Mrs. Bregg's mother. *Right*, Floating bisque bath doll. Belonged to Mrs. Laura Billings Lee of Woodstock, Vermont. *Courtesy of Mrs. John McDill, Woodstock, Vermont.*

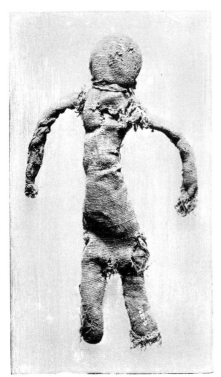
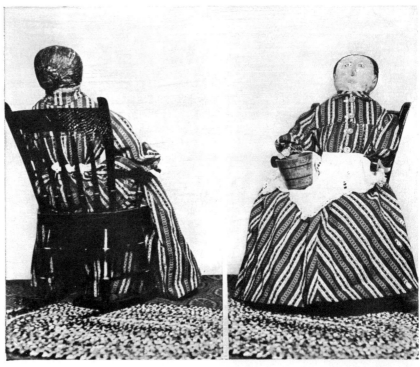

Left, Oldest rag doll in America. A Roman Rag Doll of the third century A.D. found in the tombs of Egypt. *Courtesy of the Royal Ontario Museum, Dr. C. T. Curelly, Director. Right,* "Bridget," a rag doll. *Collection of Mrs. J. J. Flynn, Williams Bay, Wisconsin*

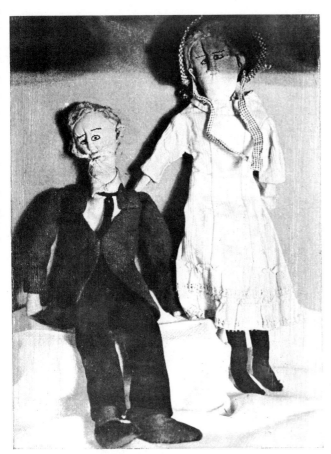

Left, Rag dolls. *Collection of Mrs. Nina Shepherd, Granville, Ohio. Right,* "Thankful," a Walker doll. Dressed by Mrs. Ralph E. Wakeman, Claremont, New Hampshire. *Collection of Mrs. George Brinton Chandler, Columbus, Ohio.*

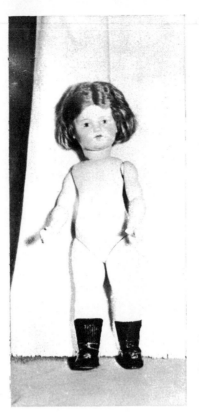

Left, Goodyear rubber head. Never used and still having label giving directions for attaching it. Lavender flowers and net molded on hair. *Collection of Mrs. Otis Carl Williams, Worcester, Massachusetts. Center,* Modern rubber doll marked *K and R Germany* (Kammerer and Reinhardt). Beautifully shaped cloth body. Rubber arms. *Collection of Mrs. Gurth Ritter, Torrence, California. Right,* Doll with celluloid head marked with Tortoise and *Germany.* Tortoise is mark of Reinesche Gummi and Celluloid Frabik Co.; date after 1898. *Collection of the late Mrs. J. D. McEwen, Wichita, Kansas.*

Rawhide doll heads by Darrow, Bristol, Connecticut, 1866. Doll on right has been repainted. Doll on left, in original condition, shows inherent weakness of type, flaking of paint from the rawhide. *St. George Collection.*

P. D. Smith dolls. *Courtesy of Mrs. P. D. Smith, now Mrs. Liddle, Los Angeles, California.*

P. D. Smith doll. *Collection of Mrs. Gurth Ritter, Torrence, California.*

Figurines by Margaret Smith, 1918.

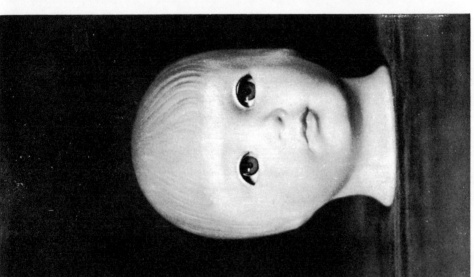

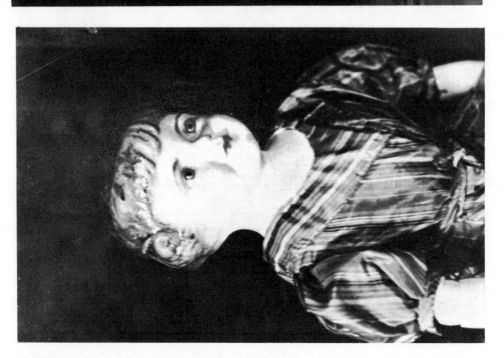

Left, P. D. Smith doll. *Collection of Mrs. Gurth Ritter, Torrence, California. Center*, Head by Grace C. Rockwell marked *Germany*, bisque. *Collection of Mrs. C. H. Criley, Los Angeles, California. Right*, "Fly-Lo Baby" by Grace Story Putnam. *Collection of Mrs. C. H. Criley, Los Angeles, California.*

"Mormon Pioneers." Made and costumed by Lewis Sorenson. In State House at Salt Lake City, Utah. *Courtesy of Lewis Sorenson, Los Angeles, California.*

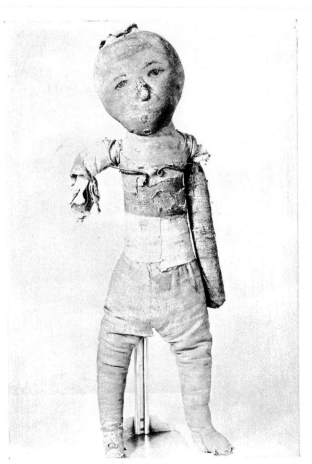

Left, "Mollie Brinkerhoff," one of the oldest rag dolls in the United States. *Courtesy of Mrs. Richard G. Miller, White River Junction, Vermont.* Right, "Sally, the White House Doll." Owned by grandchildren of John Quincy Adams. *Courtesy of Miss Mary Louise Adams Clement, Warrenton, Virginia.*

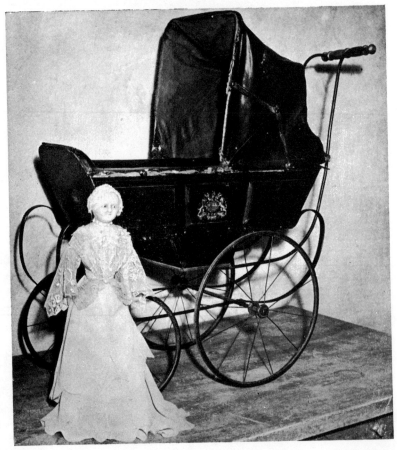

Queen Victoria's doll and doll carriage. Owned by Mrs. Marie Porter, California. Loaned to Charles W. Bowers Memorial Museum, Santa Ana, California. *Collection of Mrs. John T. Buchanan, Omaha, Nebraska.*

DOLLS

Left, "Jenny Lind," given to his kinswomen in Minot, Maine, by Crosby S. Noyes, famous editor of the *Washing Star. Collection of Mrs. William E. Briggs, Auburn, Maine. Right,* Jumeau doll brought from Paris by Col. William F. Cody (Buffalo Bill) to his daughter. *Collection of Mrs. Cyrus M. Beachy, Wichita, Kansas.*

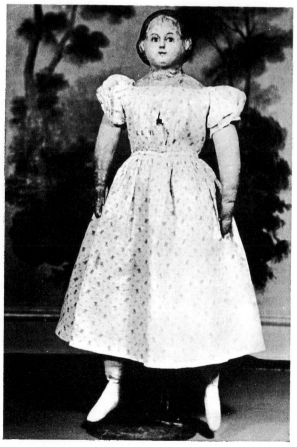

Left, "Felicia," from Brandon, Vermont, belonged to sister of Stephen A. Douglas. *Collection of Mrs. Elizabeth Fitts, Keene, New Hampshire. Right,* "Catherine Powell," the first doll that came to Omaha, Nebraska. Came from Ohio in covered wagon drawn by oxen in 1852.

"Queen Victoria" and "Prince Albert" in their wedding clothes. Papier mâché fashion dolls said to be dressed in the actual materials left from the Royal wedding garments. *Collection of Mrs. DeWitt Clinton Cohen, New York.*

Left, Old papier mâché headed doll representing "The Widow Bedotte." Maker of doll is unknown. About 1850. *Collection of Mrs. William Walker, Louisville, Kentucky. Right,* Doll given to General Eisenhower by the grateful people of Brittany, and given by him to the Children of America, Natural History Building, Washington, D. C.

Doll collection of Eugene Field. *Courtesy of Mrs. Kenneth Colburn, Pasadena, California.*

Left, Wooden doll given to Eugene Field by child in a Chicago orphanage. *Courtesy of Mrs. Kenneth Colburn, Pasadena, California. Right,* "Lucretia's Doll" belonged to Lucretia Goddard, granddaughter of William Dawes, who rode with Paul Revere, April 18, 1775. Date of doll 1828.

Left, Woman vegetable pedlar. *Collection of Mrs. DeWitt Clinton Cohen, New York.* *Right*, Fortune telling pedlar doll. *Collection of Miss Jennie L. Abbott, Westfield, Massachusetts.*

Left, Pedlar doll (Assembled). *Collection of Mrs. Velma Fuller Von Bruns, Bristol, Vermont.* *Right*, English pedlar doll. *Collection of Mrs. DeWitt Clinton Cohen, New York.*

buffalo hunter, scout, Indian fighter and great showman, was no exception to the rule. He was the father of three daughters, Arta, born December 16, 1866, Orra, whose birth date is not recorded; and Irma, born February 9, 1883.

Mrs. Cyrus M. Beachy of Wichita, Kansas, has in her collection a Jumeau doll which Buffalo Bill brought from Paris to his little daughter, Irma, on one of the occasions when his show was playing in that capital. But the daughter did not welcome the doll with the joy her father had imagined. She preferred horses and the things of the outdoor world, for she was, to quote a homely saying, "A chip off the old block," and the doll was put away, never played with, and remains as fresh as when it left the Paris doll shop—mute evidence of a shattered dream.

Of the many items associated with Queen Victoria, in existence, none is more interesting or more pathetic than the princess's doll and doll carriage, now in the Charles W. Bowers Memorial Museum, Santa Ana, Calif., loaned by Mrs. Marie Porter, who purchased it from a former custodian of Windsor Castle. The little princess seems to have everything but companionship. The carriage was made by the royal carriage maker and is so constructed as to be controlled by a mere touch of the finger. It bears the arms of the princess on each end and the coat of arms of Windsor Castle on each side.

The doll, an English made wax, has the rare violet-blue glass eyes. But, as has been said before, the Princess Victoria vastly preferred the crude little wooden "Dutch" dolls.

Another interesting Victorian association item is a pair of papier mâché dolls with kid bodies, milliners' models, which represent Victoria and Albert on their wedding day and are said to be dressed in the actual scraps left from the royal wedding garments. They were found by Mrs. Dewitt Clinton Cohen, of New York, who was in England just before the outbreak of the First World War. Unable to bring them home with her, they were left in the care of the Royal English Needlework Society until after the war.

Sometimes association interest centers in places rather than in people. Such is the interest in "Catherine Powell," a large old papier mâché doll with unusual "flirting" eyes. She was the first doll brought into Omaha, Nebr., in 1850 when it had but seven families. She came from Ohio on the "Overland

Trail" in a covered wagon drawn by oxen and crossed the Missouri River at
Council Bluffs by ferry. She is named for the little pioneer girl who brought
her. Owned by Mrs. John T. Buchanan, she is loaned to the Joslyn Memorial
Museum of Omaha.

ASSOCIATION DOLLS II

THERE ARE NO MORE interesting association dolls than the dolls collected by Eugene Field. Though he was born in Missouri and spent most of his working years as a newspaper man in Chicago, Field was nevertheless a pure New Englander and Vermont has every right to claim him as her own. His father came from Vermont. The Field family home for generations has been in Newfane, and Eugene's cousin, Charles K. Field, who is "Cheerio" of the radio, has told us that many of the family treasures are now in the Historical Society Museum in Brattleboro.

Eugene Field's brilliant father, Roswell Field, from whom he inherited both his genius and his passion for collecting, graduated from Middlebury College, Vermont, at the age of fifteen and was admitted to practice law at the Vermont bar when eighteen. Angered by the injustice he felt had been dealt him by the courts in annulling an imprudent early marriage, he left his native state and settled in St. Joe, Mo., where he made a brilliant record as an attorney. Always the foe of injustice, he fought, without compensation, on the side of the Negro defendant in the historic Dred Scott case.

When his second wife died, the two small sons, Eugene, and his elder brother, were committed by their father to the care of his sister, Mary Field

Pictures of dolls discussed in this chapter will be found following page 140.

French of Amherst, Mass. In the home of this gracious woman, the Field boys grew up, acquiring, as one writer says, "a New England bent of mind." They attended a Massachusetts boys' school and Amherst College until the death of their father in 1869, when their legal guardian took them back to Missouri and both boys graduated from Knox College in that state.

From the day after his graduation, when he and his college chum went abroad with Eugene Field's patrimony of eight thousand dollars, and he returned penniless laden with rare books and curiosities, his passion for collecting never faltered.

His marriage to a sister of this same college chum proved a happy one, although a husband who collected everything under the sun on a newspaperman's salary must, at times, have been a trial to the patience of the gentle Julia, who had to manage the family finances.

For many years they lived in a rented house in Chicago's Buena Park district, next to the vacant lot which Field has immortalized in "The Delectable Ballad of the Waller Lot." In this house, Field's friend, Julian Ralph, pictures him as "sitting down happily amid the spoils of two continents and two decades of collecting . . . from books and prints to rag dolls."

Small wonder then that Eugene Field should have understood so well the soul of the collector and written so humorously, and sometimes ruefully, of his deeds and misdeeds as he does in "The Discreet Collector," "Dear Old London," "The Bibliomaniac's Prayer" and "In Old New Orleans."

That Field was doll and toy conscious is clear from many of his child poems. He undoubtedly favored dolls that had seen much loving—dolls "in original condition" as collectors call them—such as the "raggedy home-made doll" in "Little Miss Brag" or the one in "Good Children Street":

> "And yonder Odette wheels her dolly about—
> Poor dolly! I'm sure she is ill,
> For one of her blue china eyes has dropped out—
> And her voice is asthmatically shrill.
> Then, too, I observe, she is minus her feet,
> Which causes great sorrow in Good Children Street."

144

Some years ago, his daughter Mrs. W. C. Engler (Mary French Field), of Altadena, Calif., gave part of her father's doll collection and the original manuscript of "The Duel" as a wedding gift to Mrs. Kenneth Colburn—the former Julia Rounds—of Pasadena, Calif. Mrs. Colburn's mother, Mrs. Frederick Childs Rounds is a lifelong friend of the Fields. Through Mrs. Colburn's courtesy, we have these photographs, the first ever published of the Field collection.

One of the most touching is the wooden doll in the dark suit with the ribbon across its shoulders. It was the gift of an orphan asylum child to the poet. Mr. Field had read some of his poems to the children in a Chicago orphanage and one little girl was so fascinated that with love shining in her little face she thrust into his hand her most cherished possession—the wooden doll. Eugene Field understood what was in the child's heart and gravely accepted the gift. It was dressed by the Field children.

Among the other dolls is a Sioux Indian doll with the original label written by the poet just a few days before his death, for exhibition at the World's Fair in Chicago. Another small wooden doll also has a label in his own handwriting which reads: *Whitechapel doll—London—six for a penny.*

When Paul Revere made his famous ride "through every Middlesex village and town" another man, William Dawes, rode in the opposite direction to warn the people of that region of the approach of the Red Coats. In 1819 Mehitible Dawes, a daughter of William Dawes, married Samuel Goddard whose grandfather, John Goddard, known as "John the Wagon-master" had played his part in the Revolution by keeping the supplies of food and ammunition moving to the colonial army of Massachusetts.

The progenitor of the Goddard family had come from England in 1665, just before the Great Fire of London. They were a prolific family and many descendants of this immigrant are spread over New England.

Samuel Goddard, like his uncle Nathaniel Goddard was a merchant and importer. To him and his wife Mehitible Dawes were born seven children of whom the three oldest were Louisa, born in 1819, Ann Elizabeth, born in 1821 and Lucretia born in 1823.

From a Vermont branch of the family there recently came to us an old trunk containing, among much fine needlework, six dolls belonging to these three little girls. Everything in the trunk was carefully labelled and dated so it was easy to identify the ownership and history of each item. There were the four wax penny dolls described in Chapter Seven, a pincushion doll with a wooden head of the Queen Victoria Dutch doll type; and finally, wrapped in part of an old (handmade) child's dress, was "Lucretia's doll, given to her by Mr. William Pratt of the firm of Pratt and Goddard, Pearl St., Boston, 1828."

"Lucretia's doll" is a 20-inch boy doll in page boy costume of white serge and gold braid with a red satin cape and a white satin hat with a red plume. The doll has a papier mâché head, and the feet and hands are wood, and the rest of the body is a very heavy white kid. It is unusual because only the hands from the wrists and the feet from the ankles are made of wood, with the kid used on the full length of the limbs, instead of the usual wooden arms and legs.

Whether the family respect for the donor, who for two years was a partner of Lucretia's cousin in a mercantile and importing venture, was so great, or because dolls of that type were so rare, the five-year-old Lucretia never got to play with it and the doll remains as fresh and new looking as though it had come from the store on Pearl Street but yesterday. Papier mâché appears to have been used for doll heads first in 1820 so that this is a very early papier mâché doll and it is interesting for that reason as well as for its association with two noted Revolutionary families.

Lucretia Goddard and her two older sisters, Louisa and Ann Elizabeth, were evidently good little girls in school and industrious little girls at home. The old trunk contained their unfinished samplers with threaded needles still in the work; a small thimble belonging to one or another of them; about twenty small silken bags and pincushions they had made, some worked with their cross-stitched initials. There were three needle books, evidently school prizes from a loving teacher. In Ann Elizabeth's is a card:

"Dear Ann Eliza, let this be
A token of my love for thee."

In Louisa's, a similar card reads:

"This trifle, dear Louisa take,
Accept it for the donor's sake."

There are several cards "For attention to study" and for "Meritorious conduct." Quaintest of these is Lucretia's, which reads:

"REWARD OF MERIT

Granted to Miss Lucretia Goddard for attention to study." (Below this is a woodcut of a farm yard scene with animals and within the open door of the barn, men are seen threshing grain with a flail.)

CLOSING HYMN

"Guide of our youth, to thee we pray;
Help us to tread thy holy way.
And may our whole life be past
As we would wish it had at last!

"Oh smile on those whose time and care,
Are spent in our instruction here;
And may our conduct ever prove
Our gratitude for all their love!

"Through life, may we perform thy will.
Our various duties all fulfill,
And join our friends whom we have known
In nobler songs around the throne."
"Miss A. Capen" (teacher's signature)
"Sold by N. S. Simpkins & Co., Court St., Boston."

When, where, or by whom was made the unique old character doll representing a fictional character of the 1840 and 1950 decades, "The Widow Bedotte," no one knows. She came to Mrs. William Walker of Louisville,

Ky., as a gift from a young woman to whose mother and grandmother the doll had belonged.

"The Widow Bedotte Papers" were written by a young novice writer, Miss Frances Marian Berry of Whitesboro, N. Y., who afterwards became the wife of Rev. Benjamin Whitcher of Elmira, N. Y. Mrs. Whitcher died in 1852, four years after her marriage. The papers were originally contributed to *Neal's Saturday Gazette,* a Philadelphia weekly newspaper. They were considered highly humorous and Mr. Godey of *Godey's Lady's Book,* begged the author to write for his magazine. In response to his solicitations, the sketch "Aunt Maguire's Experience" appeared in *Godey's.*

In 1854, after the author had been dead two years, Alice Neal, widow of the owner of Neal's Gazette, gathered "The Widow Bedotte Papers" into a book, of which 100,000 copies were immediately sold. The book, now almost entirely forgotten, went through five editions: 1855, 1864, 1880, 1883 and 1893. Its subject matter concerns the matrimonial ambitions of one Priscilla Bedotte, "the Widow Bedotte," relict of Deacon Hezekiah Bedotte, whose passing the widow frequently laments in verses, of which the following three, written on separate occasions, are typical:

> "I never changed my single lot—
> I thought 'twould be a sin—
> I thought so much of Deacon Bedotte
> I never got married again."

> ———

> "And since it was my lot to be
> The wife of such a man,
> Go tell the men that's after me
> To ketch me if they can."

> ———

> "And now he's dead; the thought is killing,
> My grief I can't control—
> He never left a single shilling
> His widow to console."

In spite of these protestations, she finally takes a successor, Rev. Shadrach Sniffles, and assures him in verse:

"I'll never desert you, Oh Shadrach, my Shad!"

The "Widow Bedotte" doll, which is about 12 inches tall, has a papier mâché head, with a very expressive, if not beautiful, character face; the molded hair is "slicked" back to a "washerwoman's knot" in the back; the body is cloth; the hands are kid. She wears a drab silk dress lined with brown cambric, and buttoned down the front from neck to hem with black buttons; a lawn collar edged with narrow hand-crotcheted lace and a small gold brooch complete the costume. Her tiny worn shoes are brown leather. In the ample long pocket in the skirt is a handkerchief with some only partly decipherable writing around the inside of the hem, done in India ink, apparently a quotation from the Widow Bedotte.

This amusing reminder of what a recent writer calls "the feminine fifties" could hardly have been made later than the earlier half of that decade, in the heyday of the book's popularity.

The latest, but by no means least, of Association dolls is the lovely large bisque baby doll presented to General Dwight D. Eisenhower by the grateful people of Brittany after the Americans had driven out the German invaders. General Eisenhower gave the doll "to the children of America" and it is now in the United States National Museum in Washington.

THE HUMAN INTEREST SIDE OF
DOLL COLLECTING

BATTERED AND BROKEN, the bedraggled little wax doll lay on the
heap of rubble that had once been the railway station of the doll
capital of the world—Alt Nuremburg in Germany. Someone had
tried to mend her, given it up and tossed her back on the debris.
There she lay, a poor little symbol of the civilization which Nazi greed had
wrecked—a miniature of the limp forms and broken bodies of the European
children who had perished in the War.

A young American officer, passing by, lifted her from the ruins. To
him she brought memories of home and his wife who loved and collected
dolls. He took the little wreck to his quarters, packed her and sent her to
America. His wife, Mrs. Oma Huff Mangold of Armstrong, Iowa, treasures
the gift. The little waif of Nuremburg has found a peaceful home.

Dolls are such personal possessions that not the least of the dividends paid
by a collection of old dolls lie in their associations and the memories of the
human personalities these fragile creatures have so long outlived. What tales
old dolls could tell us—and sometimes do. Often sad little stories and sometimes amusing.

Priorities and a pressure cooker brought us "Martha Victoria," a French

Picture of dolls discussed in this chapter will be found following page 188.

150

"fashion doll," a lovely Jumeau of the late 1860's. Martha Victoria has been described in the chapter on fashion dolls, but this is the story of her coming. Our neighbor, "Major John," a retired British army officer, is a bit of an epicure whose hobby is cooking wonderful dishes and canning all sorts of fruits and vegetables, the products of his Victory garden. His American wife, Martha, writes books. They are delightful and interesting friends as well as pleasant neighbors. One morning "Major John" telephoned in obvious distress and puzzlement. *Did* we know where he "might beg, borrow, buy or steal a pressure cooker?" It seemed that he had been using a pressure cooker belonging to some other friends—but now Mr. X's wife was suing her husband for divorce and Mr. X, disgruntled at the world in general and his litigating wife in particular, had come and taken home the pressure cooker she had loaned John and Martha. What to do? The Victory garden was prime for canning—and no priority for a pressure cooker in sight. What to do, indeed? At the moment we could think of no answer. Later in the day we remembered that just before the war our old pressure cooker had broken a lug, so had been replaced with a more modern type. We told the Major that if he could get the broken lug welded, he'd be welcome to use the cooker for the duration. He did get it safely repaired and then he was determined to *buy* the cooker. It was convenient to us for sterilizing jars for open-kettle canning, so we said "no," but he was welcome to use it as long as he needed it. The man persisted. (We wondered if perhaps he suspected *us* of divorce intentions!) Finally to end the discussion, we said: "Tell you what—we won't *sell* it but if you and Martha want to trade us that lovely doll you brought over for us to see the other night—it's a deal. We never dreamed of them doing *that* but he came right back: "I'll *do* it!" The next day he appeared with the doll and her outfit—dresses, umbrella, fan, toilet articles and jewels—all the impedimenta of a proper French fashion doll.

A few days later another neighbor, calling, heard the story of the doll and said: "Why I have my mother's old doll. She's something like that—if I can find it, I'll give it to you." She did. This too was a Jumeau but of a later period—1880. She was a little girl and had an elaborate little girl wardrobe of that day.

Two Jumeaus in one week in a neighborhood that boasts three important doll collectors, six antique shops and three "antique pickers!" The age of miracles is still with us.

Many elderly people give their beloved dolls—or sell them to collectors whom they know will appreciate and preserve them rather than leave them to younger relatives for whom they have no interest. Sometimes parting with such a lifelong treasure causes bitter tears to flow, and smiles that shine through the tears.

Miss Marie Ketterman of York, Pa., tells the story of the doll on the extreme right of the group of wax dolls shown following page 188: "I tried for fifteen years before I succeeded in buying the doll from a woman in California. As her owner dressed her for me to take away, tears streamed down her cheeks."

A "Bureau Drawer doll" her former owner called the wax over papier mâché which came from Maine via a "Want Ad" in the *New England Homestead*. We named her "Ginivra Augusta" for her two former owners, but most often we think of her as "The Little Girl Who Never Was a Bride." Augusta, her first owner, a young girl in a small country village in Maine was "engaged to be married" and like girls everywhere, she dreamed of having a lovely trousseau. Money was scarce in the North Country in those days and opportunities to earn it were few and far between, so Augusta went away to take a job as a waitress at a seacoast summer resort, but there she contracted scarlet fever and only came back home to sleep in the little country churchyard. Her mother gave the doll to Ginivra, the little niece of Augusta's fiancé. Put away in the top bureau drawer, Ginivra's grandmother, from sentiment or just, perhaps, pure New England "carefulness" never allowed the doll to be played with. The utmost enjoyment the little girl ever had or could have of it was that she might on Sunday morning, if she had been *very* good and obedient during the week, open the bureau drawer and peep in at the doll. A "Bureau Drawer doll," indeed—a Little Girl Who Never Was a Bride—a doll that never had the proper amount of loving! That is why, of course, that she came to a doll collector of another generation as fresh as if she had just come from the store.

Advertising for dolls in farm papers has brought many dolls out of country attics. That famous New England institution the "Swopper's Page" in the

Yankee magazine has also been a source of supply to some collectors. Mrs. Richard E. Simpson, the former Ariel Cutler, of Peterborough, N. H., obtained many dolls for her large collection, now in the town museum, through the "Swopper's Page."

A "swop" that involved orchids and a little old red high chair was ultimately responsible for the writing of this book. A potential swopper offered a little old handmade high chair in exchange for a book "Bog Trotting for Orchids." We had the book, and we like old furniture so we contacted the man. He proved to be the well-known educator and writer, J. Almus Russell. Mr. Russell wrote that, as he was leaving his summer home in New Hampshire the next day, he was "just sending the high chair along to us and if we liked it—etc."

As the crating and canvas came away, we were delighted with the quaint little red-painted chair, obviously homemade, but whose gracious curves showed plainly the hand of a master craftsman. How much more intrigued we were when a second letter came from Mr. Russell, giving the history of the chair! It had been made for his sister by their grandfather, an old Nova Scotia shipwright, who had been an adopted son of Sir Charles Tupper, one of the founders of the Confederation of Canada.

We knew all about Sir Charles Tupper, for it happened that our maternal great grandfather, Ronald MacDonald, who came from Scotland to Cornwall, Ontario, and later to New Brunswick and Houlton, Maine, was a first cousin of Sir John A. MacDonald, the first premier of Canada and the originator of the Confederation. Sir John MacDonald and Sir Charles Tupper had been throughout their entire lives, the bitterest of personal and political foes. The only subject on which they ever were known to have agreed with each other was the founding of the Confederation which made Canada a nation. Now, after so many years, the more-or-less-Tupper high chair had come to rest on the more-or-less-MacDonald hearth.

But the little chair looked empty and lonely. It needed an occupant so we bought an old doll for it—and became a doll collector. The modern all-rubber doll which now occupies it, is not that original doll. It seemed more appropriate to use a more-or-less MacDonald doll and this life-like baby belongs to our young niece, the fourth generation from Ronald MacDonald. The dress it wears is also more-or-less MacDonald—the author's "best dress" at the age of ten weeks. One sometimes marvels at having survived an 1880's infancy when babies must have wilted under the weight of dresses more than a yard and a half in length (as this one is) and long petticoats that ended in wide embroidery ruffles and nineteen quarter-inch tucks, such as is under this dress.

Sir John A. MacDonald was an unusual personality. He looked so much like Disraeli, England's great prime minister, that when he visited London shortly after Disraeli's death, his appearance on the streets startled the passersby and gave rise to a legend that "Dis'" ghost was revisiting the scene of his earthly triumphs.

When MacDonald, a young lawyer, was trying his first case in Ontario, his opponent, an old English lawyer, sought to confuse the youngster by browbeating and insulting remarks. MacDonald's patience finally gave out and the attorneys came to blows. The scandalized judge ordered the old Scotch bailiff to separate the combatants. The judge was very deaf and the bailiff was very clannish. Circling around the struggling men, he shouted loudly, for the judge's benefit:

"Order in the court! Order in the court!" adding in a lower voice:

"Hit him again, John! Hit him again! Order in the court! Order in the court! Hit him, John! Hit him again!"

MacDonald's encounters with Sir Charles Tupper, the "grandfather" of the high chair, though not physical, were often quite as colorful.

A "swop" that brought her an Indian doll and a maternal spanking is recalled by Miss Blanche Mosse of Denison, Texas. She says:

"Bannock is 14 inches high made with fawn-colored buckskin clothes, white buckskin body, black bead button eyes, beaded nose and mouth (with pink beads), two black woolen braids. Bannock is near forty years old, probably new and had known no other mistress when he came to me . . . that is when I traded my Little Red Ridinghood coat for him a little over forty years ago. My uncle was in the lumber business and had some Bannocks working for him. The Indians scared me with their queer noises and looks but I had never heard of them harming anyone, so with my cat's curiosity I slipped away to see how they

154

lived in their wigwams. When one of the squaws suggested trading my red coat for the doll, it suited me fine. Small though I was, I was tickled that I never could recognize afterwards the one with whom I traded, and when I was put before them no squaw remembered ever having seen me, so although my uncle was mad as a hatter at the Indians, nothing could be done about it. I got to keep the doll although mother spanked me and kept the doll away from me without letting me handle it for some time."

Dolls often commemorate family events. Sue L. Naysmith of Minneapolis, has a wonderful old Jenny Lind doll "loaned to me for my lifetime" that was treasured by Mrs. Sarah Bryant Smith from the day of her birth until she died at the age of eighty-seven years. After her death there was found a paper with the doll which said:

"This doll was bought for me in St. Anthony by my father, William V. Bryant, when he learned that (myself), his first child, was a daughter. Mrs. Sarah Bryant Smith."

How human a picture of the joy of the young parent, who, on learning the sex of his first child, set out immediately for town to buy her a doll?

Mrs. Louis E. Lahn of Amarillo, Texas, wrote: "I guess my two most precious dolls would not be classed as valuable antiques or collector's items. One is 'Rosebud,' an Armand Marseilles bisque, a lovely brown warm-colored bisque with brown eyes. My father who was drowned twenty years ago, gave me this doll on my first birthday. She is most precious to me because my adored father gave her to me against all advice about giving a one-year-old baby such an expensive doll that would surely be broken in a matter of days. The other is 'Baby Jean,' a Kestner baby doll that my mother gave me for Christmas when I was barely past four years of age. The doll expresses to me, more clearly than anything else the love of my mother. Times were very, very, very hard for us then, and my mother paid out fifty cents at a time for this doll so that when Christmas came, a four-year-old would not know that Santa Claus too, needed to be paid. Every time I look at her I realize how much she cost in anguish and how great is mother love."

Mrs. Huntington Brown of Minneapolis has a doll dressed in the uniform of the nurses of the Boston City Hospital which was presented to her father by the nursing staff at the completion of his internship in the hospital in 1900.

Mrs. Brown is also preparing two dolls that will be treasures for her two daughters. These are two modern bisque dolls and each time she makes dresses for her daughters she makes replicas in style and materials for the dolls, so that each girl will have a complete record of her wardrobe—a new application of the "fashion doll" idea.

Sometimes the story of the old doll is one of romance and young love. Mrs. Leo Lamb's Mary Todd Lincoln-type china doll came across the ocean from England and then overland by covered wagon across the desert to Salt Lake City with Mr. Lamb's mother when she was fifteen years old. Her father was a famous Mormon. Soon after her arrival, walking along the streets of Salt Lake City, the young girl encountered Brigham Young who stopped her and asked her who she was. When she told him, he remarked, "I will see your father tonight about taking you as my wife."

The girl had other ideas and ran to the blacksmith shop to tell the bad news to her eighteen-year-old lover who worked there. That night the two fled in a wagon train, penniless, without a dime to buy food even, but happy. They settled in Southern California and lived to acquire great affluence through oil lands there.

Another cross-country immigrant was "Catherine Powell," a large papier mâché doll with eyes that move from side to side as her body is tilted. In 1852 she came from Ohio in a covered wagon drawn by oxen and was the first doll brought into Omaha which then had only seven families. She is now in the Joslyn Memorial Museum in Omaha, loaned by her present owner, Mrs. John T. Buchanan.

Such are typical of the stories, sad, humorous or historical that old dolls might tell us, if only we could speak their language.

PEDLAR DOLLS

THE PUSHCART MERCHANTS of New York's lower east side are the modern survivals of the street merchants of England in the early eighteenth century, a day when the streets and lanes of London, narrow and dirty, were crowded with pedlars of every sort of wares, who jostled the sedan chair, borne by stout bearers, which were the taxis for people of "quality," and both jostled the passerby on foot—a day when, as Brown, a contemporary writer expressed it: "Some carry, others are carried." The air was filled with a pandemonium of hawkers' cries—"Old chairs to mend!" "Buy a fine singing bird!" "Fine writing ink!" "Old satten, old taffety, or velvet!" "Buy a white line, a jack line, or a clothes line!" "A merry new song!" "Knives, combs, or inkhorns!" "Long thread laces, long and strong!" "Holland socks, four pairs for a shilling!" "Any wax or wafers!" "Buy a new almanac!" "Pretty maids, pretty pins!" "Ripe strawberries!" "Delicate cowcumbers to pickle!" etc., etc. These were the sounds of which Addison says in the Sir Roger de Coverly papers in *The Spectator:*

"There is nothing which more astonishes a Foreigner, and frights a Country Squire, than the Cries of London. My good friend Sir Roger often declares that he cannot get them out of his head, or go to sleep for them the first week that he is in town. On the contrary Will Honeycomb calls them the

Pictures of dolls discussed in this chapter will be found following pages 140 and 188.

Ramage de Ville, and prefers them to the sounds of Larks and Nightingales, with all the Musick of the Fields and Woods."

Through the countrysides of England too—just as in our American country districts two or three generations ago—folks bought their notions, and small merchandise from wandering pedlars. In England these pedlars were often women and were called "Notion Nannies."

It is not strange that old dolls which so often reflect the social customs of their day should sometimes have taken the form of these pedlar women or "Nannies" and should carry on their trays miniatures of the multiplicity of wares they sold in real life.

Pedlar dolls were made in England during the eighteenth century and to about 1860 in the nineteenth. The dolls were usually of wood, but occasionally one sees a wax doll dressed as a pedlar. Some have thought them homemade, but the early English wooden pedlar dolls look too carefully finished for amateur manufacture.

Seventeen-eighty is the date of the wooden pedlar sent from England in 1944 by Staff Sergeant Charles Mears of Springfield, Vt. He found her standing under a vitrine (glass globe) in a small antique shop in Lancashire, the same shop in which he bought the two so-called "pre-Victorian fashion-plate dolls" described in the chapter on "Milliners' Models." The proprietor of the shop later wrote that her husband had bought the doll at a farm auction in a small thatched stone cottage in Nottinghamshire where it had belonged to the same family for several generations.

Nannie is about 12 inches tall, a wooden doll with painted hair. Her arms are jointed but her legs are inserted in the round wooden base of the vitrine which covered her. Her costume consists of a black dress, a white apron, and a long red wool cape. Under her black silk bonnet, with its somewhat forlorn-looking feather, she wears a white mob cap. The flat wicker basket which is suspended about her neck contains an array of miniature wares as many and as varied as the cries of London.

The U. S. Army postal authorities refused to allow the glass cover to be shipped with her which is probably as well for had it broken in transit her quaint, cheerful little face might not be as unmarred as it still remains after about 165 years of life.

An interesting variation of the old wooden pedlars is a "Fortune Telling" pedlar belonging to Miss Jennie L. Abbott of Westfield, Mass. This also dates about 1780.

Antique pedlar dolls are rare. Mrs. DeWitt Clinton Cohen of New York City who has the most notable collection of them in America says she has been collecting them for thirty years, here and abroad, yet her collection numbers only eight specimens. Among these are a Russian lace pedlar, a man, with lace over his arm and a pack on his back. Another is a Russian woman vegetable pedlar, seated, with baskets of vegetables around her and a basket of eggs in her lap. There is also a Welsh yarn pedlar who knits placidly on a tiny sock as she waits for customers.

Of the English pedlar dolls, "Mrs. Diggs of Threadneedle Street" is a very elaborate specimen in figured bombazine with quilted petticoats underneath and the money bags flung over her arms. Another Nannie, less elaborately dressed boasts 125 tiny articles in her wicker tray.

One of the most interesting of the English dolls is about eighty years old. This pedlar in real life was once a familiar sight on the streets of London—a crippled veteran of the Crimean campaign, he was given a license to peddle. The replica of this familiar figure is dressed in the colorful uniform and displays his license on his box as required by law.

Some American collectors have dressed their own pedlar dolls, using old wax dolls and assembling a supply of miniature articles, with surprisingly good results. An interesting example is shown in the doll dressed by Mrs. A. M. Fuller and her daughter Mrs. Velma F. Von Bruns of Bristol, Vt.

Some of the cities of our own deep south—such as Charleston, South Carolina, and New Orleans have had their picturesque pedlars and the street merchants' cries of Charleston are almost as famous and as colorful as those of Queen Anne's London. This phase of our country's life which is passing is well worth memorializing. Comparatively modern is the Negro flower vendor that turned up in Harriet's Doll House, Springfield, Mass., this winter. She is a spirited and intriguing figure made of black linen and clothed in gay flowered garments. Who made her or where she came from we do not know.

Some years ago, Mrs. Harriet McGee bought the entire stock of a New York doll shop and doll hospital. It was an enormous stock and there are still several hundred boxes that have never yet been unpacked. Out of these boxes, which Harriet opens a few at a time as she needs the stock for her shop, almost any treasure may turn up unexpectedly and often does. The Flower Merchants is one of these finds.

CRÈCHE FIGURES AND DOLLS IN
RELIGIOUS DRESS

CRÈCHE DOLLS are really not *dolls* at all but should be classed as art figures or statues. The men who made them were artists and many of the figures, especially those of the period of the Italian Renaissance, are of great beauty and skilled workmanship. Why should they not be? Italy is the land of great art and her artists have always given their best to the service of the Church. Here the lesser artists who made the crèche figures—and *were* they all *lesser* artists?—had models of the utmost beauty in the church frescoes to guide them. The earlier figures were of carved wood and were dressed by the nuns and ladies of the nobility in garments of rich and beautiful materials. Later wax and other mediums were used for the figures.

From Italy the idea of the crèche spread north to Switzerland, France, Holland and Germany—the land of skilled wood carvers.

We would like to believe that the gentle St. Francis of Assisi was the originator of the Christmas crib, as many have thought, but we learn from Max von Boehn's *Dolls and Puppets* that the scenes of Our Lord's birth depicted in figures were much, much older than St. Francis—as old, indeed,

Picture of dolls discussed in this chapter will be found following page 188.

161

as the Christmas festival itself which was first established by Pope Liberius in the year A.D. 354.

Just as the Church used the Miracle Plays, so it used the Christmas Crib or Crèche at the holiday season to visualize things spiritual to the people.

Quite often rich figures were given as an atonement for sin and they frequently represented the donors, just as the pictures of the wealthy donor and his family were often painted as worshippers, spectators, or other supplemental figures in some of the great religious paintings. Animals too, appear in the crèche groups: the ox and the ass in the stable and richly caparisoned horses or camels in the trains of the Wise Men from the East.

Today these old figures are sought by doll collectors and many of them have found their way into American museums and into private collections. One of the best collections of crèche dolls is that of Mrs. John B. Yerkes of Philadelphia, Pa.

Dolls dressed as monks or nuns sometimes appear in eighteenth-century pictures of children as in Greuze's painting of a little girl holding a monk doll (1760), and Chardin's portrait of the daughter of M. Mahon, with a doll dressed as a Carmelite nun (1741).

The Catholic University in Washington, D. C., and The Little Flower Mission Club in New York have collections of dolls dressed as nuns; but by far the largest, finest and most complete collection of the kind in existence is a private collection, that of Mrs. John Sahli of Hays, Kansas. It numbers over 200 dolls and is constantly growing.

Mrs. Sahli's dolls are interesting because each of the dolls has been dressed by nuns of the order it represents in the actual materials used by the order and is correct in the most minute details. Each doll has its tiny rosary and insignia or emblem when such are part of the garb of the orders. The exact type of head-dress is faithfully copied and many of the dolls are fitted with rings of gold and silver according to the regulations of the orders using rings. To make the dolls more realistic, about twenty-five of them have been fitted with miniature spectacles especially made to order for Mrs. Sahli by a Kansas City optical firm.

Mrs. Sahli began her collection in 1936 with just one doll dressed by the sisters of St. Agnes of Hays, Kansas, where Mrs. Sahli attended school. Large imported bisque dolls have been procured and sent to the different convents in the United States, Canada, Mexico and even India, to be dressed. Often prolonged negotiations have to be carried on beforehand, as in each case permission to dress the doll in the habit must be obtained from the mother-house of the order. In one instance, during the war, eighteen months elapsed before permission could be received, as the mother-house of this particular order was in France.

The dolls vary in size, the average being 26 inches tall, some smaller and the largest is 40 inches.

Shortly after Mrs. Sahli started her collection, she learned that the wife of a distant cousin in Akron, Ohio, had the same hobby. When this cousin died in 1938 her collection came to Mrs. Sahli. There were about one hundred dolls in this group but many had become soiled or were mussed in shipping them, so for eight months the basement of Mrs. Sahli's home was turned into a dry-cleaning establishment and laundry. Every doll was washed, clothing cleaned, collars, head-dresses laundered, starched, ironed and cellophane covers made for each of the dolls.

Each doll in the Sahli collection, which is the only private collection of its kind, is accompanied by a card giving the history of the order the doll represents and pointing out interesting differences in its habit.

This group of dolls show the interesting possibilities for the collector in specializing in any particular type of doll.

An interesting old doll in Quaker garb is in the museum in Philadelphia and there are many more modern dolls dressed as Quaker maids.

The picturesque garb of the various sects of "plain people" in Eastern Pennsylvania, the Mennonites, the River Brethren and other sects have been copied on dolls. These, we think, would be better had the dolls used been more in keeping with the types they portray. The whiskers of the eastern Pennsylvania Patriarchs on the baby faces of small bisque dolls seem utterly incongruous. One would much prefer character faces such as Lewis Sorenson has created for his "Mormon Pioneers."

At the Eastern States Exposition, Springfield, Mass., in past years, one

found interesting handmade rag dolls in Shaker garb at the booth displaying work of the then flourishing religious sect, but these dolls belong to the
past. Being a celibate sect, the Shakers have almost died out since young
recruits in the form of converts have not been coming. The once large colony
at Enfield, N. H., became so small that a few years ago the buildings were
sold to a Catholic monastery and school of the La Salette Fathers, and the
few remaining members of the Shaker group joined the colony at Canter-
bury, N. H. Here there remain now only about eight women members of
the original Shakers. The once prized Shaker products are now "gone modern" and are factory made. There are still "Shaker dolls" but they are no
longer what they were. Now they sell a rather cheap type of bisque doll,
factory dressed in grey crêpe de chine, cut in the Shaker style. They are worth
adding to one's collection of modern dolls, but they are not now the handiwork of the Shaker women.

In the collection of antiquities in the Royal Ontario Museum in Toronto
is a touching little object which requires no stretch of one's imagination to
class as a religious "doll." It is a terra-cotta head broken from a figurine of
the Greek god Apollo and into the hollow neck has been thrust the end of a
stick draped in a rag. One sees in it a pathetic relic of ancient Greek childhood.
It brings the picture of a child picking up from somewhere the head of a
broken votive statuette and, after the manner of children everywhere, making
its poor wee self a doll by thrusting in the stick for a body and seeing a
sumptuous robe in the bit of old rag tha has outlived its small owner many
centuries—just as the terra-cotta head ha survived its artist creator.

NEGRO DOLLS

THERE IS SOMETHING very appealing about "little brown babies with sparklin' eyes," as Paul Laurence Dunbar, the Negro poet, calls the little human Negro babies. A collection of Negro dolls would be both interesting and fascinating.

In modern dolls there is one wholesale firm in New York which makes and sells only Negro dolls for Negro children. Rosa Wildes Blackman of Louisiana, wholesale maker of handmade dolls has created some interesting and truthful types of Negroes of the deep South. There was also a firm in Louisiana, apparently no longer in business, that, under the sponsorship of the Louisiana Travel Bureau had done not only white historical dolls such as Evangeline and the "casket girls" but many of the gullah Negro types as well.

Over a hundred years ago, there came to New Orleans from Mexico a 'teen-age youth named Francesco Vargas trained by the Church in the art of making religious statues from beeswax. Mexican waxwork was and still is very fine. He plied his trade and art successfully in New Orleans for many years.

In the year 1884, when the Cotton Centennial Exposition was held in Mississippi, Francesco Vargas was commissioned to make a 30-foot wax statue of King Cotton, and his daughter created four life-size Negroes kneeling at his feet offering him brimming baskets of cotton.

Picture of dolls discussed in this chapter will be found following page 188.

THE DOLLS OF YESTERDAY

Francesco Vargas died in his nineties, passing on the knowledge of his art to his daughter, and she, in turn, passed it on to her children. It is believed that now only two people in the United States possess this knowledge. They are his granddaughter, Mrs. Lucy Vargas Resado of New Orleans, now herself a grandmother, and her son. Since he is a career man in the U. S. Department of Health, she is the only one practicing the art. Whereas Vargas created saints and religious figures, his granddaughter is known for her figures of the South, the Negroes of New Orleans, Louisiana and Mississippi in their colorful garments and the implements of their various trades.

Her figures are all made of beeswax mixed with some ingredient which prevents them from melting, and their faces have almost the texture of human skin. They are about 8 inches high, and she usually starts with a wood base and wire frame.

Mrs. Resado has never studied art and she does not sew. The colorful prints in the tiny garments are impregnated with wax and stuck on the figures while the cloth is warm.

Old Negro dolls may be found in many sizes and many materials. There are some little black "penny" dolls in china not more than an inch long that look like licorice candy babies one used to buy; Moorish dolls, also in "penny class" with colorful wee fezzes and modesty draperies, on up to the fine Simon and Halbig German bisques of thirty inches or more.

A rare old wooden Negro boy with set-in button eyes from the collection of Miss Alma Robeck, Annapolis, Md., is said to have been for a time in the old Salem Museum at Salem, Mass.

Unique is Mrs. Nina Shepherd's Negro boy with papier mâché head, black kid body and wooden arms and legs—the whole doll similar in type to the so-called "fashion-dolls" or "Milliner's models" described in another chapter. He is 10 inches high.

"He came from Wiscasset, Maine," writes Mrs. Shepherd, "from the Hubbard home. They seemed to be selling many things and I am under the impression that they were breaking up the home because of age and ill-health. Mr. Hubbard was a close friend of ex-Governor Carleton. (The unusual Bath, Maine, bridge is named for Governor Carleton.) I asked Mr.

Hubbard if he didn't have any dolls. He answered 'No' and then disappeared, later appearing with this Negro doll, asking if I called *this* a doll. Indeed I did and he wanted to give it to me but I could not accept it that way. The Negro doll has on a faded straw hat with green ribbon tying it under the chin; khaki trousers; a green and white checked shirt with beautifully made button holes. A find!"

Germany has made some lovely brown bisque dolls. Mrs. Rose Parro of Waterbury, Vt., has a large and handsome one—about 33 inches tall with a sweet face and lovely eyes. The composition, jointed body is also brown and beautifully finished. The doll is supposed to have been brought from the Philippine Islands about fifty years ago—if so, it is an illustration of the care and effort the German doll merchants used in catering to their customers in lands where there were brown-skinned races. The doll is marked *Heinrich Handwerk, Simon and Halbig, 7.*

Not so large, but equally lovely is a similar brown bisque doll belonging to Mrs. Louis E. Lahn of Amarillo, Texas, given to her when she was a child.

Very black bisque is the mammy doll who guards the Bye-Lo baby in the old Maine cradle. This Bye-Lo Baby is one of the rare "first edition" for which Kaestner in Germany made composition bodies. These proved too expensive and were discontinued in favor of the soft cloth bodies found on most Bye-Lo Babies.

Mammy's body is all black cloth—her bald head is concealed by a gay bandanna and the dress is of black cotton gaily flowered in fuchsia red— earrings, brooch and shoe ornaments are colored synthetic ivory in the form of fuchsia blossoms. Nothing is known of the age of this doll or of its maker.

Quaint little "Vestine Alberta" who stands at the foot of the cradle was a pitiful little wreck when she came in a box of old dolls, from Plymouth, N. H. One foot was broken off and there was a great gaping hole in the side of her cheap little plaster of Paris body. She had no wig but the little brown bisque face and dark eyes had the same appealing sweetness that was found in the faces of the large bisque dolls of Mrs. Parro or Mrs. Lahn, so one could not resist having her repaired. A bit of crêpe hair supplied the missing wig.

167

Tony Sarg, the puppeteer, created a Negro mammy doll with white nursling for "Derby Day Doll" which was sold in Lexington during the race season of 1938. . . . This doll was better "Tony Sarg" than it was "Southern Mammy" and had something of the flippancy of an *Esquire* illustration.

Much more of the real spirit of the South is found in Ida M. Chubb's cloth doll, "Mammy and Mose" which is in Mrs. John T. Buchanan's collection on exhibit at the Joslyn Memorial Museum, Omaha, Nebr. "Mammy and Mose" are illustrations in one of Ida M. Chubb's books of Negro rhymes.

"The Emperor Jones," from the stage play of that name, is a recent creation of Gertrude Florian of Detroit. The Pullman porter hero is shown in the full panoply of his glory as an Emperor in the Jungle—meticulously clad in scarlet trousers, blue coat and much gold braid and gold epaulets. His papier mâché pistol is black and silver, leather boots and holster, black. He is on exhibit at the Kansas City Art Museum but is owned by Mr. Theodore Redwood, New York City. The whole doll illustrates the careful attention to detail which makes all Gertrude Florian's doll work so outstanding. "Emperor Jones" in spite of his glorious raiment still somehow suggests the knight of the clothes brush and the shoe polish, and that is real artistry.

BABY DOLLS, BOY DOLLS AND
STORY BOOK DOLLS

MADAME AUGUSTA MONTANARI of London, is credited with the introduction of child and infant types to the doll world in 1851, when her remarkable exhibit of dolls in appropriate settings and accessories at the Crystal Palace Exposition in London, included wax dolls representing all ages from infants to adults. This exhibit was something of a sensation because prior to that time, dolls had been depicted as adults only.

Grace Story Putnam's Bye-Lo Baby of the early 1920's still further interested doll markets in favor of infant dolls.

Today, by far the majority of all dolls manufactured represent infants or small children. There are babies of every sort—smiling, laughing, crying babies, and cunning pickaninnies as well. They come in every sort of material: rag, rubber, wood, bisque and a variety of compositions. Such a collection of them as that of Mrs. Rose Parro, Waterbury, Vt., suggests an interesting specialty for collectors. Among the possibilities would be examples of such American doll-makers as Chase, Smith, Schoenhut, Putnam, and Mme. Alexander; dolls by foreign makers, particularly the fascinating toddlers of Kathe Kruse and Mme. Lenci.

Pictures of dolls discussed in this chapter will be found following page 188.

THE DOLLS OF YESTERDAY

China heads do not appear in modern *baby* dolls and only rarely in old dolls. One of these rare babies with china head is in the collection of Mrs. Huntington Brown of Minneapolis. By the style of its original clothing, this seems to date about 1880. The body is kid and the head is entirely bald, as representing a very young infant.

Of approximately the same date is "Victoria," the wax Montanari owned by Mrs. William Walker of Louisville, Ky., which is discussed under the wax Montanari dolls.

Bisque "Baby Otto, the Wonder Baby of 1910," a crying baby, is in the collection of Mrs. E. James of Worcester, Mass. Mrs. William J. Connors of Dorchester, Mass., has a bisque baby dressed as a Brittany baby, which resembles the doll given to General Eisenhower by the people of Brittany.

Prior to the Second World War there were all-rubber baby dolls—often life-size—with a satiny skin that made them appear very life-like. Occasionally, however, the surface of these dolls tended to warp and curl. Recently a much finer doll was sent to Humpty Dumpty Doll Hospital for attention, marked *Kammerer and Rinehart*. The head, forearms and lower limbs are of rubber, as firm and fine almost as bisque; the other parts, of cloth, are also beautifully modelled and very firm. It is a little masterpiece from a firm that has always made exceptionally fine dolls. No other example of this particular model has come to light.

The "Dydee Doll" was a pre-war novelty which was rubber-lined, drank from a bottle and wet its diaper. This was one of a series of novelties, mostly designed by Mme. Alexander, which included the Dionne Quintuplets at various ages; motion picture child actresses such as Shirley Temple and Jane Withers, and the quaint little *McGuffey Reader* doll, "McGuffey Ana."

The thousands of composition dolls that have been made and are still being made annually, are, for the most part, not durable and seem unlikely to outlast the generation for which they were created, much less live to be handed down to subsequent generations as have the papier mâchés, bisques and china heads. Nevertheless, many of these dolls are collectors items because of their originality and life-like charm.

In the early 1900's, Kathe Kruse of Germany, created a sensation with her child dolls which she first created for the entertainment of her own children. She is at her best with toddlers, both boys and girls.

Men and boy dolls are rather rare, and are most often found in bisque and Parian. Bisque is the boy in the collection of Mrs. Henry Hepple of Fredonia, N. Y., and bisque, also is the "Choir Boy" owned by Mrs. John T. Buchanan of Omaha. This lad is particularly interesting because of the correctness of his costume in every detail.

Looking much like a real boy is a bisque in the collection of Mrs. William J. Connors of Dorchester, Mass. He is weeping bitterly because of the broken balloon which he holds in his hand. The Scotch lad in the same collection looks very intriguing with sporran and plaid.

There are several types of boyish heads found in old china dolls. One of the most unusual is Mrs. William Walker's "Ned" or "Edward Dade Conway," named for the brother of the woman who gave him to Mrs. Walker. "Ned's" costume is copied exactly from the old daguerreotype of his namesake. The material of his suit was woven by hand by a friend of Mrs. Walker. A quaint straw hat, copied by Mrs. Walker, and a hoop, complete the doll.

Miss Jennie L. Abbott of Westfield, Mass., the librarian of Doll Collectors of America, owns a Parian lad, apparently in his teens which is typical of the Parian men and boy dolls.

A boy doll that one sometimes sees, is chiefly notable for the combination of cloth and composition in its body. The head and pelvis and lower legs and hands are composition and the rest is cloth. The purpose of the combination, no doubt, is to allow flexibility for sound contrivances. The dolls are comparatively late and seemingly of German manufacture.

The Schoenhut factory in Philadelphia turned out many types of wooden boy dolls intended purposely for boys, it seems. A promotion picture from one of the firms early 1900 catalogues shows small boys playing with them. The two boys who are in the picture are George W. Schoenhut and Norman E. Schoenhut, grandsons of the inventor of the Schoenhut all-wood dolls.

From dolls representing children, it was a logical step to create dolls representing their favorite story book characters. *Alice in Wonderland* was published in 1865 and was followed by *Through the Looking Glass*. "Alice" dolls with circular combs came out soon after and have been made of various materials down to the present time. One of these earlier "Alice" dolls is a china head which Mrs. Cyrus M. Beachy calls "Katy Opplebaum" because she found it in the Pennsylvania Dutch section near Philadelphia.

A much older doll on which a Parian "Alice" head is a replacement of the original head, came to Clarendon, N. H., from California recently. The doll is a family heirloom and its present owner is the fourth generation to possess it.

"Little Lord Fauntleroy," "Little Red Ridinghood," and the girls of Louisa May Alcott's *Little Women* are among the favorite storybook character dolls, although, in truth, these are more often a matter of costuming only. More recent successful storybook dolls have been "Raggedy Ann" and "Raggedy Andy," in cloth; Mme. Alexander's "Snow White," "Pinnochio" and "Jiminy Cricket." Walt Disney's "Ferdinand the Bull" in rubber, for a time bade fair to rival the popular "Teddy Bear."

Rachel Field's "Hitty" was never a commercial doll. The picture following page 188 is of a larger version, an individual doll carved for Mrs. Cyrus M. Beachy by Mrs. Roy Williams of Augusta, Kansas, and finished and painted at Humpty Dumpty Doll Hospital. The pictures were posed and taken at Humpty Dumpty. This doll is 10 inches tall. Hitty in the story was but 6 inches tall.

A similar doll in Mrs. Beachy's collection is the "Little Girl with a Curl Right in the Middle of Her Forehead."

Dolls with two or three faces turning under a hood and each expressing a different mood, are of German origin. Generally the faces are bisque, occasionally wax. There is a metal hood, concealed by a bonnet, and the head is turned by means of a metal ring at the top, bringing the faces into view in turn, laughing, crying or sleeping, according to the whim of the small owner of the doll.

The most unique of these three-faced dolls is also a storybook doll, "Little Red Ridinghood." The heads represent the little girl, her grandmother and the wolf. The first two are of the usual bisque and then one is surprised by a papier mâché wolf. Its owner, Mrs. John H. Lewter of Houston, Texas, found

172

this interesting doll in a shop in Illinois some years ago. The body is in two sections, divided just below the bust and is joined together with transparent tape.

On the back of the body is a label reading *Geschutzt*. The doll is 13½ inches tall. The eyes of the grandmother and Red Ridinghood are set-in eyes of blue glass. The eyes of the wolf are painted.

JOEL ELLIS DOLL CARRIAGES AND TOYS
Other Doll Carriages, Little Girls and Their Dolls

A PRESIDENT OF THE UNITED STATES, in his infancy, was wheeled about in a baby carriage made by Joel Ellis of Springfield, Vt. Since Plymouth, where President Calvin Coolidge was born, is not far from Springfield it was natural that the Coolidge carriage should have come from there. It has been said that Joel Ellis made the first baby carriages in America. If this be true, possibly it was the only source from which it could have come.

Through the kindness of Mrs. Grace Coolidge, we have this charming picture of their son, John, in the President's baby carriage.

"My husband gave the carriage to Mr. Henry Ford," writes Mrs. Coolidge, "and I believe it is now in the Ford Museum at Dearborn."

The manufacture of these carriages gave their maker the nickname "Cab" Ellis. The factory catalogue of 1869, loaned by his son, Herbert Ellis, shows that the baby carriages came in two- three- and four-wheeled designs, some thirty types in all, selling wholesale for from $3.50 to $25 each. The Coolidge carriage is a three-wheeled model. Very different in their springless discomfort from the luxurious baby coaches of today, they were no doubt considered to be the very acme of luxury and smartness in their time.

Pictures of dolls discussed in this chapter will be found following page 188.

From the left-over materials from these carriages, Ellis made doll carriages and gigs in the same designs. The catalogue says of the doll perambulator:

"This is a new and elegant toy, which has met with an extensive sale for a new article, amounting to 3,262 perambulators during the season. The wheels are five inches in diameter, and the body is sufficiently large to contain the largest sized doll. The bottom is padded, and it is nicely

Courtesy of Herbert Ellis.

Joel Ellis doll carriage. Catalogue of 1866.

painted a dark color, like the large carriage and neatly ornamented. We put them up in cases containing one dozen each, or they may be packed with toy gigs of the same size. Price $17.50 a dozen.

"LARGE TOY GIGS—These are the same as the perambulators, with the handle in front instead of behind. It is a nice saleable toy. Our sales of them last season amounted to 2,865. They are put up one dozen in a box. Price $14.00 a dozen."

There was also a smaller size of this gig.

Courtesy of Herbert Ellis.

Joel Ellis doll carriage from 1866 catalogue.

"TOY GIGS FOR DOLLS—This is a very attractive and saleable toy. We sold last year 8,676 of them. They are neatly painted and ornamented in assorted colors. Have spoked wheels nine inches in diameter made of wood. We put them up in boxes containing one or two dozens each. Price $8.00 a dozen."

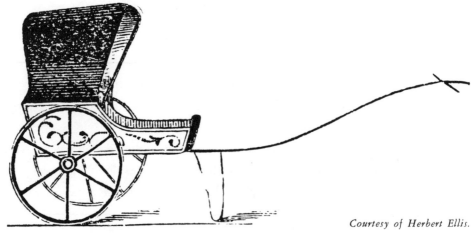

Courtesy of Herbert Ellis.

Joel Ellis doll carriage. Catalogue of 1866.

176

These catalogue descriptions and pictures should be a help to collectors in identifying the Ellis doll carriages when found. Note that in the pictures the small gig is shown to have six wheel-spokes while the larger ones have eight spokes.

Joel Ellis made a toy piano finished in rosewood coloring, that was described as "two feet high, and two and a half feet wide and sixteen inches high with a capacity of three octaves." The wholesale price of piano and stool was twenty dollars. At least one of these pianos has survived the years. It is owned by Miss Eva Mary Baker of Springfield, Vt., who is said to have found it in a coal shed in the town. Imitation of rosewood was also the finish of the other toy furniture made by Ellis: a bed, dining table and chairs and a doll's rocking chair.

Small leftovers of wood were thriftily made into building toys, log cabins and rail fences shown in the reproductions from the catalogue. Note the quaint costume of the little girl who is building the log cabin. This catalogue of 1869 was entirely written and arranged by Joel Ellis himself, says his son Herbert Ellis. These Ellis pictures were taken from the illustrations in the catalogue.

Following the Ellis carriages, subsequent doll vehicles varied in materials, styles and tops from the three-wheeled wicker carriage taken from a *Godey* fashion plate of 1873 sent in by Mrs. R. E. Dimick of Corvallis, Oregon, through the quaint wooden carriage of 1869 that belonged to Anna Jameson of Albany, N. Y., and her French fashion doll, whose elaborate trousseau is described in another chapter, and the large wicker carriage wheeled by the little girl of 1908 who is now Mrs. Robert H. Carey of Worcester, Mass. A number of other interesting carriages are in the collection of Mrs. Maude S. Post of New Milford, Conn., many with the surrey type of canopy.

A large and interesting Vermont carriage, which may have been a baby carriage, has the front wheels set in out of line with the rear wheels and a surrey top edged with fringe. It was found in Burlington by its present owner, Mrs. Rose Parro of Waterbury, Vt.

A more luxurious carriage occupied by the "Little Annie Collins" doll was formerly in the collection of the late Mrs. Edward S. Lane of Bristol, Vt., and is now owned by the author. The ceiling of the canopy is painted a celestial blue with gold scroll work and with decalcomania cherubs floating about. Similar scrolls and cherubs decorate the sides of the carriage.

The ultimate of doll luxury is found in the coach made by the royal carriage maker of England for the little Princess Victoria, afterwards Queen Victoria. The coach is so perfectly constructed and balanced that it moves and turns with a mere touch of the finger. The arms of England are painted on the sides, and those of the little princess on the ends. The carriage and the wax doll with the rare "violet-blue" eyes were purchased some years ago from a custodian of Windsor Castle by Mrs. Marie Porter of California, who has loaned them to the Charles W. Bowers Memorial Museum, Santa Ana., Calif.

Very quaint, and no doubt homemade, suggesting the sedan chairs of the days of Queen Anne, is the closed-in doll sleigh from Maine, in the collection of Mrs. Earle E. Andrews, Winchester, Mass., President of Doll Collectors of America, Inc.

From decade to decade, fashions in dolls have changed as much as fashions in doll carriages. Fashions in the clothes and manners of little girls have also changed, as seen in the series of pictures of little girls and their dolls.

In 1867 the solemn-faced tot, Annie Collins, clutches a china head doll of the Mary Todd Lincoln type. All we know of Annie Collins is penciled on the back of her small *carte de visite* photograph taken by a New York photographer:

> *"Annie Collins died March 16, 1867. Aged two years, 3 months and 45 days."*

For eighty years, the inanimate doll creature has survived its frail and pitiful little owner.

In the early 1860's, Mrs. Mary Millard of Cuba, Illinois, who was ten years old, had been ill a long time when her mother went to Chicago and brought back to her the large china head doll, now known as the "Dollie Madison type." This doll is the model that Mrs. Emma C. Clear used for the modern "Dollie Madison," made at Humpty Dumpty.

In 1869 and the early seventies, French dolls, usually Jumeaus, rivalled the

178

china head doll in the affections of children whose parents had friends making "The Grand Tour" which always included Paris. Such a doll is the one shown with little Anna Jameson of Albany, New York. The doll's remarkable wardrobe is described in another chapter.

The doll in the *Godey* picture of 1873, might well be a papier mâché, possibly a Greiner, since Greiner had just renewed his patent for composition doll heads. The elaborate furbelows worn by the child are worthy of notice.

By 1885, when ten-year-old Sarah Miles of Boston, now Mrs. Smith of Fairlee, Vt., received her Christmas doll, the wax doll was the popular type. The doll was dressed by Sarah's grandmother assisted by a neighbor who was a member of the Proctor family of Vermont—a family which has given the state two governors. The red morocco shoes, which the doll wears over its painted composition ones, are stamped *Jumeau* on the soles, indicating that the house of Jumeau in Paris probably sold doll accessories for exportation as well as dolls. Since this doll is obviously not French, the shoes must have been purchased in a Boston store.

Sarah Miles was a niece of Sara Swan Miles Sweetset of Worcester, Mass., the original owner of the Mystery doll in Chapter Eleven. The wax doll has recently come to join the Sara Swan Miles doll in the author's collection.

Coming down to 1898, the doll over which Baby Margaret smiles so happily is a German bisque as is the doll in the 1909 picture of the same Margaret. Bisque dolls were the popular type in those years. Margaret is Mrs. Robert H. Carey of Worcester, Mass.

30

MANY MATTERS

CARE OF WAX DOLLS

Temperature Control: A Vermont collector was heard to remark: "I don't think Mrs. X does a good job of rewaxing dolls. She did one for me last fall and this spring the wax was all cracked off."

"Where was it stored through the winter?"

"Out in the shop which was closed."

"Was the shop heated?"

"No, it wasn't."

"That is what is the matter with your doll, then. Wax dolls will not stand extremes of either heat or cold. Sub-zero temperatures or being left on top of a radiator or too close to an open fire are equally disastrous. Wax dolls should be stored at ordinary room temperature."

Another type of doll that is sensitive to extremely low temperatures is the little "Milliner's model" doll with a papier mâché head, kid body and wooden limbs. If shipped in sub-zero weather, the cold will cause the surface of the face to crack and curl and the doll will be utterly ruined. Apparently many collectors are unaware of this fact. It may be also that exposure to extremely low temperatures would have a similar effect on Greiner or other large

180

papier mâché dolls. I cannot say as to this, but I have twice seen the milliner's model so spoiled.

Cleaning wax heads: Do not use water to clean wax heads. Unsalted butter should be used. One collector reports having had good results with Johnson's liquid floor wax.

Removing Wax: A good commercial solvent, such as Gem Solvent, will remove wax from the waxed papier mâché head preparatory to rewaxing, says Mrs. Emma C. Clear.

Rewaxing: Rewaxing doll heads is a highly technical job and should not be undertaken by an amateur. The head must be dipped only once and this calls for an uneconomical amount of materials needed unless one is doing several heads at a time. An expensive laboratory thermometer is necessary as the temperature of the wax must be exactly right. The formula for waxing contains a number of items which are expensive and not easily available everywhere. In the end, the result may not be what you planned. A head that is well done is a lovely thing and is worth the expense of having it done by a professional.

If one really wants to undertake such work, they will do well to work for some time as an apprentice in a studio and learn the correct way by experience. Many jobs of doll repairing may be successfully done by an amateur but waxing is not one of them.

Some amateurs have attempted to wax doll heads with ordinary paraffin but this gives the head a dead, pasty look.

Useful Materials for Repairing Dolls: For repairing china heads one may use Tracy's China Cement. Duco is also good.

Wood flour, which is mixed with water in small quantities, as needed, is useful for repairing cracks in papier mâché heads, or for building up feet or small missing parts. It should be kept on hand. A few tubes of oil paints in suitable colors, artists brushes, together with some refined linseed oil and turpentine for thinning the colors will prove helpful.

Wig Making: Human hair doll wigs are a technical job that is best done by a professional. Your hairdresser, if friendly, is usually a good source of supply for material, and often will be on the lookout for suitable hair and save it for you. Mrs. Clear warns that hair which has had permanent waves or been treated with chemicals is not suitable for doll wigs as it will break and will not last. Naturally curly hair is the best to use. Hair that is not naturally curly will require occasional recurling on the doll's head. An electric curling iron is good for this purpose.

Mohair for wigs may be purchased in various colors at the Humpty Dumpty Doll Hospital at twenty-five cents per skein. A skein will make a small wig; larger wigs require from two to six skeins.

The following directions for making mohair wigs have been generously furnished for this book by Mrs. Emma C. Clear.

DIRECTIONS FOR MAKING MOHAIR WIGS

"Match the mohair with soft cotton or silk material. Glue the material on the head to any desired hairline. Let dry. When dry, spread your mohair and plan your wig. There are two ways to make a part. The simplest is to spread the mohair and stitch to a bit of the cap material. The better way, called 'invisible part': Spread two layers of mohair with a layer of paper between. Spread in opposite directions, and press the part with the point of an iron. Tear out the paper. Make either part about one inch longer than wanted to allow enough to turn under at each end.

"Large curls are made with an ordinary curling iron. Miniature ones on a heated ice pick or any small bright metal rod. Use a piece of white cloth to test for heat. Be careful not to burn it.

"Spread paste over the cap about as you would butter bread. Place the mohair in position, pressing down into this paste. Butter the underside of the part and lay it in place. Bind a soft cloth tightly around the head. Leave overnight.

"The next day it is finished but it may need a bit more curling.

"The mohair may be spread and stitched to strips of the cap material. It is laid on the head in glue, like shingles on the roof. It requires two rows of stitching to hold it tight. Made this way it may be combed and brushed like a woven wig.

"Mohair may also be ventilated and woven like human hair. It is preferred to human hair for tiny dolls. Instructions for weaving may be found in most libraries."

Moth Prevention: Clothes moths are an ever present hazard for dolls with wigs. Such dolls may be kept under glass or cellophane covers with a few crystals of paradichlorobenzine sprinkled on the wigs.

Mrs. R. P. Fitts, a New Hampshire collector, finds an annual spraying of the wigs with kerosene effective. She states that it does not harm the wigs and soon evaporates. Clothing is removed from the dolls before spraying, of course.

Doubtless some form of the new DDT sprays will solve the problem in due time.

Doll's Eyes: A collection of doll's eyes prepared for Doll Collectors of America, by Mrs. Emma C. Clear is most interesting. It includes early English, French and German glass eyes as well as modern American metal eyes.

The English eyes are probably the oldest and are familiar to collectors in the earliest papier mâchè and wax dolls. The deep-blue eyes are somewhat less common than the dark eyes. Neither color shows any clearly defined line between the iris and pupil which are inclined to blur and fuse into each other. This is especially true of the blue eyes in which Mrs. Clear finds the same pigments used in the old blue Staffordshire china. This seems to confirm the English origin of the eyes. The brown eyes are often almost black. There is no sign of threading in the iris of either color.

The early French and German eyes were oval and show fine threading in the iris which is clearly defined and has a greater depth than in other eyes. The deep center had to be sacrificed when eyes were made round, when moving eyes came into use. The oval glass eyes were used in Parians and blonde bisques and are found in the early Jumeau dolls which are notable for their soulful eyes.

In early English wax dolls with sleeping eyes, some have the blurred quality of the early eyes and these were undoubtedly made in England. Others have the fine threading of the French and German eyes and were probably imported.

The sleeping eyes were mounted in pairs with various types of counter weights. The very earliest of the English dolls with sleeping eyes had the eyes moved by means of a wire which came out of the body at the waist line. Such eyes appeared about 1825. The use of counter weights for moving the eyes was of a later date. Later the dolls with so-called "flirting" eyes were invented, each eye having its own weight and mounted separately from the other.

Artificial eyes for human beings were first made at the end of the sixteenth century in France it is said. Various materials—bone, ivory, etc., were used before glass. Louis Bossard of the George Borgfeldt Corporation of New York, is authority for the statement that German glass doll eyes were made in the same town, Lausha, Thuringia, Germany, where glass eyes for humans were made, and that years ago it was an enormous industry.

Many terms and classifications of eyes used by collectors have little authority or foundation in fact. "Spun glass eyes" is a pet term which seems to be fanciful. Borgfeldt's say: "We never heard of 'spun glass eyes'." Certainly this author does not know of any dolls having eyes that could be so classified.

Those collectors and writers on dolls who talk of "spun glass eyes" in early French and German dolls do not seem to be able to tell you where, when or by whom such eyes were made. On the other hand, consulting such authoritative sources as the Baker Memorial Library at Dartmouth College, the Smithsonian Institute in Washington, the Metropolitan Museum of Art in New York, and the Research Department of Steuben Glass, we find they all agree with Steuben Glass who write thus:

"We have found no record of any such use having been made of spun glass or fibre glass."

This, it would seem, also has its origin in some collectors' fancy and not in fact.

"Paper weight" eyes seems to refer to the old oval glass eyes which were very high in the center. Even here, "oval glass eyes" would seem a better term.

Very occasionally one finds in a china-head doll a painted eye that has a luminous quality clearly achieved by the use of ebanel. These are usually in brown-eyed dolls.

The first American made sleeping eyes were printed on celluloid and pasted on metal with the printed side down. Various devices were used to attach them.

American made winking eyes, which bear the patent date, *August 10, 1915,* were mounted separately, each with its own weight attached. They opened and shut independently of each other. The German made "flirting" eyes were made earlier than this.

In the best American made pre-war eyes the iris and pupils were printed under plastic lenses, giving depth to the eyes. The lashes were set in slots in the eyelids. American made double-action eyes of the pre-war period were much simpler than the German winking eyes.

A set of double-action, American made eyes from a "Dy-dee Baby" which is in the collection, shows a possible disadvantage of the use of metal eyes in that they may rust badly when they come in contact with water, as they are in some danger of doing when used in a doll that drinks from a bottle.

Shipping Dolls: Dolls may be safely shipped by express or insured parcel post if they are packed in stout paper cartons and surrounded by plenty of crushed newspapers. Most dealers prefer shipping dolls by express. Careful wrapping of the head and breakable parts in soft tissue paper or cotton wadding, and protecting with corrugated paper before packing in the carton will pay dividends in safety.

If the doll has sleeping eyes, lift the wig and pack a moderate amount of tissue paper under the counter weight of the eyes and pack the doll *face-downwards.*

Doll Stands: Workable stands for small or medium-sized dolls (if they wear long dresses) may be simply and inexpensively made from what the manufacturer calls "shipping tag stock," the material from which shipping tags are cut. It comes in sheets 24 by 24 inches which sell for five cents a sheet at wholesale houses. One sheet makes several stands. *Method:* Cut a rectangle of the stock the desired height and at least twice the circumference of the doll's body. Fit the upper end around the doll under her skirts, spreading the lower end to make a firm base. Fasten the paper in place with strips of cellophane tape or with metal paper fasteners. Three and five pound cereal boxes may be used as doll stands also.

Hat Blocking: Mrs. William Walker of Louisville, Ky., wished to make a doll hat from an old leghorn hat. She took it to the man on the corner who cleans and blocks men's hats.

"Yes, I could do it all right," he said, "but none of my blocks are small enough for the crown."

"Couldn't you block the crown over a tomato can?" she suggested.

He could and did. The suggestion is passed along to other collectors.

Mrs. Walker is very skillful in making hats for her doll collection and has many interesting ideas for handling materials, such as soaking refractory straw braids under water for several days to make them easier to work with.

Doll Shoes From Glove Fingers: Mrs. Ralph E. Wakeman of Claremont, New Hampshire, has a method of making small doll shoes from old kid gloves. The two middle fingers of the glove are used. These two fingers are in four sections: one serves as the sole of the shoe, two serve as sides, and the top section the vamp. The tip of the finger is the toe of the shoe. One simply cuts the two fingers the length of the foot, rounding it some for the heel. Leaving the sewed edges for strength, cut the top of the finger back towards the finger end, leaving it the right length for the vamp, shaping it to your fancy. Sew up the heel end, add a tiny buckle or bow, and presto! One has a good representation of the Empire slipper.

A Picture Book of Dolls and Doll Houses is published by the Victoria and Albert Museum of London and is obtainable for fifteen cents at the offices of the British Information Services, 30 Rockefeller Plaza, New York 20, N. Y.

Cleaning Doll Bodies: Kid bodies may be successfully cleaned with any preparation for cleaning white shoes.

MODERN COMMERCIAL DOLL-MAKERS

THIS BOOK is primarily for collectors of antique dolls so one need not do more than touch upon the commercial doll of modern days in this and other lands.

The British Information Services, 30 Rockefeller Plaza, New York 20, N. Y., furnishes the following list of English Doll-makers:

Miss Ruth Allen, 29 Glenthorne Road, London, W.6

Artistic Dolls, Ltd., 144 Holland Park Ave., London, W. 11

Be-Be (Dolls), Ltd., 63 Avenue Chambers, Vernon Place, London, W.C. 1

British National Dolls, Ltd., Acton Lane, London, N.W. 10

B.U.T., Ltd., 518 Caledonian Road, London, N. 7

J. Cowan (Dolls) Ltd., 10 and 20 Tabernacle St., London, E.C. 2

Doll Industries, Ltd., 148 and 150 High Road, Willesden Green, London, N.W. 10

Mrs. Edith Houghton, 16 Penton St., London, N. 1

Motriz and Chambers, Ltd., 80 York Way, London, N. 1

Max Moschkowitz, 2, 4, and 4a Chillingworth Road, London, N. 7

Pictures of dolls discussed in this chapter will be found following page 188.

THE DOLLS OF YESTERDAY

Pomsons Dolls and Toys, Ltd., 27–31 Willesden Lane, London, N.W. 6

L. Rees and Co., Ltd., 16–30 Provost St., London, N. 1

J. Sear, Ltd. (soft—wholesale and export) 61a Fortress Road, London, N.W. 5

Sharp and Akis, Ltd., 125 Westbourne Park Road, London, W.C. 2

Made before the war, the English "Coronation dolls," accurately costumed replicas of the Royal family and others taking part in the coronation ceremonies, were popular with collectors.

During the war years, Norah Weilings' dolls representing British Tommies, Sailors, Aviators, Red Cross Nurses, and Gremlins have been of considerable interest. So also have been Violet Powell's dolls representing Isle of Aran peasant types. These Irish dolls, dressed in Irish tweeds, are accurate representations of national character.

The reports of the British Patent Office—those from 1890 to date only being available in printed form—show a rather prolific invention of dolls but these are largely mechanical toys—walking, talking dolls.

One of the most ingenious of these designs was the subject of two patents, the first granted to William Henry Haughton, 9 Warsham Court Road, Carshalton Beeches, Surrey, April 29, 1937, and the second, an improvement, granted July 7, 1938, to William Henry Haughton and John Gordge. The primary purpose of the doll—and the idea could be applied to toy animals—was for the production of animated cartoons without the necessity of making thousands of drawings, as is generally done.

According to this invention, the process of producing the animated cartoon film consists in employing a subject, such as a doll, puppet, toy animal, constructed so that parts can be moved to various positions, the parts being moved between each exposure, so that in the finished film, the effect of animation is obtained.

The doll, puppet or toy animal or the like is preferably constructed from lead wire or strip of suitable thickness as the foundation of the device, the wire or strip being encased in a suitable padding or wrapping, and the

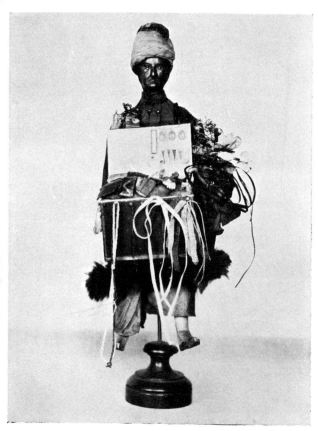

Left, Pedlar doll, veteran of Crimean War. *Collection of Mrs. DeWitt Clinton Cohen, New York. Right,* Negro flower vendor. (Linen.) Origin unknown—may be Charleston, S. C. *St. George Collection.*

Left, Crèche doll, brought from Italy by soldier of Second World War. *Courtesy of B. H. Leffingwell, Rochester, N. Y. Right,* English wooden pedlar doll. Found in Lancashire antique shop. Date about 1780. *St. George Collection.*

The wax doll at extreme right caused tears to flow. *Collection of Miss Marie Ketterman, York, Pennsylvania.*

Left, The doll that caused a spanking. *Collection of Miss Blanche Mosse, Dennison, Texas. Right,* "Baby Jean," bought on the installment plan "That a four-year-old might not know—" *Collection of Mrs. Louis E. Lahn, Amarillo, Texas.*

Left, the more-or-less-McDonald doll in the more-or-less-Tupper high chair. Modern life-sized rubber baby doll, old baby dress. *Right,* "Martha Victoria," French Jumeau doll, 1869. Traded for a pressure cooker.

"The Little Girl Who Never Was a Bride."

Group of old Crèche dolls. *Collection of Mrs. John B. Yerkes, Philadelphia, Pennsylvania.*

Nun dolls. From the more than 200 correctly garbed religious orders in collection of Mrs. John Sahli, Hays, Kansas.

"The Emperor Jones," created by Gertrude Florian, Detroit, Michigan. *Collection of Mr. Theodore Redwood, New York City, New York.*

"Mammy and Mose," created by Ida M. Chubb. *Collection of Mrs. John T. Buchanan, Omaha, Nebraska.*

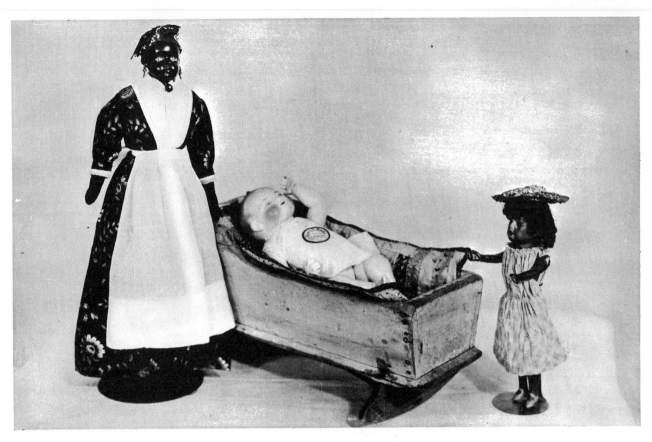

"Mammy" and "Vestine Alberta" with original Bye-Lo Baby. They all have bisque heads. *St. George Collection.*

Left, Very rare old papier mâché Negro doll found in Maine. Kid body, wooden arms and legs. *Collection of Mrs. Nina Shepherd, Granville, Ohio. Right*, Brown bisque doll made for the Philippine Islands. *Collection of Mrs. Rose Parro, Waterbury, Vermont.*

Top, Collection of baby dolls. *Collection of Mrs. Rose Parro, Waterbury, Vermont. Bottom.* Rare china head baby about 1880. *Collection of Mrs. Huntington Brown, Minneapolis, Minnesota.*

George W. Schoenhut and Norman A. Schoenhut, grandsons of the maker, playing with Schoenhut wooden boy dolls.

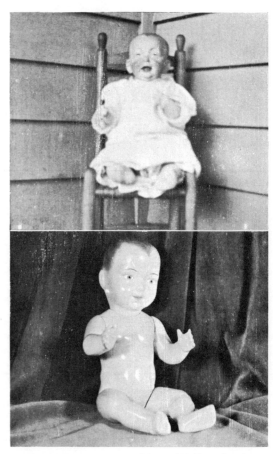

Left, "Ned," china boy doll dressed after old daguerreotype picture. *Collection of Mrs. William Walker, Louisville, Kentucky. Right, top,* "Baby Otto," the 1910 Wonder baby. *Collection of Mrs. E. James, Worcester, Massachusetts. Below,* All-metal baby doll of First World War period. Maker unknown. *Courtesy of Humpty Dumpty Doll Hospital.*

Collection of boy dolls—English Schoolboy, **American** Schoolboy, Beau Brummel, and Tommy Tucker. *Collection of Mrs. Cyrus M. Beachy, Wichita, Kansas.*

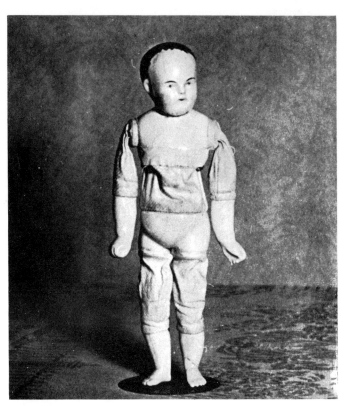

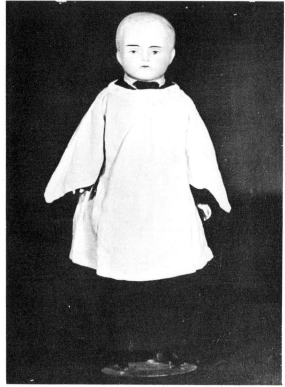

Left, Boy doll—combination of composition and cloth. *Collection of Mrs. Henry Hepple, Fredonia, N. Y.*
Right, Choir Boy, fine French bisque, complete in every detail. *Collection of Mrs. John T. Buchanan, Omaha, Nebraska.*

Unusual three-faced doll—Red Ridinghood, Grandmother and the Wolf. *Collection of Mrs. John H. Lewter, Houston, Texas.*

Left, "Hitty," wooden doll after Rachel Field's *Hitty. Collection of Mrs. Cyrus M. Beachy, Wichita, Kansas.*
Right, Wooden doll—"There was a little girl and she had a little curl." *Collection of Mrs. Cyrus M. Beachy, Wichita, Kansas.*

Left, Little Annie Collins and her doll, 1866. Old carte de visite photograph is inscribed on the back: Annie Collins died March 16, 1867. Aged 2 years, 3 months, 45 days. *Right,* Little Annie Collins' doll has survived its pathetic owner by 80 years. Still in original condition except the dress, which is a copy of original.

Left, Anna Jameson, Albany, New York, with French doll and doll carriage, 1869. *Courtesy of her daughter Mrs. C. L. Mitchell, San Antonio, Texas. Right,* Mrs. Mary Millard, 1860, and her china doll which is the original copied by Mrs. Clear in making the "Dolly Madison" doll. *Courtesy of Mrs. Mary Millard, Cuba, Illinois.*

Little girl and her doll and carriage from *Godey's Lady's Book, 1873. Courtesy of Mrs. R. E. Dimick, Corvallis, Oregon.*

Left, John Coolidge as an infant in the President's baby carriage, made by Joel Ellis, Springfield, Vermont. Now in Ford Museum, Dearborn, Michigan. *Gift of President Coolidge. Picture by courtesy of Mrs. Grace Coolidge, Northampton, Massachusetts. Right,* Doll Sleigh found in Maine. *Collection of Mrs. Earle E. Andrews, Winchester, Massachusetts.*

Left, Baby Margaret and her doll, 1899. *Courtesy of Mrs. Robert H. Carey, Worcester, Massachusetts. Right,* Mrs. Robert H. Carey as a child, and her doll carriage, 1909. *Courtesy of Mrs. Robert H. Carey, Worcester, Massachusetts.*

Left, Doll dressed as "A Lady of the gay nineties" by Mrs. Carrie A. Hall. *Right,* Wax doll, 1885. A childhood portrait of Mrs. Sarah Smith and her doll. *Courtesy of Mrs. Sarah Smith, West Fairlee, Vermont.*

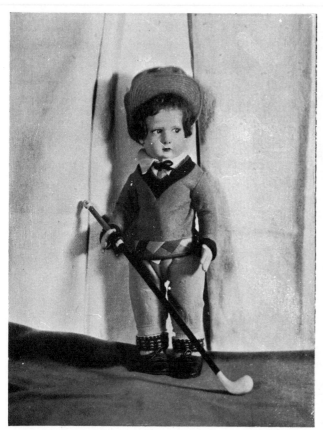

Dolls by Mme. Lenci, Italy. *Courtesy of Humpty Dumpty Doll Hospital.*

Left, A Leprechaun—Violet Powell, Ireland. Dressed in Irish homespuns. *Right,* Baby Doll—Kathe Kruse, Germany. *Collection of Mary Howe, Wichita, Kansas.*

Dolls created by Mrs. Emma C. Clear prior to World War II. Exhibited at Annual Doll Show, Charles W. Bowers Memorial Museum, Santa Ana, California. *Collection of Mrs. Gustav Mox, Santa Monica, California.*

Clear dolls: Jenny Lind, Martha Washington, and Biedermeier doll. *St. George Collection*.

Left, Jumeau doll dressed as French fashion doll. Dress and hat of green and gold changeable taffeta. *Right,* Old materials were used—gray-blue surah silk with cut velvet—in dressing this doll. Both dressed by Mrs. Ralph E. Wakeman, Claremont, New Hampshire.

whole enclosed in a covering shaped to the form of the device to be constructed.

The foundation of lead wire or strip may be made up to suit the form of the device intended to be constructed, and such wire may be employed for use with the ears, nose and mouth of the device.

By the employment of lead wire or strip as the foundation of the device, the body . . . and other parts of the device may be bent to any desired shape or contour, the alteration being effected by pressure of the fingers of a person without fear of the wire breaking.

The American rights to these patents were purchased by certain Hollywood producers, who brought the samples to Mrs. Emma C. Clear of Humpty Dumpty Doll Hospital to estimate on making the figures. Mrs. Clear took one of the figures apart to study the construction and found it to be extremely ingenious. She reported back that she could make them, if desired, but to date no use seems to have been made of the figures for the purpose for which they are intended.

These patents are one example of the many uses that dolls have served through the ages.

The classified business section of the New York City telephone directory lists fourteen firms making doll's clothes; forty firms making doll's parts, such as eyes, and wigs and doll accessories, such as hats and shoes, and there are seventy-two manufacturers and wholesalers of dolls. New York is the center of the doll-making industry of the United States and these figures give some idea of the extent to which it has been developed. This of course is the commercial side of it. In addition there are hundreds of individual American doll artists who are scattered all over the country and who work on a small scale.

Prior to the war, Germany, with its long experience and cheap labor, and skilled workmen, led the world in output and quality of dolls.

Bernard de Ravaca, long an outstanding French doll-maker and creator of wonderful peasant types, is now established in New York. His most recent creation, a mechanical organ-grinder doll, has been featured by the well-known music house of Schirmer.

In Italy, Mme. Lenci was the prominent doll-maker in pre-war days. She was an artist as well as a creator of dolls and her "Madonnas" have attracted much attention in the world of art. She turned her attention to the making of dolls, it is said, after the death of her only child. Mme. Lenci's creed in doll-making was summed up in her reply to a query as to the secret of her success: "One must always use supremely good taste." That she did so is clear from the pictures of a group of dolls recently found in a storage warehouse and sold by the Humpty Dumpty Doll Hospital.

How much of the European doll and toy industry has survived the war is still problematical. We must also wait to see what will be the trends of the industry if it is revived.

HUMPTY DUMPTY AND SOME
JENNY WRENS

EVEN THOUGH HUMPTY DUMPTY in the nursery rhyme was "a good egg," there would seem, at first glance, to be little connection between poultry and dolls, but the famous Humpty Dumpty Doll Hospital at Redondo Beach, California, was once a chicken house—and "thereby hangs a tale."

Emma C. Clear, head surgeon of Humpty Dumpty Doll Hospital and creator of the first American made china doll as well as of many other china, Parian and blonde bisque beauties, was born in St. Louis, Missouri, where her father was engaged in buying and selling cattle. When she was a year old, the family moved to Buffalo, N. Y. In a family of comfortable means, she enjoyed the advantages of education and travel. She graduated in commercial law and then attended Vanderbilt University.

Gifted with extraordinarily skillful fingers and an artistic eye for beauty and fitness, a visit to the Chicago World's Fair where she was fascinated by the sculptures, fired the teen-age girl with an ambition to study sculpture. Later, these same gifts suggested a surgeon's career, still later she thought of writing. How was she to know then that her life work would be in a profession that combined all three.

Pictures of dolls discussed in this chapter will be found following page 188.

THE DOLLS OF YESTERDAY

Shortly after college she married, and a son was born to her. This first marriage was soon ended and she was faced with the necessity of finding something to do to earn a living for her son. Taking tea with a friend one afternoon, the two women were discussing her problem. They paid no attention to the hostess' nine-year-old son who was playing on the floor with the visitor's baby boy, until the youngster intervened with the remark: "Wouldn't it be nice if we could only make a living doing the things we *like* to do?"

"Well, why not?" thought the guest. As a child she had mended all the broken dolls in the neighborhood and she loved doing it. Why not? Here was work in which she could be happy. So she and her sister opened a doll specialty shop and doll hospital in downtown Buffalo. The business grew and was highly successful for several years. Then they separated, the sister keeping the shop in Buffalo. Emma moved to Cleveland and later to Los Angeles, locating on Hill Street and then on Broadway between Fifth and Sixth.

In California, she met and married Wallace C. Clear, a native of Tennessee. Mr. Clear had always been a farmer, so, after twenty years in the doll business, the doll shop was closed and the dolls packed away. Mr. Clear owned a poultry ranch at Redondo Beach, on a country road some twenty miles from Los Angeles.

A poultry ranch with two thousand layers and a house to build kept the Clears busy through one prosperous year and then came the depression of 1929 and the bottom dropped out of everything. In common with millions of other American families, the Clears saw hard times—very hard times—during the following three years. First the chickens went, then piece by piece, the poultry equipment had to be sold at a loss to keep going. They had long since cashed in life insurance policies, lost their city property, mortgaged the ranch. When they had to apply for relief, Emma Clear fell ill, dangerously ill, for the first time in her life. The doctors gave no hope for her recovery, but a country physician managed to save her. As she lay, too weak to move, her mind attacked the problems of the future. They would go back into the doll business, she decided.

The doll collecting hobby was rising fast in America. They had the molds and equipment to make doll parts that could not be procured from Europe. They had a stock of pre-war imported dolls. They had the skill and the knowledge. The problem was that of location—which it was impossible to change—that they would have to make do. Advertising? No money. Not even a five-dollar bill in the house. That indeed was a problem.

"Mama" Clear, as she is affectionately called by thousands of doll collectors, climbed out of bed despite the doctor's orders, to set her plans in motion. The empty two-story laying house would serve as their factory and workshop. She cut a large stencil reading, "Doll Hospital," and suggested to "Papa" Clear that he scrub some of the dropping boards and make signs. There was paint and there was scrap iron to make the supports.

"Papa" Clear did not have much faith in the venture, but he loyally co-operated. More dropping boards were scrubbed to make work tables and display tables. Dolls were unpacked and given beautiful costumes from "Mama's" old party dresses. A couple of good dolls were traded to a local newspaper editor for advertising. The place was busy as a beehive.

Three days after the signs went up, the first out-of-state car drove in. They were delighted with what they found. The doll-collectors' grape-vine telegraph spread the news of the discovery and other cars continued to roll in. They beat a path to the erstwhile chicken ranch that branched off to farthest corners of the United States. Boxes of dolls poured in by express and mail. Business became so heavy that in order to get the work out, they had to close the Hospital to visitors except on Saturdays when they keep open house. The Clears came back from the depths of the Great Depression in a big way.

In England they often speak of "a gentleman's gentleman." Humpty Dumpty might be called "a doll hospital's hospital," for doll hospitals everywhere send here their critical cases to be restored; dealers all over the country send their dolls for attention and collectors know that no wreck of a doll is too hard for the Clears to restore.

Wallace Clear, as we have said, was a farmer and so, as all farmers know, had to be able "to turn his hand" to a great variety of occupations. The training helped him in the doll business, but here he developed quickly a versatility of talents which surprised even himself. He can fill in at any job in the place, when help is scarce. He invented a machine for filling the doll bodies with sawdust. His packing department is a marvel—no doll is ever broken in ship-

193

ment when he has packed it. Opening one of "Papa" Clear's doll packages is about as easy as breaking into the Philadelphia sub-Treasury, but the dolls ride safely in them.

"Mama" Clear tells one amusing instance of his resourcefulness. One of his newly discovered talents is wood-carving. The problem on this occasion was to supply new feet on a carved wood monk doll. No sculptor's model for the bare feet could be found; time was pressing, so "Papa" Clear solved the matter by simply removing his shoe and sock and using his own bare foot for a model as he carved.

Prior to the First World War china doll heads were made only in Germany. Skilled in ceramics, Emma C. Clear created the first American made china doll, a replica of the old Jennie Lind doll of the 1850's. It is very beautiful and comes in three sizes in white, pink and rose luster. Other china and blonde bisques followed, so beautiful that a group of the Clear dolls are found in most good doll collections. By far the finest of their dolls are the blonde bisque George and Martha Washington, designed by that talented American sculptor, Martha Oathout Ayres. These exquisite dolls rank with the best of the old Dresden, and will undoubtedly continue to be sought by connoisseurs in future generations.

The Second World War with its shortages of labor and materials, its restrictions and red tape, and the endless reports required by the Government, greatly handicapped the output of work at Humpty Dumpty and made necessary the limiting of the dolls to be handled to the chinas, Dresdens and bisques. Few new dolls were made during the war. When materials have become available, no doubt new types will be created.

No account of Humpty Dumpty Doll Hospital would be complete without a mention of the efficient secretary whom most know only as "Rose" and to whom Mrs. Clear always refers as "My precious little Rose." Rose keeps the office work running smoothly, checks in the orders and checks them out; handles routine correspondence and in a thousand other ways saves the Clears for more important work. In private life, Rose, who is a Bohemian-American is the wife of a young mechanical engineer and the mother of five interesting children.

Her great love for her work and forty years of handling all types of dolls, thousands of them every year, have made Emma C. Clear the foremost authority on the subject in the world today. Her knowledge is equalled only by her generous willingness to share what she knows with others. She always has time to answer a question by any collector. Without her co-operation, no book such as this could be written—nor ever has been in recent years. All doll collectors hope for the day when Mrs. Clear will take time out to write the greatest of all books on the subject. Only she can do this.

THE JENNY WRENS: One of the most beloved of Charles Dickens' characters has always been "Jenny Wren," the little dressmaker for dolls. With the increased interest in old dolls during the recent past, a considerable number of women are making a profession of dressing dolls. One of the most skilled of these and a pioneer in the field is Mrs. Ralph E. Wakeman, of Claremont, N. H. It began as a hobby about twenty years ago but soon grew into a profitable and absorbing business. The fine workmanship and good taste which made her a successful dressmaker for women has been equally valuable in dealing with miniature people.

Dolls are first studied and typed to determine the correct period; often they are repaired, new bodies made for them, and then they are dressed in old materials. These materials are gathered from many sources: antique "pickers" bring in old Civil War costumes, old wedding dresses, discarded evening dresses, old handmade baby clothes, fine underwear, and other costume items of other days. Neighbors, breaking up housekeeping sell the contents of old trunks in their attics; auction sales yield treasures, and stocks of old stores, closed for decades, have been purchased. He. accumulation of twenty years can be depended upon to yield any necessary item: flowers, feathers, whalebones, anything at all necessary to complete a costume correctly.

A characteristic story of Mrs. Wakeman's meticulous attention to detail is told by her sister: "When we were children and used to play with 'penny' dolls, Bernice could make the most wonderful dresses for hers—she put *sleeves* in them and used to *turn* the sleeves. She did it with the head of a pin!"

When Mrs. Wakeman was called upon to dress a doll representing Queen

Elizabeth, the present Queen of England, in coronation robes, it is said she first wrote to the Royal Mistress of Robes at Windsor Castle to find out how many petticoats Her Majesty wore on the occasion.

Many California collectors send their dolls to New Hampshire for costuming, and dolls she has dressed have been exhibited in many doll shows.

Another dressmaker who turned her experience to dressing dolls, is Mrs. Carrie A. Hall of North Platte, Nebr. Mrs. Hall was once the leading modiste of Kansas City and it is said more than two hundred thousand gowns, for the women of Fort Scott and the southwest, were made in her shop. She is the author of two books, one on old pieced quilts and the costume book, *From Hoopskirts to Nudity,* mentioned in an earlier chapter.

It takes real courage for a woman of seventy-three to face the world alone and make a new start at earning a living. Mrs. Hall was that age when her husband died. The dauntless little lady started to dress dolls for collectors; and to make soft toys for children. Her business has grown and each year she sells hundreds of these dolls: "Maggie," the lady elephant, "Maggie's Man," "Mrs. Roo" and her son, "Sydney," the kangaroos and others, to New York specialty shops. She has created many character dolls for collectors: "Buffalo Bill," "Susan B. Anthony" and many other famous women; also dolls representing famous paintings—among the most popular of which are "Whistler's Mother" and Gainsborough's "Blue Boy."

Most dressmakers can turn out a doll dressed in Civil War or 1870 styles, but not everybody can do a correct coat suit or Gay 'Nineties costume. In this period, Mrs. Hall is an expert.

APPENDIX

THE MANUFACTURE OF DOLLS

From *Harper's Bazaar*

AUGUST 18, 1877, pp. 523–524

By courtesy of Miss A. Blanche Edwards, Abilene, Kansas

GERMANY, Switzerland and France are the principal storehouses of toys, but the manufacture of the wax doll is a specialty of England, France being the only rival in this respect. The French dolls, however wide their reputation for beauty and tasteful dress may have spread abroad, are not fancied by the English children, who wish their toys for playthings and not for ornaments.

Even in this small matter, the characteristics of the two nations are very apparent. The English doll is substantial and well-made, can be dressed and undressed, is plain in her attire, and dressed like a child; very different from her fine furbelowed French sister, arrayed like a marquise in silks and satins, with her eyeglass and poodle dog.

The number of people employed in the manufacture of dolls is astonishing, and in large establishments nearly all the work takes place on the premises, every person having his or her own particular work or specialty. In some of these wholesale establishments in London thousands of dolls are turned out in the course of a week.

The work of one man is the making of the head. This is done by pouring melted wax into a mold or cast of the head and features. Some of the wax, however, is poured off before it has time to become all perfectly solid. In this way, the more expensive ones are made. The others are of composition or paper coated over with wax and are much more generally used, as they are less expensive, and are not so easily cracked or broken. Another man's entire work is to put in the eyes. With a sharp knife he cuts away the wax for the sockets; after properly adjusting the glass eyes, he fastens them in by pouring a little melted wax in the skull, which, coming in contact with the glass, cools and keeps them in place. With more expensive dolls he models the eyelids and eyebrows with his hands. This requires considerable skill and long practice to accomplish successfully.

These little glass eyes are imported from Germany. Hundreds of gross of them, assorted in sizes and packed in large cases, are sent over to England annually.

When the eyes are inserted in the head, the next point is the putting on of the hair. This is an important consideration of the manufacturer, being the most costly part of the whole toy. In many of the best dolls, the hair and its insertion cost as much as the rest of the head put together, for no doll would be considered perfect unless the hair were natural, that is, unless it could be combed and brushed without injury. This work is all done by women. The head to be adorned is placed on a block and the operator holds

197

in her left hand the hair, carefully combed and cut in a uniform length; in her right hand a dull knife, with which she lifts a small piece of wax, and pushes the hair underneath. When she has finished this process by inserting only two or three hairs at a time, she takes an iron roller and gently. but firmly rubs it over the surface, thus fastening the hair securely on the head. This is a very tedious process and used only on the more expensive dolls. In the less expensive or composition ones, a deep groove is cut completely through the skull along the top of the head where the parting is to be and the uncurled ends of the ringlets are pushed in with a blunt knife, and then fastened down with paste.

Black hair, which is seldom used for dolls, is almost entirely human, and is imported from the Continent, while the flaxen locks so universally preferred are made of mohair. This material is especially manufactured for the purpose and there is one house in London that supplies nearly all the English as well as the best of the French and German makers. It is of a remarkably soft and silky texture and is sold in little bundles of different lengths.

Having finished the doll's head, the body is now to be considered. Upon this a number of people are employed, chiefly women, assisted by the younger members of their families, each of whom takes one special part. The manufacturer gives out so many yards of cotton and he knows to an inch how much material each dozen dolls will require, according to their size. The body-maker takes it home and accomplishes the work in the following manner: One person cuts out the body of the doll, another sews it, a third rams in the sawdust, a fourth makes the joints and in this way a family will produce many dozen in a week. The payment for this work is by the piece.

The arms form another branch of the manufacture, upon which certain persons are almost exclusively employed. Except for the very commonest class of dolls, the arms are made of kid below the elbow and cotton above; and in every case there is an attempt at fingers, although their number may not always be correct. The price paid for these arms complete is incredibly small. The workwoman furnishes the kid, cotton and sawdust and for large arms about six inches long receives $6\frac{1}{2}d$. for a dozen pairs, or thirteen cents in American money. Small arms for cheaper dolls are supposed to be worth only $1\frac{1}{2}d$. a dozen pairs, or three cents. As these poor people furnish the material, it must be difficult to keep starvation from their doors, unless they have other means of support.

The putting of the head and arms together is the last process. This is done with glue and thread. The doll is then wrapped in tissue paper and is ready for the market.

At least twenty different people are employed in making a doll, not counting those who manufacture the raw material, that is, the wax, the eyes, the cotton and the hair. In London there are sixteen wholesale establishments or manufacturers, and as for the retail dealers, it is impossible to calculate their number, as there are so few who make toys a specialty, they being generally sold with other things. This will give an idea of the number of people employed in England alone in manufacturing these apparently trivial articles. Still, trifling as they are, toys are supposed to be the necessities of children, and in Europe, where labor is cheap and plentiful, so much skill and time are bestowed on these Lilliputian articles that they have attained a high degree of perfection.

INDEX

INDEX

INDEX

Field, Mary, aunt of Eugene Field, 143
Field, Rachel, *Hitty,* written by, 172
Field, Roswell, Eugene Field's father, 143
Fifield, Ila, *Alice in Wonderland* characters, 26
Fiscus, Robert G., Mrs., doll of, 115, 116
Fitts, R. P., Mrs., doll collector, 140, 183
Flanders, Helen Harkness, editor of *Vermont Folksongs and Ballads,* 42
Florian, Gertrude, doll-maker, 134, 168
Fly-Lo Baby, designed by Mrs. Putnam, 133
Flynn, J. J., Mrs., doll collector, 72, 127
Ford, Henry, Ellis carriage sent to, 174
Fortune Telling pedlar doll, 159
Foster, Abbie, wax doll owned by, 90
Foster, H. A., Mrs., Paul Revere doll made by, 25
France, ivory doll, 55; milliners' models, 70; dolls from, 74, 75; fashion doll, 76–79, 81, 151; wax doll, 89, 96; Jumeau doll, 112–118; Bru doll, 118–119
Frances Dee, doll, 102
French, Mary Field (*see* Field, Mary)
French fashion doll, 70, 74–79, 81, 151
Frieda von Schall, Dresden doll, 104
From Hoopskirts to Nudity, by Carrie A. Hall, 87, 196
Frozen Charlotte, made in Germany, 39; description of, 40; name derived from ballad, "Fair Charlotte," 41
Fuller, A. M., Mrs., pedlar doll of, 159
Furniture, toy, 12, 177
Frye, Katherine, Mrs., dolls owned by, 90, 125

Garland, Grace, Mrs., doll collector-dealer, 60
German doll-makers, 58, 59, 169
Germany, 57, 61, 71, 81, 84, 99, 112, 119, 121, 122, 123, 131, 133, 139, 150, 167, 172, 189; wooden dolls of, 31; Frozen Charlottes of, 39; fashion dolls, 77; wax dolls, 89, 96; china head dolls, 5, 98, 99–105; Dresden (Parian) dolls, 2, 84, 106–111; bisque dolls, 120–123
Gibis, F. R., Mrs., china dolls of, 5
Glasshouse, cemetery, 54, 55
Goddard, Ann Elizabeth, dolls of, 145, 146
Goddard, Louisa, dolls of, 145, 146, 147
Goddard, Lucretia, dolls of, 145, 146, 147
Goddard family, 41, 145
Godey's Lady's Book (1831–1898), 4, 40, 59, 60, 70, 71, 80, 86, 87, 148, 177, 179
Goldsmith, Mrs., maker of wax figures, 88
Goldsmith, Philip, doll-maker, corset on doll, 103
Good Will Industries, Louisville, Ky., 68
Goodyear, Charles, inventor, 128
Gordge, John, doll inventions by, 188
Gould, S. Baring, *Strange Survivals,* by, 55
Graffly, Charles, art teacher, 32
Graziano, doll heads made by, 32
Greiner, Ludwig, doll-maker, 57, 58, 60
Greiner doll, 2, 61, 62, 64, 81, 179, 180
Groshong, Edith, Mrs., dolls of redwood, 26, 27
Gussie, wax doll, 97

Hairdress, doll, 58, 59, 71, 72, 73, 80, 100, 107, 110
Hale, Lula M., director of "Homeplace," 25
Hale, Sarah Josepha, quoted, 62
Hall, Carrie A., *From Hoopskirts to Nudity,* by, 87, 196
Handwerck, Heinrich, German bisques marked, 121
Harding, Winifred, Mrs., antique dealer and doll collector, 3, 18, 58, 109
Harvey, William F., Mrs., Lincoln doll sold by, 22
Haughton, William Henry, doll inventions by, 188
Hayes, Helen, American actress, 60
Heads, doll, Greiner's method, 60, 61

Heppel, Henry, Mrs., doll collector, 68, 171
Histoire des Jouets, by Henry d'Allemagne, 77, 81, 82, 92, 112, 118
Historic Costume for the Stage, by Lucy Barton, 86, 87
Historic Dress in America, by Elizabeth Mc-Clellan, 87
Historical dolls, 139, 165
Hitty, Rachel Field's, 172
Hobbies, magazine for collectors, 1, 62, 89
Holtz-Masse doll (mystery doll), 63, 64
Home Magazine, 140
"Homeplace," E. O. Robinson Mountain Fund, 25
Hubbard, Mr., Wiscasset, Maine, doll given by, 166, 167
Humpty Dumpty Doll Hospital, Redondo Beach, California, owned by Mr. and Mrs. Clear, 5, 46, 47, 57, 71, 96, 99, 170, 172, 178, 182, 190, 191–195
Huret, Calixto, Mlle., Parisian doll-maker, 83

Ida Mae Russ, Parian doll, 84
India, native doll of, owned by Mrs. Winifred Harding, 18
Indian doll, 21; redwood, 26; Sioux, 145; Bannock, 154, 155
Indiana, gas days in, 54
Infant dolls (*see* Baby dolls)
Irish dolls, airplane carriers, 46, 49; Violet Powell's, 188
Isabeau, Queen, of Bavaria, fashion dolls from, 76
Isabella, Queen of Spain, fashion doll for, 76
Italy, wax figures, 89; doll-making in, 190
Ivory doll, found in Dordogne, France, 55

James, E., Mrs., doll collector, 170
Jameson, Anna, doll carriage belonging to, 177, 179
Jamison, Anna V. A., doll wardrobe belonging to, 83
Janet, wax doll, 95
Japanese, Dickinsons and, 50, 51
Jaques, Rupert, Mrs., cloth doll belonging to, 68
Jenny Lind, Swedish singer, 138
Jenny Lind doll, 101, 138, 139, 155, 194
Jenny Wren, Dickens' character, 195
Joel Ellis doll (*see* Ellis doll)
Johl, Janet P., *The Fascinating Story of Dolls,* by, 132
Johnson, C. C., doll-maker, 14, 16, 17, 18
Joslyn Memorial Museum, Omaha, 94, 96, 102, 142, 156
Journal of American Folklore, 41, 52, 54
Jumeau, M., French doll-maker, 112; inventions of son, 115
Jumeau doll, wardrobe, 82; Janet, 95, 96; characteristics of, 113, 114, 115, 117; Buffalo Bill brought from Paris, 141; Martha Victoria, 151; shoes, 179

Kaestner, doll-maker, 167
Kammerer and Reinhart, doll-making firm, 122, 170
Katy Oppelbaum, Pennsylvania Dutch doll, 102, 172
Keller, Lillie, dolls belonging to, 95
Kentucky, poppets from, 24, 25; Louisville dresses, 95
Ketterman, Marie, wax dolls owned by, 97, 152
Keys, Frances Parkinson, Mrs., doll collector; "Dixie Doll, the," by, 140
Kimport dolls, State dolls, 27
Kingsley, Charles, *The Lost Doll,* by, 72

201

INDEX

INDEX

INDEX